AF473789

Liotard

A Portrait of Eighteenth-Century Europe

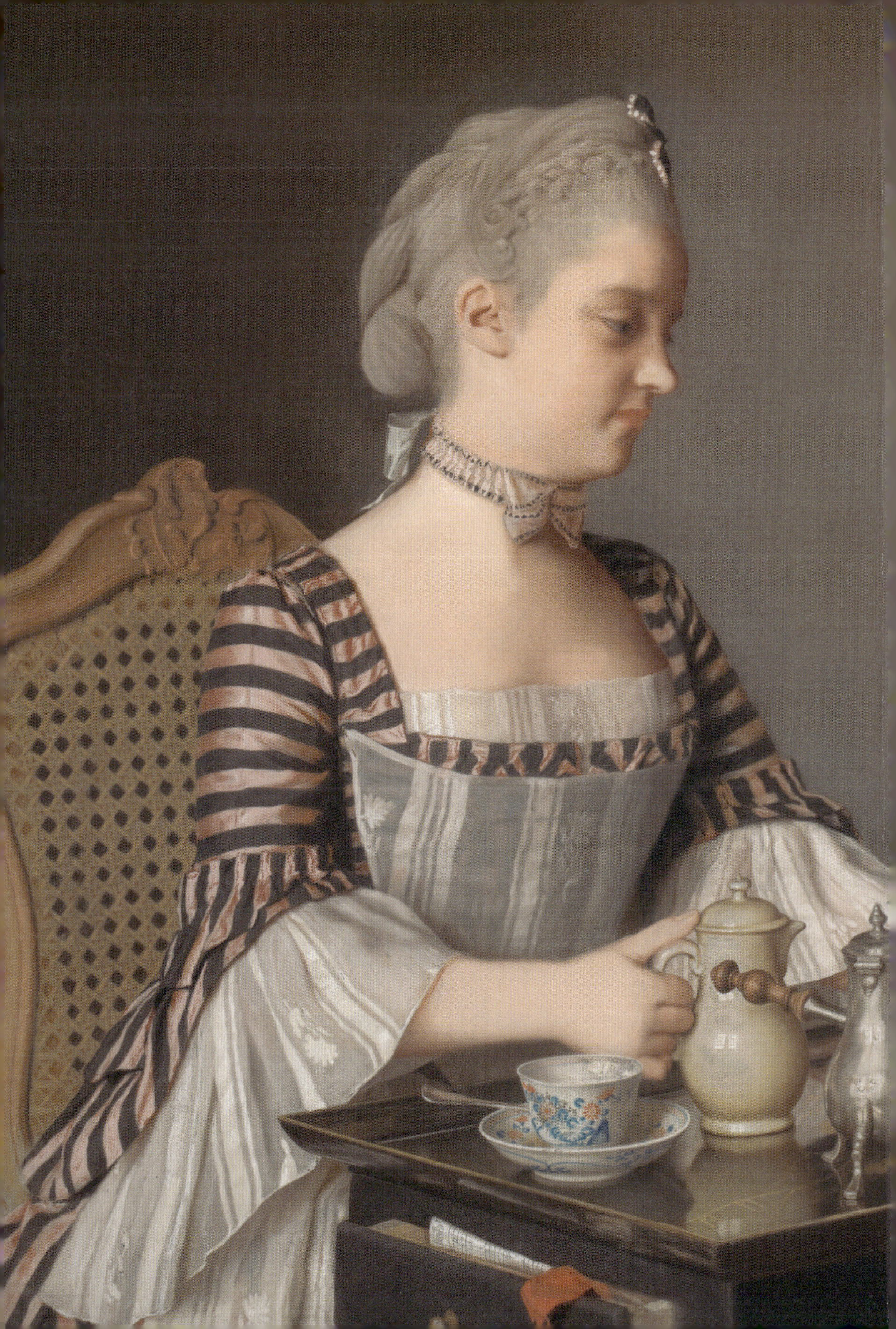

Liotard

A Portrait of Eighteenth-Century Europe

Christopher Baker

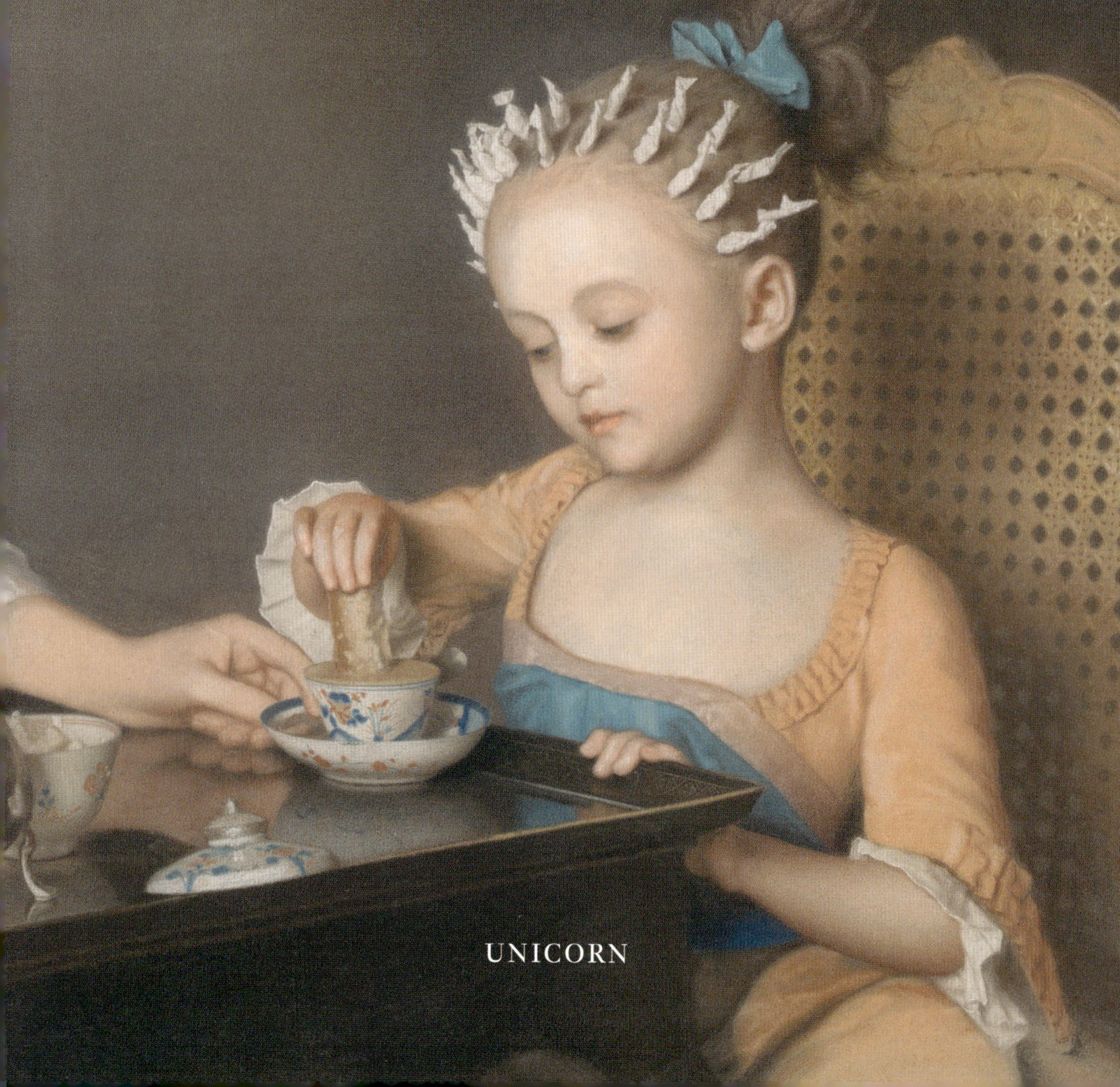

UNICORN

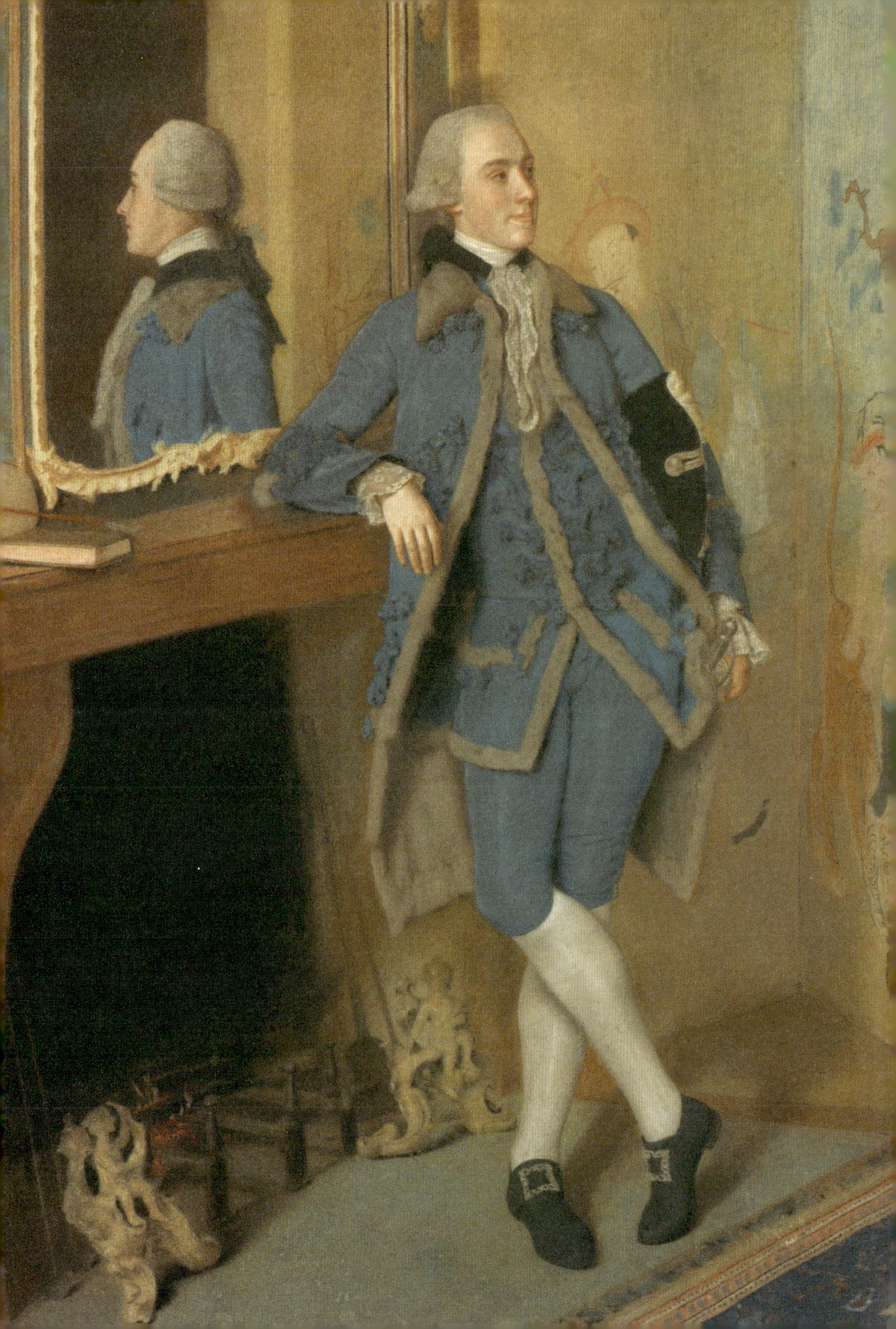

Contents

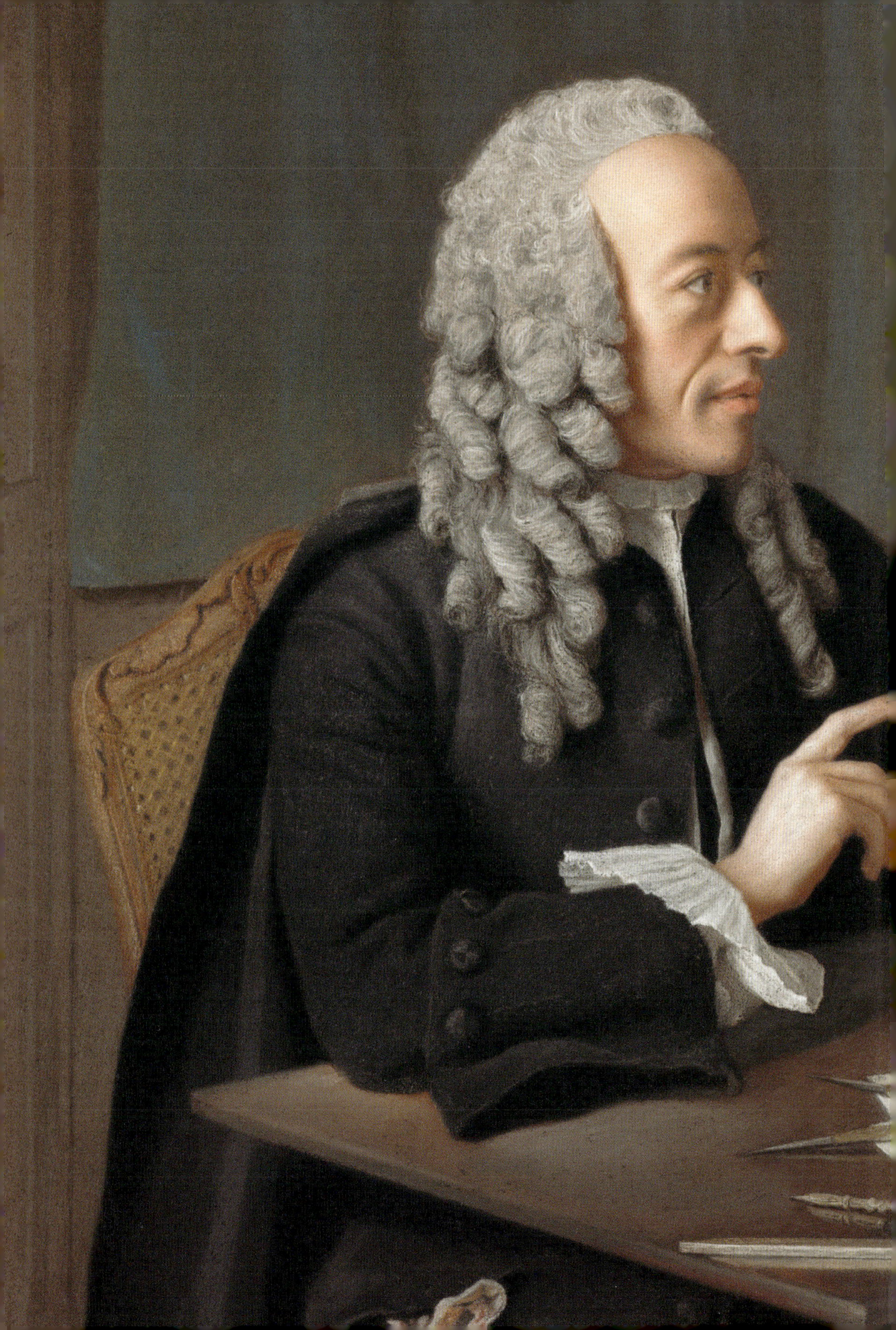

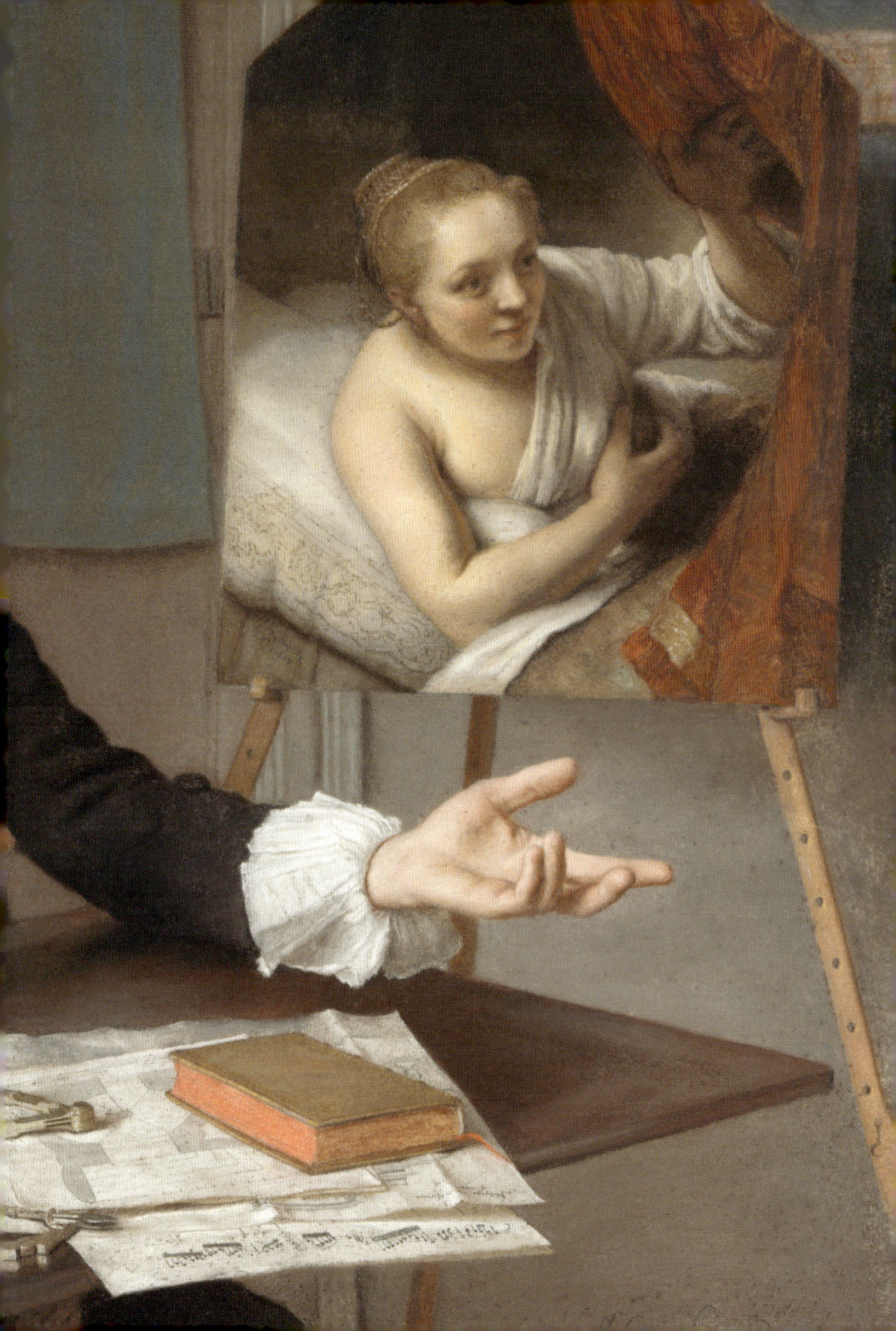

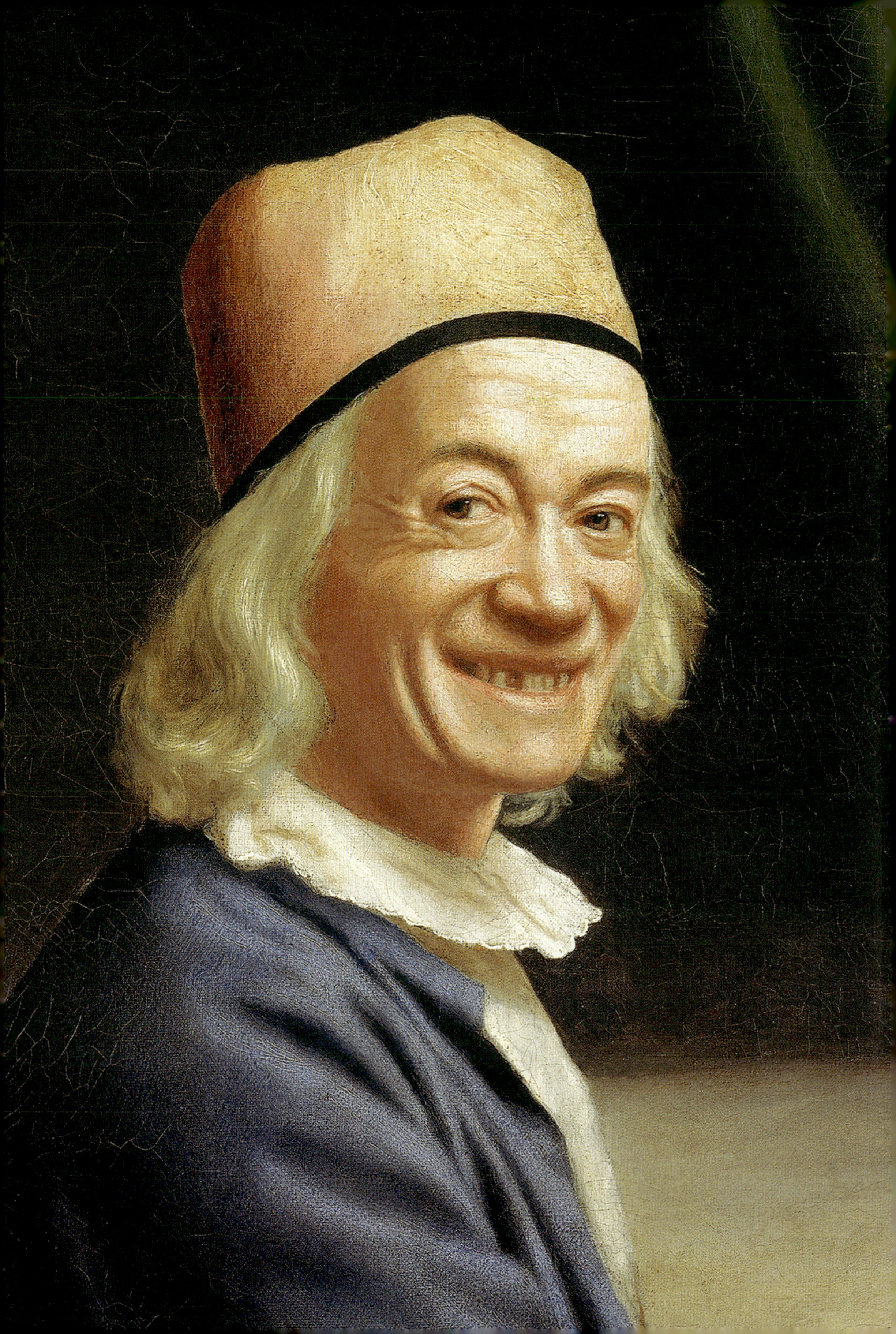

Introduction

IN ONE OF THE STRANGEST PAINTINGS of the eighteenth century a grinning man in his late sixties stares at us and points emphatically to the right, past a curtain [FIG. 1]. This is a startling self-portrait by the artist Jean-Étienne Liotard (1702–1789); he depicts himself with remarkable candour and appears to be encouraging you to follow him as he has wonders and curiosities to share. As well as being a mercurial, highly accomplished and quirky artist, Liotard was something of a showman. The discoveries he revealed through his career were the people he encountered and commemorated in his portraits: imperial and royal families, philosophers and collectors, travellers, diplomats, actors, citizens and servants, as well as members of his own family – an extraordinarily rich and diverse pageant of European society. The world he depicted was the pre-revolutionary *ancien régime*; it was a precisely stratified society, the social barriers of which were hard for most to cross. However, as Liotard's remarkably successful professional life was to prove, an artist with great talent and precocious skills to sell could deftly navigate it.

Smiling as Liotard is here, was a new, if not radical development in late eighteenth-century portraiture, especially in France. Licence to smile in painting came with the wider cult of sensibility which encouraged more natural forms of expression and emotion. It was in many ways, however, for Liotard an especially appropriate development in his invariably daring art, as he had both a lot to smile about because of his considerable reputation, but also because he had never shied away from depicting people as they are, rather than as they would hope to be seen. So much portraiture of the eighteenth century was propogandist, public and unremittingly serious, whereas Liotard's work was in many instances the opposite of this – private and stunningly candid, as well as often affectionate in tone.

Detail, FIG. 1

The politician, writer and arbiter of taste Horace Walpole (1717–1797) wrote that Liotard's 'likenesses were as exact as possible, and too like… Freckles, marks of the small-pox, everything found its place… Truth prevailed in all his works, grace in few or none.' Truth was certainly what the artist aimed for but even the briefest glance at a book like this or a catalogue of Liotard's works demonstrates he also had a profound sensitivity to qualities of grace – if by that we mean elegant compositions and the subtle language of gesture, as well as the sensory appeal of beautiful clothes and possessions.

The pointing self-portrait illustrates characteristics that recur in many of Liotard's depictions of others: a novel honesty and lack of idealisation, which is particularly notable here in terms of his own dentistry, and at the same moment a fascination with dress and fashion and the ways in which it can convey status. In this case the artist wears a hat of a type he acquired when he travelled through the Levant or eastern Mediterranean and later used in order to emphasise his adventurous and exotic credentials. The portrait may brilliantly encapsulate characteristics he sought to promote though his art, but it has a slightly hard, brittle quality; it is one of his rare oil paintings and this choice of medium and the precision with which he applied it explains its appearance. Liotard was certainly skilled as an oil painter but he chiefly specialised as an artist who used pastels in order to record and celebrate both his own appearance and that of his eclectic range of clients.

Pastel as a medium for portraits enjoyed an extraordinary vogue during the eighteenth century and was employed by some outstandingly talented artists, such as Liotard's great contemporary Maurice-Quentin de La Tour (1704–1788). It resulted in works of novel immediacy and vibrancy and Liotard's mastery of the medium is illustrated especially well by other examples of his self-portraits – including one he made about twenty years before the painted depiction of him pointing, which shows the artist not just inviting us into his studio and world, but actually at work [FIG. 2]. Here once again he looks directly at the viewer utilising a mirror to scrutinise his features, and the precision of the depiction is so specific that you can see points of light reflected on his piercing brown eyes. A luxuriant beard falls down across his chest; the grey and whitening hairs on it are individually drawn. A brilliant scarlet jacket lined with blue silk seems to be a rather grand garment to wear when you are working as an artist; if, however, we imagine ourselves as a client, then he is setting out to impress, through his persona, his fashion sense and the radiant skill he could bring to his mimetic art. In this case Liotard was also seeking to secure the approval and admiration of fellow artists, as the portrait was exhibited at the Académie de Saint-Luc (the guild of painters and sculptors) in Paris in 1752. It is one of a sequence of self-portraits by Liotard which extends across his career that were executed in a variety of media and formed part of a sustained campaign of self-promotion and self-scrutiny for which there are few other parallels in the eighteenth century.

How could such virtuosic effects be achieved? Pastel remains for many an unfamiliar medium and so a brief account of its characteristics and challenges helps deepen an understanding of the work of a brilliant practitioner like Liotard.

Pastels are made of ground up colourful pigments bound together with a filler by a binder and then shaped into small sticks or crayons. The pigments might be from mineral or organic sources and the fillers, which give the crayons their solidity, could be made of different materials, such as plaster of Paris, clay and chalk. The binder that coalesced these ingredients was usually made from gum Arabic extracted from Acacia trees. There were different recipes that provided variations on these basic components and would alter the texture and nature of the pastels and consequently the effects that might be achieved with them; for example, binding could be provided by olive oil or honey.

It was the high concentration of rich pigments that resulted in the stunning colours of eighteenth-century pastel portraits, such as Liotard's. He was very aware of the chromatic brilliance and subtle effects that could be achieved with them and evangelised about their attributes, writing in 1762 that 'For its beauty, vivacity, freshness and lightness of palette, pastel painting is more beautiful than any other kind of painting.' The pigments in pastels were similar to those used in dyes employed to colour fabric and so were especially appropriate to replicate the wonderful hues which are such a notable feature of the clothes worn by many of his subjects.

Treatises which provided advice about how pastels might be made in the studio were available to artists; however, ready-made pastels could also be bought from specialist suppliers: the maker most highly regarded across Europe during Liotard's lifetime was a man called Bernard-Augustin Stoupan (1701–1775) who worked in Lausanne. His pastels were distributed by agents in France and England. A London dealer called Pache & Davis is recorded in 1760 as selling on Stoupan pastels to

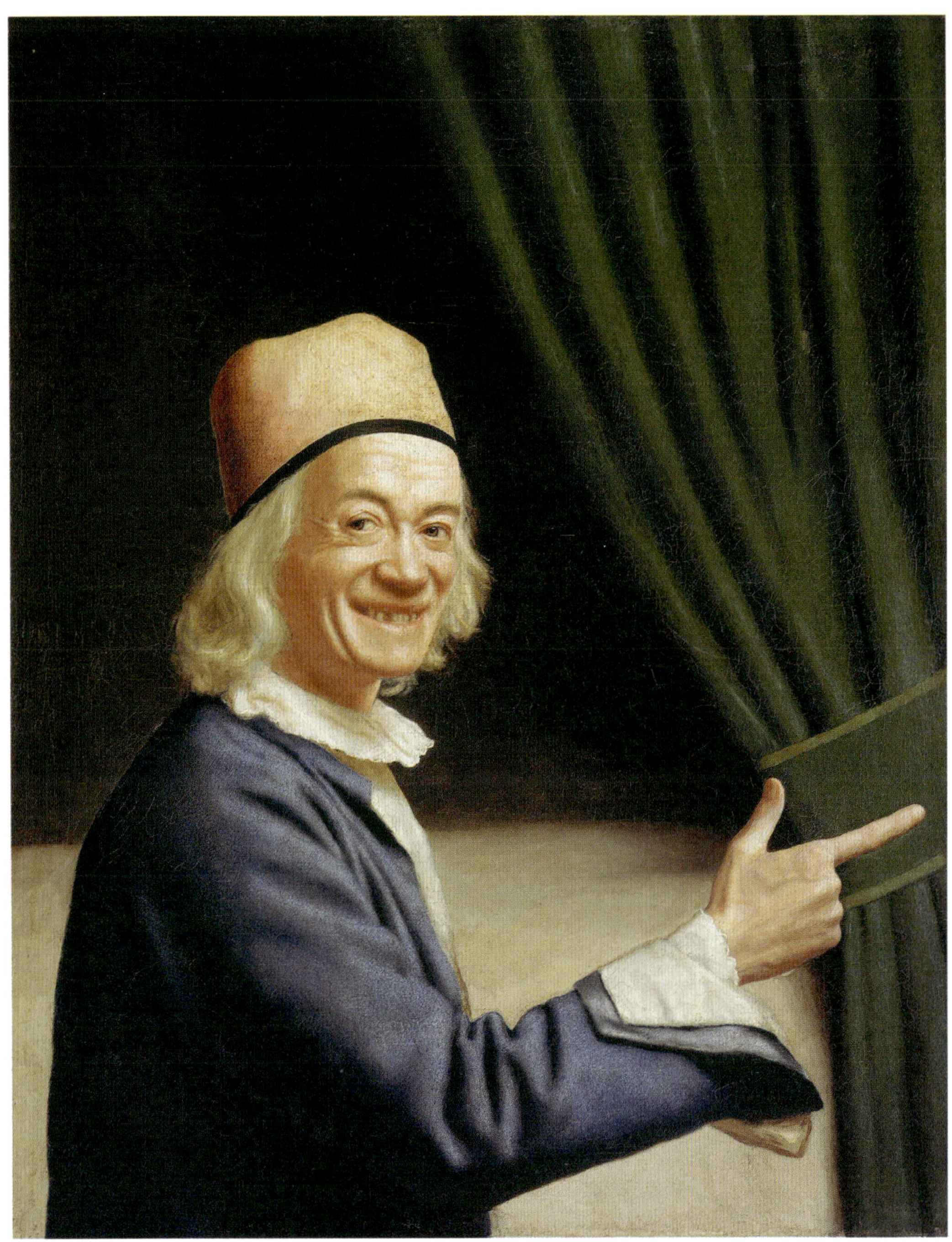

FIG. 1
Jean-Étienne Liotard
Self-Portrait Laughing
c. 1770
Oil on canvas, 84 × 74 cm
Musée d'Art et d'Histoire, Geneva
Inv. 1893–9

artists, as recommended by 'that famous painter Liotard.' This was six years after the artist's first visit to the city and so conveys an impression of both his enduring fame and how it was linked to a mastery of pastels.

Pastels, such as those made by Stoupan, could be held in the hand and used directly or placed in a 'porte-crayon' – a wooden tool or holder which meant the pastel did not rub off on to the artist as it was used. Liotard delicately holds just such a tool in the 1752 self-portrait, with a bluish-grey piece of a pastel secured at the end of it. Such pastels were usually used on paper, which in the eighteenth century was hand-made from rags, although other smooth supports such as vellum (made of calf skin) could be worked on and Liotard favoured this for some of his finest works. If paper was employed by pastellists they particularly liked selecting blue-grey sheets although other colours could of course be chosen. As you placed the crayon or stick on the paper or vellum and gently applied pressure some of the pastel was directly transferred. The resulting marks could be made in a linear manner, or different colours might be layered and rubbed and mixed on the surface of the work. Gentle rubbing of the pastels could create very subtle variations of tone and hue, in order to evoke, for example, the sheen on silk or the bloom of skin. Blending pastels in this manner might be done by hand but was often undertaken with the use of a 'stump' – a term used to describe a rolled up piece of paper or leather. The remarkable ability of pastel to replicate the appearance of the face and features of a sitter had a profound dimension for some: the philosopher and art critic Denis Diderot (1713–1784) referred to the dusty medium of pastel as reflecting the nature of mankind 'who is nothing but dust.'

Occasionally very large pastel portraits were created in the eighteenth century and Liotard made splendid contributions to this development, but far more frequently they were relatively small works, intended for intimate, domestic display. The paper or vellum they were executed on was usually adhered to a canvas, which was secured to a wooden stretcher and then framed and glazed. The glazing protected the surface of the pastel, which was vulnerable to abrasion and damage. If a large work was to be made, sheets of paper had to be joined together.

Pastels are fundamentally both a dry and a portable medium. This means that an artist like Liotard, rather than travelling with all the complex paraphernalia that an oil painter would require, could move around with less luggage: a box in which to store his pastels and other drawing equipment and perhaps rolls of paper were essentially all he required. There was also no necessity to wait for the pastels to dry (as you have to with oil paint), so the process of execution and completion of a work could be relatively quick. The medium also allowed for the creation of a work to be interrupted easily and re-activated at a later moment – if other commitments intervened – so it was very accommodating in a social sense. Before committing to an ambitious work in pastel drawings could be made to establish the pose of a subject and this was certainly a tactic Liotard employed for especially complex works.

These characteristics were all attractive both to the sitter and artist, especially as the equipment of the studio might easily be brought to the sitter rather than vice versa. Having said that, clients sometimes went to the temporary studios Liotard established in his lodgings and more than one sitting would usually be required in order to achieve the level of finish and refinement that he sought. The limited evidence we have which documents his interaction with his sitters illustrates this. For example, when he was creating a pastel portrait of the celebrated actor David Garrick (1717–1779) in Paris in the early 1750s there were five sittings spread over a week. The two men appear to have enjoyed each other's company and more than once Garrick remained in the studio to dine with Liotard. Other types of companionable activity were also recorded on at least one occasion in the context of his studio: the 3rd Earl of Bristol (1724–1779) sat for a now lost portrait the year before Garrick and used frequent visits to Liotard's studio as a cover for trysts with his lover Susanne-Félix Lescarmotier (1730–1786). This sounds like an episode from the later novel *Les Liaisons Dangereuses* (1782). However, most of the surviving information about Liotard's studio life suggests the activities there were chiefly confined to matters of art and business and propriety.

Artists who used pastels came to establish their own styles of work – as is the case with every medium. But in very broad terms there were two distinct approaches that might be applied to the use of pastels for

FIG. 2
Jean-Étienne Liotard
Self-Portrait at the Easel
1751–2
Pastel on several sheets of paper, 97 × 71 cm
Musée d'Art et d'Histoire, Geneva
Inv. 1843–0005

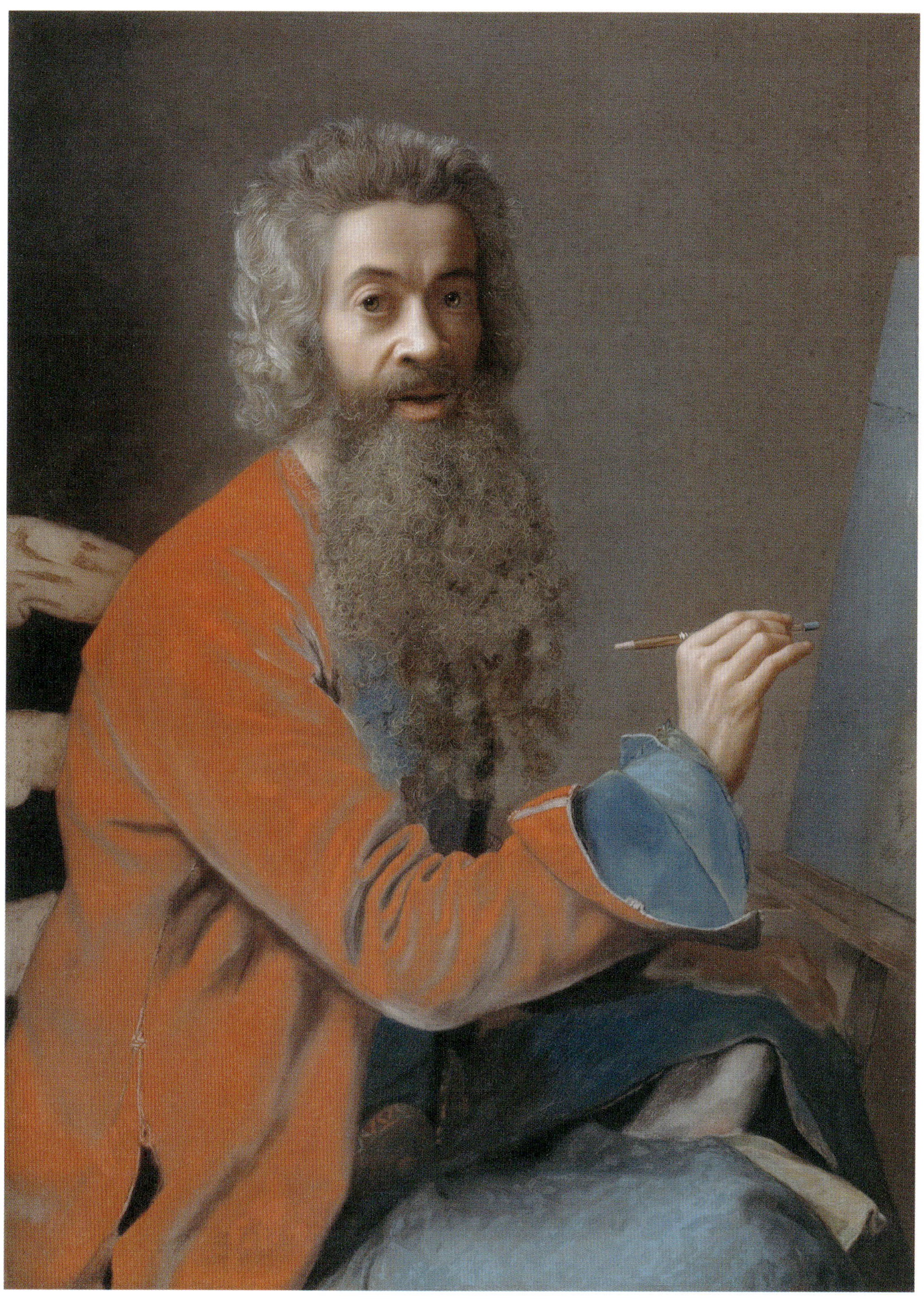

portraits. You could work in a manner which both depicted a sitter for a portrait but made it clear that the portrait was a work in pastel – in other words the medium was allowed to remain apparent, through perhaps a linear style with visible hatching or feathery mark making. This approach was developed, for example, by the great Venetian pioneer of pastel portraiture Rosalba Carriera (1673–1757), whom Liotard met and with whose work his was sometimes compared and contrasted by contemporaries. Alternatively, an artist might meticulously seek to replicate the direct experience of looking at the face and clothes of their subject and create an illusion of, or approximation of, reality. This was the mature approach of Liotard, which his subjects found extraordinary, and which means that his works still often convey an uncanny and at times unnerving sense of the presence of an individual at a particular moment in time. Such an impact was the 'truth' described by Walpole. It has been seen as being aligned with theories that were expounded about the role of portraiture in the eighteenth century: for example the artist and critic Roger de Piles (1635–1709) in his *The Principles of Painting* (1708) stated that '... in portraiture resemblance is paramount... one must imitate defects as well as beauties...' It might seem reasonable to suppose Liotard was adhering to this strategy as an Enlightenment artist – a maker of portraits in the age of reason and observation, who applied empiricism to his work. He certainly did theorise about his practice, but only at the end of his career. His skills appear to have evolved gradually into the realist or observational nature of depiction he excelled at, rather than it being part of a pre-determined philosophical agenda; it had the distinct benefit though of amazing his clients and leading on to more and more illustrious commissions.

Liotard combined these remarkable artistic skills with an awareness of how beneficial it was to be the latest sensation – by moving across Europe and further afield he both gradually built his reputation and inspired fresh waves of curiosity and admiration. This was achieved in his native Geneva and in Rome, Paris, Constantinople, London, Amsterdam and Vienna. He repeatedly became the 'new' man in the cultural worlds of the great cities he temporarily resided in during his picaresque career and cleverly through such appearances maximised both his status and the impact of his hypnotic art. His travels especially during the first half of his career were not however part of a pre-planned campaign; rather they formed part of a search to find new professional, artistic and ideally financial opportunities.

Liotard was not alone in employing this mode of work, as his younger contemporaries included some of the most prodigious cultural travellers of the eighteenth century; at a time when undertaking journeys across the continent was relatively slow, dangerous and costly, it is interesting to consider the adventures of men such as Wolfgang Amadeus Mozart (1756–1791) or Giacomo Casanova (1725–1798) alongside Liotard. Mozart travelled great distances to perform and hopefully secure patronage, most especially in the 1760s, when as a child genius he was paraded around the palaces of Europe, being seen and heard in Munich, Vienna, Prague, Mannheim, Paris, London, The Hague, Amsterdam, Utrecht and Zurich. He later wrote to his father: '... without travel we... are miserable creatures... a man of superior talent... deteriorates if he remains continually in one place.' Casanova was a charismatic polymath who journeyed even further than the other two men, in pursuit of new cultural and financial opportunities as well as amorous liaisons, but also sometimes fleeing from the threat of imprisonment. Just to take the 1760s again as an example, he visited during that decade Cologne, Stuttgart, Marseilles, Genoa, Florence, Rome, Naples, Modena, Turin, London, Warsaw and Spain. Travel at this time may have been fraught with difficulties, but since the mid-seventeenth century it had become more systematically organised, so you could gallop across Europe using established networks of public coaches, the timetables for which were often advertised in advance.

The benefits in terms of professional opportunities and income that came from having skills that you could travel with were clear. Such journeys also though encouraged the acquisition of knowledge about different cultures. This was considered a highly desirable ideal in eighteenth-century Europe; it meant you were aspiring to be a cosmopolitan 'citizen of the world.' Such status might be partially gained at home in the confines of a library where you could meander between books, engravings or collections of curiosities, but the reality of direct experience and an international outlook was highly valued in certain circles: Diderot wrote to the Scottish philosopher and historian David Hume (1711–1776) in February 1768, asserting '... I pride myself on being, like you, a citizen of that great city, the world.' As Liotard acquired his knowledge of cities, courts, fashions and intriguing personalities he could impart gossip about them at his next stops, so enriching further the service he offered patrons who were hungry for information, a steer over matters of taste or tittle tattle. The renowned salons of

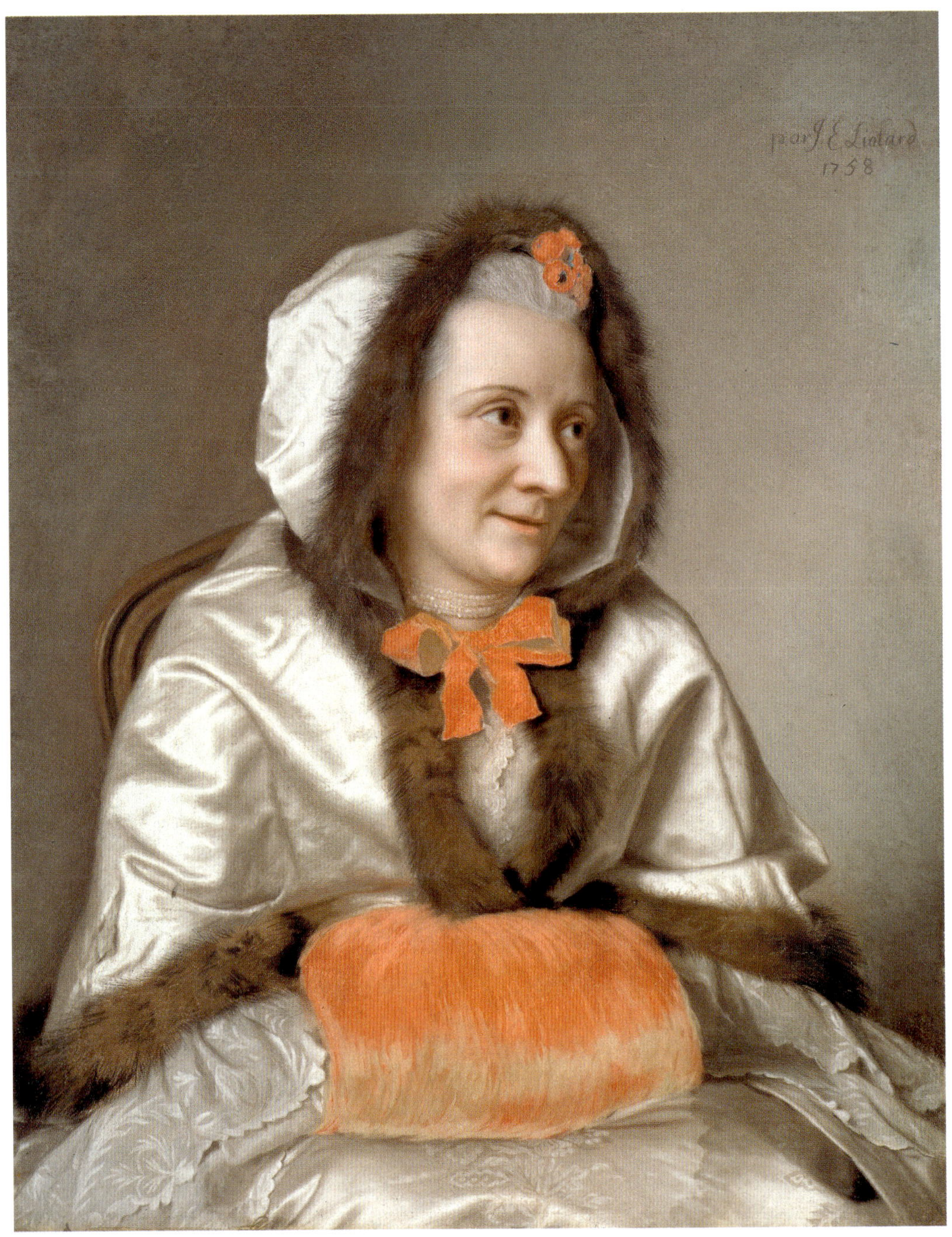

FIG. 3
Jean-Étienne Liotard
Madame François Tronchin 'Dressed for the Cold'
1758
Pastel on vellum, 68 × 55 cm
Musée d'Art et d'Histoire, Geneva
Inv. 1985–42

mid-eighteenth century France were the epitome of social gatherings where intellectual innovation and an international outlook was fostered; more informal spaces, like artists' temporary studios, could serve you well however. Once again, as was the case with Liotard's empiricism, it would be quite wrong to suggest he had a long-term, serious agenda to become some sort of European intellectual, but the richly varied opportunities he seized meant that he certainly came into contact with a number of contemporaries who nurtured such ambitions and he contributed to their status through commemorating them.

Liotard did not just move across Europe, he also ascended and descended its social hierarchies. He came from a relatively modest artisan background and his most famous work is a depiction of an anonymous servant carrying chocolate in a wealthy household; the pastel was though acquired by a king. Liotard was entirely at home depicting the bourgeoisie and intelligentsia of his home city of Geneva, but he also secured direct access to the private spaces of the grandest of all households and, for example, acquired not just patronage from Empress Maria Theresa (1717–1780), who ruled the vast Hapsburg dominions, but also her trust and a degree of intimacy with her family. Such social fluidity was due certainly to the prodigious skills he displayed and the value that was attached to fine portraiture, but it must also have been related to his personality and charm. In addition, it is noteworthy that a time when Europe was riven by religious divides Liotard also seems to have crossed these without any problems; so, for example, he secured commissions from many Protestant sitters, whose background and faith was similar to that of his own family, but also depicted the Pope (a portrait that is sadly lost) and Maria Theresa, a vehement defender of Catholicism. He also worked with apparent ease in the Islamic culture of the Ottoman Empire and must have avoided any provocative discussions around religion.

The shifting political and economic backdrop to his career brought with it new opportunities. When Liotard started his training as an artist in the 1730s Europe was chiefly a pre-industrial society ordered according to traditional hierarchies, focused on courts, municipalities and landed estates. Most people did not travel far beyond their villages or towns. He died however just before the French Revolution and seismic changes had by then been experienced by many. Increasing mobility occurred not only for artists, as people migrated from the countryside to the expanding cities to work, and opportunities for securing wealth and education particularly benefited the growing middle and professional classes, from whom many of Liotard's clients when he was a mature portraitist were drawn. There was also a significant evolution of how art was commissioned, displayed and distributed during the eighteenth century, as local guilds were to some extent superseded by state sponsored academies, which had rigorous agendas about teaching and exhibitions, and arguably did not accommodate the type of more idiosyncratic service an artist like Liotard offered.

Whether he was depicting those at the apex of eighteenth-century society or more humble subjects, there is in Liotard's work an enduring interest in material culture and the ways in which it can be replicated in pastel. He was fascinated by the specificity of clothes and so has undoubtedly done a great favour to later historians of fashion. The remarkable observational skills he applied to the faces of his sitters were carried over to the minutiae of the silk, lace, cotton, wool or furs they wore. A splendid example of such interests is his sensitive portrayal of *Madame François Tronchin* [FIG. 3] from 1758, who is shown 'dressed for the cold' in a manner that allowed a dazzling display of silvery light falling on white silk, fringed with fur. Liotard was not alone in exploring such preoccupations – Maurice-Quentin de La Tour, for example, also brilliantly rendered ornate fashions in pastel. Clothing could of course signify status and wealth and international connections and these issues were an important strand of Liotard's output as well as the expectations of his subjects, such as Madame Tronchin, who lived an affluent life in Geneva and whose father had been a Director of the French East India Company.

There are though wider cultural issues being reflected here as there was a widespread contemporary fascination with, and analysis of, the manufacturing arts, which were both a source of pride and beauty but also economic power. It is no accident that the years of Liotard's maturity as an artist when he excelled at depicting luxurious and beguiling dress were those when Diderot's *Encyclopédie, ou Dictionnaire raissonné des sciences, des arts et des metiers'* (Paris, 1751–72) was published. The *Encyclopédie* took a close and unprecedented interest in the origins and crafting of an extraordinary range of fashionable products and illustrated them with precise engravings. It included over three thousand entries related to clothing. A similar didactic role was also adopted by the *Encyclopædia Britannica*, which was first published in Edinburgh (1768–1771). As well as having this intellectual backdrop to his fashionable preoccupations, Liotard was undoubtedly always keeping an eye on promoting what could be achieved with his chosen medium of pastel. Contemporaries were both aware of what might be done with it, but also how challenging it was. So, for example, the British pastellist John Russell (1745–1806) wrote in 1772 that drapery was very difficult '... to execute with Taste; merely to give the effect of Silk, Satin, or Cloth... is not the point...; but to make the folds give grace and dignity to the figure, to cloath[e] it uninfluenced by prejudice... or caprice... requires the fullest exertion of true genius.'

If Liotard was a 'true genius' and so remarkable and successful as an artist why is his work not widely known beyond the realm of specialists, and why do many feel that they are making a special discovery when they come across it now? The answers lie partly in the nature of his chosen medium and partly in the nature of his career. Pastels are admired but have never become a strong feature of displays in museums and galleries, because so many examples still remain in private collections. They have been considered a tributary alongside the main stream of oil painting which dominates the narratives of eighteenth-century art. In addition to this challenge Liotard in particular, because of the nature of his international practice, does not lend himself to the conventional ways in which art histories are plotted. In the late eighteenth and nineteenth centuries, for a variety of reasons, national pride came to form a powerful force in the defining of cultural history – so the distinctive nature of French, British or German art for example was celebrated and discussed. This had many benefits, but it did not easily accommodate a creator of portraits who worked in many different cities and kept moving on. The result was that Liotard was given a small role in a number of different narratives and had to wait until the twentieth century to benefit from detailed and fulsome scholarly attention.

He compounded these confusions about identity not merely through his travels but also by adopting exotic Levantine clothing when he was traversing Europe, following his visits to the Ottoman Empire. This was not merely an instance of dipping into a dressing up box for a brief episode of entertainment, but became a sustained and successful strategy which gave Liotard a professional edge in what was already a quite fully populated world of portraiture. When, for example, he arrived in London in the mid-eighteenth century around two thousand people in the city were said to be engaged in the business of making portraits in every conceivable medium. In such a context standing out from the crowd, wearing scarlet robes and a long beard, caught the attention of the press, the public and patrons. Most of them were not disappointed when they saw the work that this strange, mercurial, artistic magus produced.

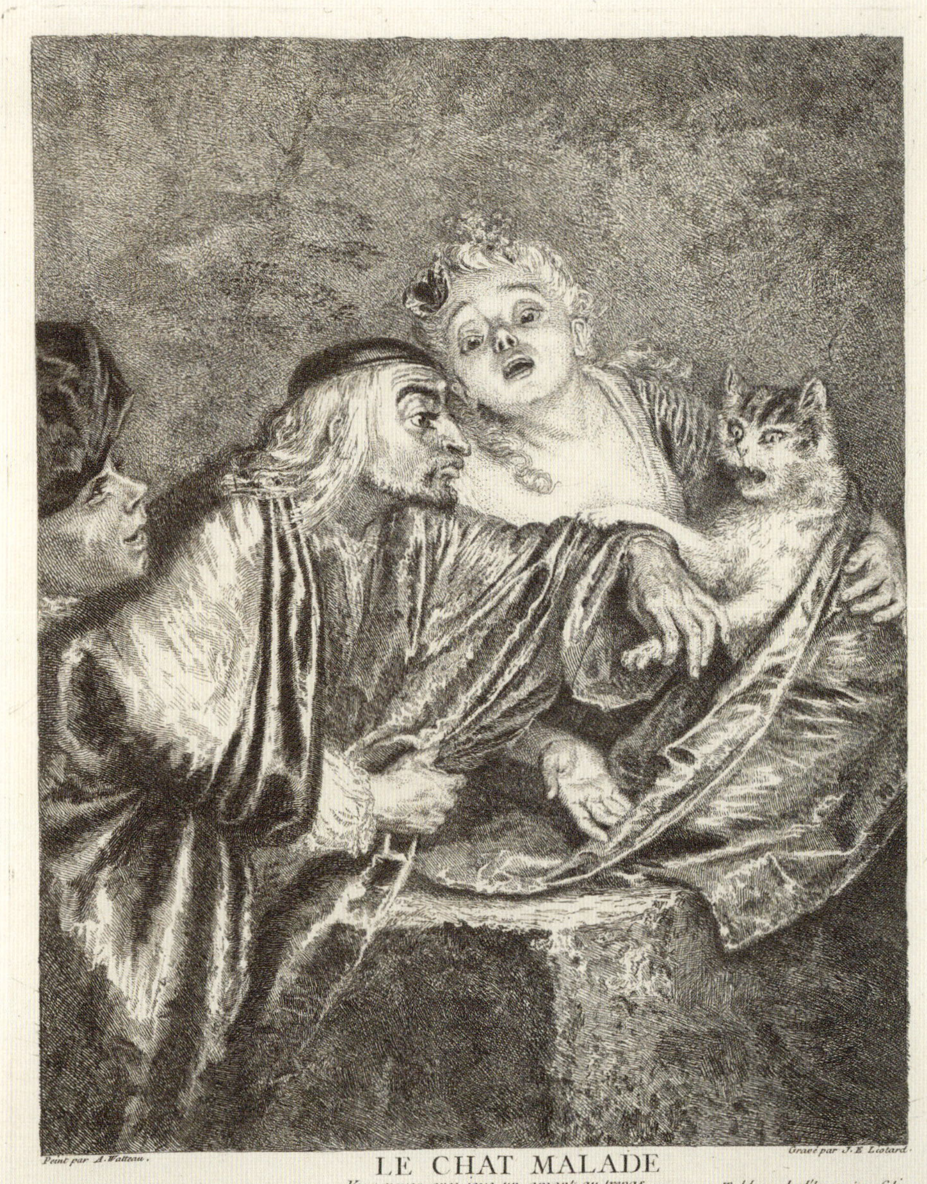

FIG. 4
After Jean-Antoine Watteau (1684–1721)
by Jean-Étienne Liotard
Le Chat malade
1731
Etching, 380 × 278 mm
The British Museum, London
(1838,0526.1.32)

1 Geneva and Paris
Family and Training

JEAN-ÉTIENNE LIOTARD was born in Geneva on 22 December 1702; he lived to the age of eighty-seven – a considerable and rare achievement in the eighteenth century. His twin brother, who was called Jean-Michel, exceeded even this, however, and reached his ninety-fourth year. The twins were the youngest members of a family of fourteen children; their parents were Anne Sauvage and Antoine Liotard, who was a tailor and dealer in textiles from Montélimar, south of Lyons in Provence.

The family were Huguenots, Protestants who fled from France following the revocation of the Edict of Nantes in 1685, which meant they were no longer protected from persecution. The Liotard family found sanctuary in Geneva and was granted citizenship there in 1701. The Huguenot community became dispersed extensively across Europe and was especially renowned for its mastery of a wide range of artistic and craft skills in different media. They notably established a reputation for brilliantly working with silver and silks, but also proved to be outstanding jewellers, furniture makers and designers in many other fields. This vibrant creative heritage was not merely a matter of historic interest to Liotard, but had a direct bearing on his family life, opportunities for work and subject matter. When he visited relatives in the Netherlands, Venice and Lyons, for example, these encounters were to result in important artistic projects, sales and commissions, as well as more personal liaisons.

Geneva was a relatively small independent city state, a republic, from the mid-sixteenth century up until 1798 when it was annexed by France. It later joined the Swiss Confederation following the fall of Napoleon. During Liotard's life it grew as a successful mercantile city with a liberal reputation; its most famous son in the eighteenth century was the brilliant progressive philosopher Jean-Jacques Rousseau (1712–1778), whose work was profoundly influential across Europe. In spite of the enlightened status such figures suggested, Geneva was not always stable in political terms, as there were tensions between a wealthy elite who dominated the councils – the ruling bodies of the republic – and working-class activists. This led to riots in the 1730s and much later, in 1782, a brief revolution, which attempted to expand the franchise, but was suppressed. Although Liotard travelled extensively his connections with Geneva remained strong throughout his career and some the greatest of his mature portraits were created there; he also returned to live near the city at the end of his life.

Liotard served an apprenticeship in the city from the age of thirteen in the studio of the miniaturist Daniel Gardelle (1679–1753), to whom he was distantly related and who was chiefly known for executing work in enamel. This was a technique Liotard certainly mastered and later employed in his career, although it did not come to dominate his practice. His time with Gardelle was short, lasting only four months. However, it provided Liotard with an important formative experience of working in a technically very demanding workshop environment.

Enamel portraits of the type made by the Gardelle and Liotard, consisted of paint made from ground glass being fused to a support of metal, through firing in a kiln and therefore heating at high temperatures. Such works required considerable knowledge and finesse and evolved in particular from the skills of goldsmiths, snuff box makers and watch-makers. The metal support for enamelling a portrait on usually consisted of a thin plate of copper, hammered to create a slightly curved surface, which prevented warping during the firing process. The great heat involved in firing might result in cracking but the risks were minimised if the work was small. Later Liotard, who was always trying to push back boundaries, created an exceptionally large enamel portrait of Empress Maria Theresa; however, most of the works of the type he created were conventionally small in scale and brilliantly coloured (see FIGS. 21 and 24).

The enamel paints he would have used were made from glass, coloured metal oxides and a medium, such as sandlewood oil or lavender oil. A layer of white base enamel was applied to the support and fired before the coloured paints were used. The colours could only be employed one at a time as different colours had different melting points and those that needed the highest temperature to fuse had to be employed first. So an artist had to know about the different chemical properties of the colours as well as employ extraordinary levels of manual dexterity and care on what were invariably detailed and miniature works. Although Liotard mastered the technique, it was restrictive and did not, because of all the equipment and time required, lend itself to the peripatetic life he came to favour. Whereas pastels undoubtedly did. There was some common ground though between the two techniques as, when brilliantly applied, they both resulted in works of glorious colour and exquisite detail.

Daniel Gardelle came from an artistic dynasty of miniature and enamel painters: he collaborated as an artist with his brother Robert Gardelle (1682–1766), who painted in oils but was primarily a printmaker. They were related to Theodore Gardelle (1722–1761) who, as a travelling miniaturist from Geneva, in some respects anticipated aspects of Liotard's future career. He trained as a painter and enameller and visited Paris. He is, however, not chiefly remembered for artistic achievements, but rather acquired a quite different type of notoriety for having murdered his landlady Anne King in London, and attempting to destroy and hide her body. He was executed at Haymarket.

The type of richly coloured small scale works Daniel Gardelle created were very refined objet d'art produced for a wealthy clientele – and so Liotard immediately, albeit briefly, entered a sector of the art market that specialised in intimate luxury items that linked the skills of painters with jewellers and goldsmiths. The greatest centre for such work in the eighteenth century was Paris and expanding his artistic horizons, in terms of techniques and clientele, Liotard next travelled there at the age of twenty-one in 1723. He took up his second apprenticeship, a contract for which is dated to 27 April. Liotard trained this time in the studio of Jean-Baptise Massé (1687–1767), who was a miniature painter and engraver. The apprenticeship was to last three years; he was to be taught 'the art of painting', serve his master and lodge in Massé's house on the Place Dauphin. Neither party was required to make any payment. This arrangement may have been offered because Massé was a Protestant, no doubt a key consideration of Liotard's family.

The Place Dauphin, which was laid out at the beginning of the seventeenth century, is at the west of the Île de la Cité, so Liotard was based for this important formative period in the heart of the city. This was the Paris of Louis XV (1710–1774), who had succeeded his great-grandfather Louis XIV in 1715. Louis was then only five years old and France was ruled by the Duke of Orléans (1674–1723) as Regent. The Orléans collection of paintings, among the greatest in Europe, was housed in the Palais-Royal and easily accessible for artists, amateurs and tourists. The year Liotard arrived was a key moment for Louis XV as he reached his maturity and made the decision to move the court from Paris back to the Palace of Versailles. The Regency had been a period renowned for pleasure, if not hedonism, and this was now to be succeeded by more traditional and staid conventions for elite life. Arguably the defining moments in cultural terms during Louis XV's reign arrived later – with the brilliant Enlightenment publications from the 1740s onwards of Diderot and Voltaire (1694–1778), the magnificent patronage of art and music by the King's mistress Madame de Pompadour (1721–1764), and Louis's own support in particular of architecture and city planning.

Massé had been taught by Louis de Chatillon (*c.* 1639–1734) and in 1717 was elected a member of the Académie royale de Peinture et de Sculpture. He became a notable figure in the Parisian art world, in 1759 being appointed keeper of paintings in the Royal Collection. It was in the middle of the period of Liotard's apprenticeship that Massé started work on what was to prove to be his most significant commission: a major series of engravings after painted schemes at Versailles, in the Grande Galerie, the Salon de la Guerre and the Salon de la Paix. The project involved collaboration with a number of other draughtsmen and printmakers and was finally completed in 1753. It is unclear what if any contribution Liotard made to this important undertaking, but it must have been the subject of much discussion in the Massé household, and we know that later Liotard's brother Jean-Michel, who established himself as an engraver, did make prints after the Versailles decorations. It seems highly likely that it was at this point that Liotard learnt about the techniques of printmaking, so adding more techniques to his growing repertoire. Only a small group of prints executed by Liotard survive; however, they demonstrate considerable accomplishment with the intaglio processes of engraving and mezzotinting. The latter was in Liotard's day a still relatively novel technique especially in France, having been invented in mid-seventeenth century, and signifies his evolving interest in artistic innovation.

Liotard may have been gradually acquiring a knowledge of printmaking, painting and enamelling all of which would serve him well. But there remains an as yet unresolved mystery at this formative point in his career: where and from whom did he learn the art of using pastels, with which he was to excel? Liotard later claimed that early in his career in Geneva he was working in pastel, but there were no obvious mentors or teachers in the city, so it seems more likely to have been in Paris that his enthusiasm for the medium was acquired. His Paris years (1723–35) followed a key moment in the growing vogue for pastels, when the Venetian artist Rosalba Carriera visited the city (1720–21), creating something of a sensation and making the commissioning and production of pastel portraits a fashionable pursuit. She used it to cut across social barriers as Liotard was later to do. Carriera portrayed the King and Regent, members of the nobility and fellow artists, such as Jean-Antoine Watteau (1684–1721). Earlier figures who had employed the medium with some success in Paris include the late baroque portraitist Joseph Vivien (1657–1735), who came from Lyons and was received as a member of the Académie royale. The apparent absence of formal training in the use of pastel, which is such a peculiarity of Liotard's career, may help explain to some degree the idiosyncratic nature of his work, which through its intense naturalism and veracity cut through many of the polite conventions of eighteenth-century art; it was perhaps the achievement of an autodidact.

According to a biography written by his son, Liotard considered Massé an excellent painter but was disappointed by both the work he had to undertake and the teaching he received during his apprenticeship. There may well though have been other benefits that accrued from the time spent in his home, as Massé built up a collection which Liotard would have had access to; along with miniatures by artists such as Carriera, it included Flemish, Dutch and French oil paintings by Sir Anthony Van Dyck (1599–1641), Rembrandt (1606–1669), Jean-Marc Nattier (1685–1766), Jean Siméon Chardin (1699–1779), François Boucher (1703–1770) and Watteau.

As we will see, artists such as Rembrandt and Chardin were to have a significant influence on Liotard's future work and taste as a collector; Watteau also provides at this formative stage a fascinating connection with his commissions. Some while after his apprenticeship, in the 1730s, along with his brother, he was engaged to contribute to an engraving project by the renowned collector Jean de Jullienne (1686–1766) who engaged artists to make a series of prints after Watteau's paintings. Liotard produced one engraving for it in 1731, called *Le Chat malade* (*The Ill Cat*) [FIG. 4]. The Watteau painting it is based on is lost and the ambiguous verse beneath Liotard's print does not provide a clear explanation of the action, which appears to be theatrical and satirical, perhaps highlighting the foolishness of both being too attached to

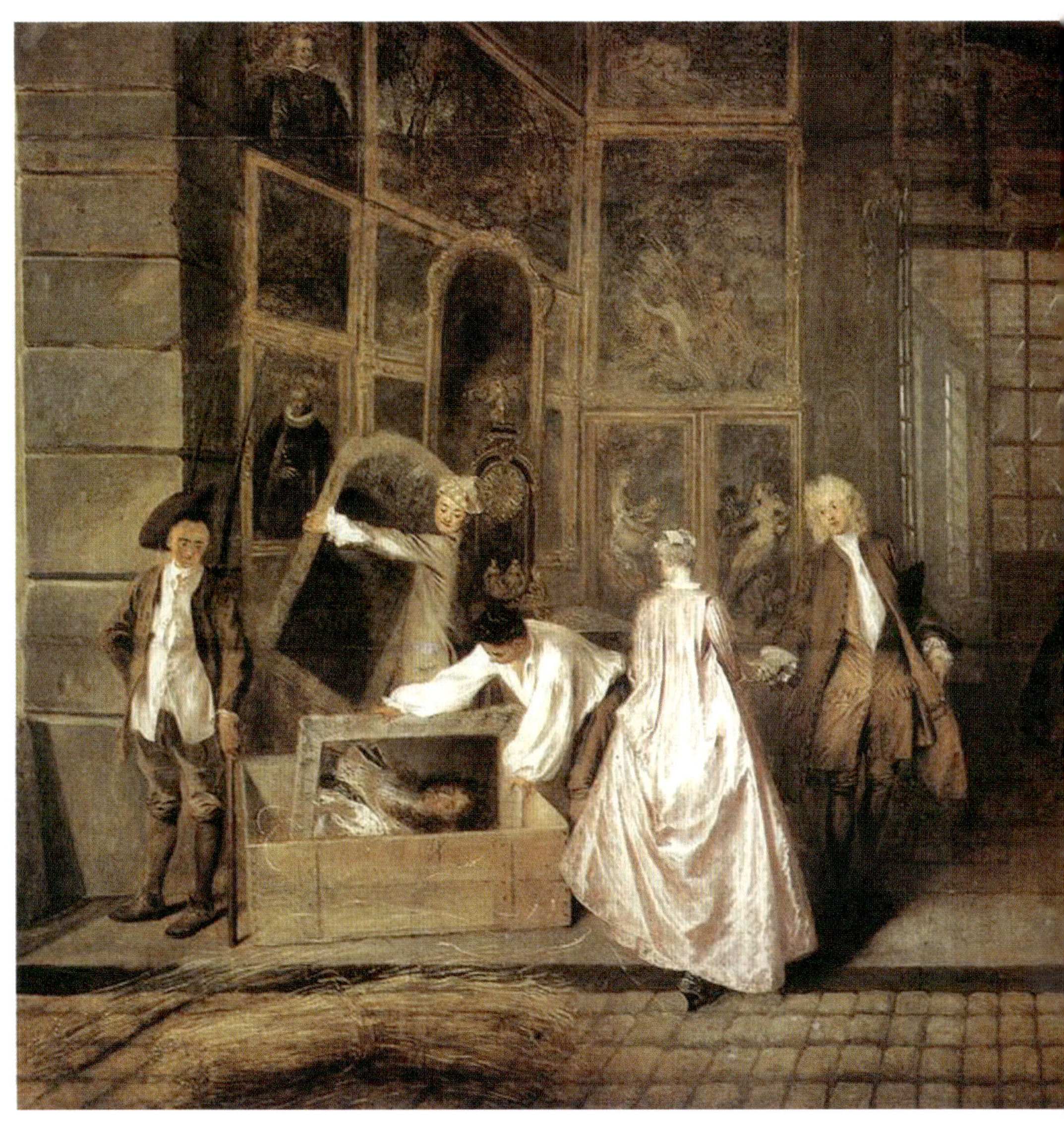

FIG. 5
Jean-Antoine Watteau (1684–1721)
L'Enseigne de Gersaint
(The Shop Sign of Gersaint)
1720
Oil on canvas 163 × 308 cm
Charlottenburg Palace, Berlin

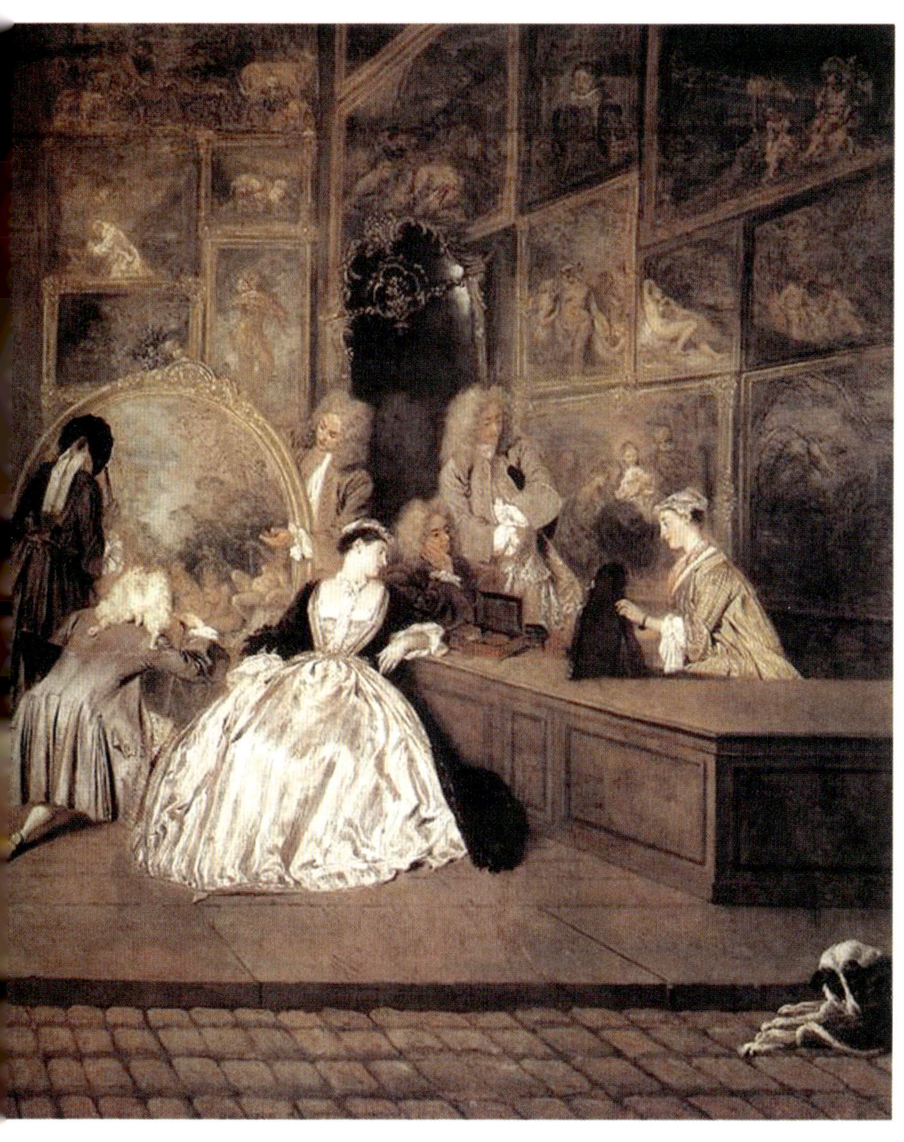

cats and of a doctor attempting to cure one. The elements of dramatic, slightly preposterous expression and humour seem to be the key appeals of this work, which is early evidence of the printmaking skills Liotard had learnt with Massé. His brother produced five engravings for the series.

The evolving nature of Paris's art market at the outset of the eighteenth century which Liotard formed part of is evoked by Watteau's exquisite final painting, *L'Enseigne de Gersaint* (*The Shop Sign of Gersaint*) [FIG. 5]. Edme François Gersaint (1694–1750) was a 'marchand-mercier' – an entrepreneurial merchant who specialised in selling works of art and luxury goods. His small shop was on the Pont Notre-Dame, a couple of minutes' walk from the Place Dauphin where Liotard lodged, and he was a great innovator, as he created catalogues that described works of art and provided biographies of artists. Watteau's painting depicts an elegantly dressed clientele scrutinising and discussing works of art, surrounded by pictures, mirrors, clocks and smaller *objects de luxe* to tempt a sale. Art is explored as a fashionable pursuit and subject of discourse in an intimate space, available to the bourgeoisie as well as traditional aristocratic patrons – this was the fluid class-crossing world Liotard had entered. Gatherings such as the one depicted by Watteau provided an informal and delightful arena for refining your critical faculties and were quite distinct from the grand formality of Paris's Académie royale, which had been founded in 1648. It was the most prestigious institution for the teaching and exhibiting of art and the font of most royal commissions. From 1667 onwards it hosted the Salon – an exhibition every year or two at which success was necessary in order to either establish or further your career.

In 1732, the year after his Watteau-inspired engraving was made, Liotard submitted an oil painting in an attempt to win the prize for history painting at the Académie royale. He was not, however, successful in his attempt to have his work accepted and in fact never became a member of the Académie. This was a rare moment of difficulty for Liotard in an otherwise remarkably successful career and it may not have been helped by the fact that he did not retain connections with his master Massé who could have influenced the outcome. It's also possible that even at this relatively early stage in his professional life his non-conformist, idiosyncratic characteristics were coming to the fore both as a man and an artist and they were not considered compatible with the conventions of the artistic establishment. He was perhaps more at home in the informal and fluid commercial world evoked by the *L'Enseigne de Gersaint*.

The painting he submitted is lost but known through old photographs. Its subject was an almost wilfully obscure theme specified for the competition – 'David and Abimelech'. This Old Testament story described how David was given by the priest the sword of Goliath, whom he had defeated. Such a history painting was considered the most testing for an artist according to the traditional hierarchy of the genres (or subject types) which dominated the academic perception of art in the eighteenth century, most especially in Paris. Portraiture sat below history painting, with landscape painting and the creation of genre (everyday life scenes) and still lifes further down the ranking of subjects according to this rigid scheme. Later in his career Liotard brilliantly experimented as we will see with genre, landscape and still life – so he most unusually touched on the full spectrum of possibilities available to an artist. But portraiture came to dominate his practice after his failure with history painting and was the key to his success.

Following his apprenticeship with Massé, Liotard journeyed back and forwards between his home in Geneva and Paris twice, probably engaging in family discussions about what form the next stage in his career should take. He seems to have been attempting to forge a distinctive artistic role; so, for example, in 1735 an advertisement appeared in Paris for a technique of colour printing that he had apparently developed – it was claimed to have the freshness of pastels and the strength and durability of painting in oil. This attempt at eye-catching marketing seems, however, to have little substance behind it. It might though have been inspired by the sort of works pioneered by an artist such as Jacob Christoph Le Blon (1667–1741), who is chiefly remembered for inventing a colour mezzotint printing process. Le Blon had settled in Paris by 1735 and two years later was awarded a twenty-year patent for his invention. A decision had to be made by Liotard to seek opportunities elsewhere and he made a risky but ultimately inspired move south.

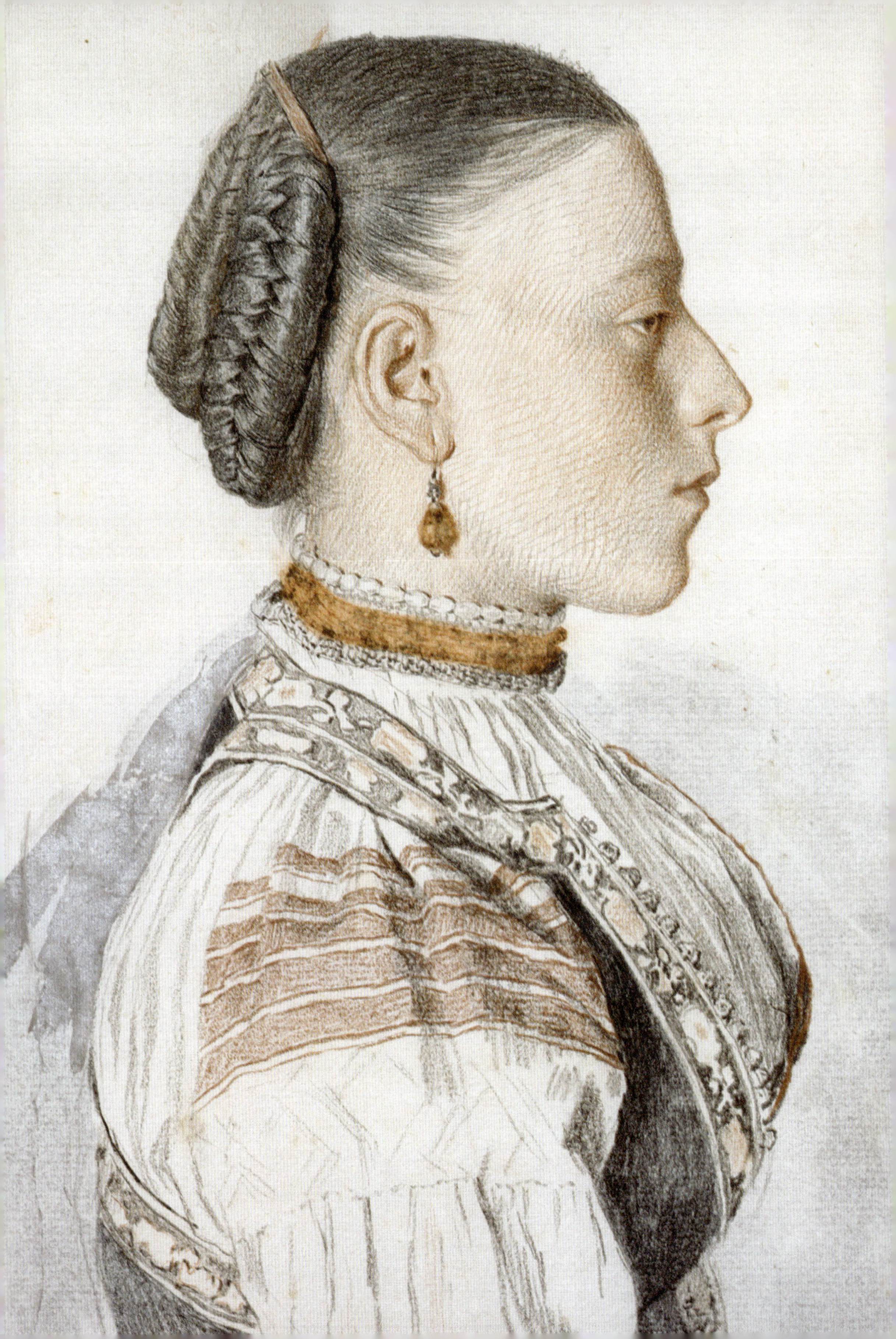

2 Italian Encounters

ITALY SEDUCED MANY TRAVELLERS from northern Europe in the eighteenth century who were drawn to admire its classical heritage and Renaissance glories. The motivations that drew them south beyond these broad inducements varied greatly and included trade, banking, education, entertainment, scholarship and the possibility of making acquisitions as a Grand Tourist. In Liotard's case it was a diplomatic connection that enabled him to undertake the journey, which resulted not in an illuminating study of Italian art but important opportunities that led to adventures and patronage as the prize.

The political map of Europe was being re-drawn repeatedly, with competing dynasties vying for land, prestige and wealth. Naples was conquered by a Spanish army in 1734, so the Kingdom was no longer a possession of the Austrian Holy Roman Emperor, Charles VI. In 1735, Charles, Duke of Parma, son of Philip V of Spain, was installed as King of Naples and Sicily. It was against this background of shifting alliances that in 1735 Liotard, aged thirty-three, travelled to Naples. He departed on 1 October and accompanied Philogène Brûlart, Count of Puisieux (1702–1770), a diplomat who later served as France's Foreign Minister. The Count had been appointed the new French ambassador to the Kingdom of Naples in July. Such travellers often employed an entourage, which might include valued companions – such as a doctor, guide (cicerone) or artist.

Naples, where Liotard stayed for four months, offered, as well as a strategically significant court, remarkable natural and man-made wonders to enjoy. Set in its magnificent, curved bay in the shadow of Vesuvius, you could explore ornate churches and a dense urban fabric; and journeys might be undertaken north to the royal palace at Caserta and perhaps further south to view classical splendours at Herculaneum (although Pompeii was not rediscovered until 1748). The city may have

Detail, FIG. 7

been the initial goal in Italy for Liotard, but in the following year, 1736, he returned north to Rome and Florence, so turning a diplomatic journey into a more conventional Grand Tour, which involved the great centres of Italian culture. We do not unfortunately have surviving drawings that documented what he saw, admired or indeed ignored. There is though a hint in one of his early and now rather abraded pastel self-portraits (Musée d'Art et d'Histoire, Geneva); it was created in Florence in 1737 and includes in the foreground a stone ledge, of a type used in fifteenth-century Italian portraits, that may imply Liotard spent some time looking at such paintings in the city's collections. It was an intriguing moment to be admiring works of art in Florence, as in 1737 Grand Duke Gian Gastone (1631–1737) died without heirs and the powerful Medici dynasty came to an end; it was agreed, however, that the family's great collections should remain in the city. The Grand Duchy of Tuscany then passed to Francis, Duke of Lorraine, who was to later become a significant patron for Liotard. The artist might have learnt a little from Renaissance art during his Florentine interlude, but it was Rome above all that offered enticing opportunities for new commissions.

The Papal States were at the time ruled by Pope Clement XII Corsini (1652–1740). His papacy was marked by some significant contributions to the cultural enrichment of Rome, including completion of the façade of the church of San Giovanni in Laterano, restoration of the ancient Arch of Constantine and acquisition of classical sculpture from Cardinal Alessandro Albani (1692–1779) for the Capitoline collections. When Liotard was in the city work was underway to construct one of its most joyous monuments, the *Fontana di Trevi*, although it was not completed until many years later.

Clement XII was painted by artists such as Agostino Masucci (1691–1758) and sculpted by the Frenchman Edmé Bouchardon (1698–1762). He was also depicted somewhat surprisingly by Liotard, whose now lost portrait was executed in pastel on vellum and based on two sittings. It would be fascinating to see how the artist might have added to the pontiff's iconography and what level of candour he could have applied as an ambitious but still largely unknown portraitist to an illustrious sitter in his eighties.

The papal portrait may not survive, but in Rome Liotard was also introduced to distinguished foreign residents in the city, most notably the Stuart Court in exile. He produced refined miniatures in watercolour and gouache of Prince Charles Edward Stuart (1720–1788) [FIG. 6] and

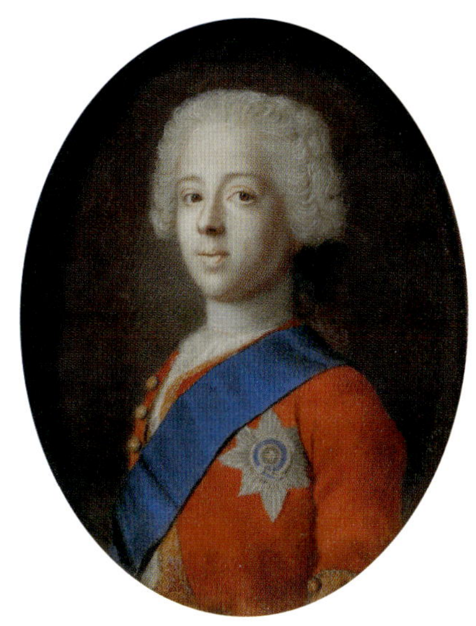

FIG. 6
Jean-Étienne Liotard
Prince Charles Edward Stuart
1737
Watercolour and gouache on vellum, 7 × 5.5 cm
Private collection
ACTUAL SIZE

his brother Prince Henry Benedict Stuart (1725–1807) – the first of his royal patrons. Portraiture always had a propagandist role in courts, conveying messages of continuity and legitimacy and this was especially the case with the exiled Catholic Stuarts, who used it to garner loyalty and support for their never to be realised claims on the thrones of England, Scotland and Ireland. A number of Italian and international artists supplied works to strengthen their cause and its visibility and Liotard's surviving contribution to this strand of employment demonstrates his ability to bring dignity and sensitivity to the portraiture of young regal sitters, which would later prove to be a key accomplishment that he could employ in London and Vienna. The sons of the 'Old Pretender' James Francis Edward Stuart (1688–1766) were depicted by the artist with some skill: Prince Charles Edward Stuart ('Bonnie Prince Charlie') was portrayed, at the age of seventeen, wearing a bright red coat and the Order of the Garter, eight years before his ill-fated attempt to reinstate the Stuarts which was thwarted at the Battle of Culloden. His younger brother, Prince Henry Benedict Stuart, was twelve when Liotard encountered him and is more soberly dressed in his miniature, although also wears the riband of the Order of the Garter – the oldest of England's chivalric orders and a key signifier of the brothers' claims. Eleven years later, in recognition of his sustained devotion rather than military ambitions, Henry Benedict became a cardinal. Larger pastel portraits of the brothers

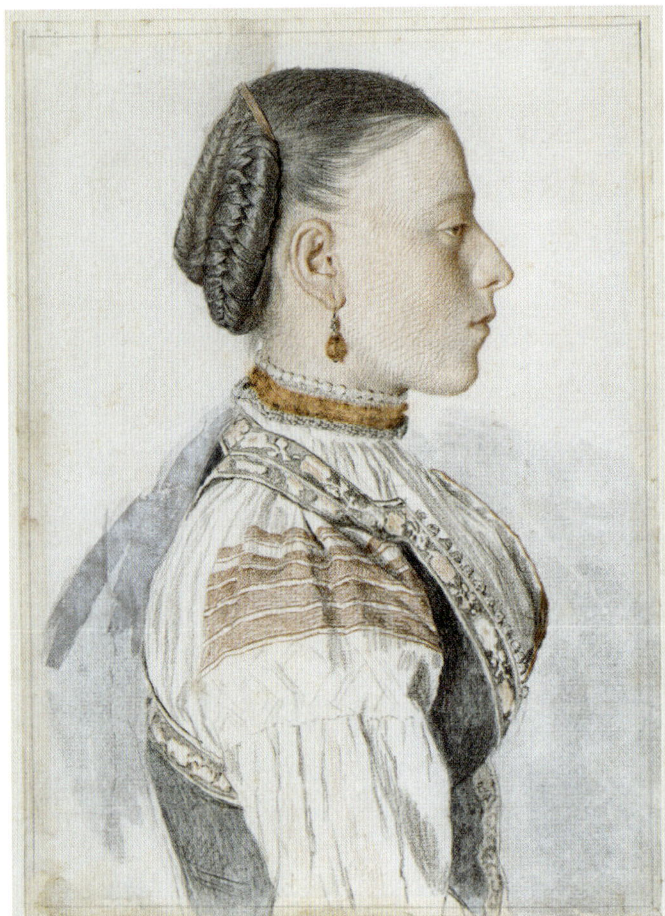

FIG. 7
Jean-Étienne Liotard
Young Roman Woman in Profile
1737
Black and red chalk with watercolour and pastel highlights on paper, and watercolour on the verso, 20.6 × 15.6 cm
Musée du Louvre, Paris, Département des Artes graphiques
Inv. RF 1386

were also supplied by Liotard, but the originals of these are now lost. James Stuart considered the portrait of his son Charles by Liotard a better likeness than the one supplied by Rosalba Carriera.

Few other works survive from Liotard's Italian period. We can deduce though that he visited the Borghese collections as he created a pastel after Gianlorenzo Bernini's (1598–1680) celebrated white marble *Apollo and Daphne* sculpture which was displayed there. Such baroque splendour did not, however, have any discernible influence on his later work. He also stood apart from the contemporary Roman artistic milieu, as he did not, for example, become a member of the artistic academy in the city, the Accademia di San Luca. His skills were nonetheless maturing, as one notable drawing amply illustrates because of the sophistication of its technique and subtlety – his depiction of a young Roman woman in profile [FIG. 7]. We do not unfortunately know the identity of the model, who is precisely individualised, although the drawing of her seems to be as much a study of costume and hairstyle as character. The artist used here an idiosyncratic approach which he was later to employ for other portraits on paper: on the back of the sheet he applied watercolour to plot the essential elements of the composition, with ochre for the face and blue for the outline of the dress. These colours in a very subtle way are just visible on the front of the drawing, as they can be seen through the semi-transparent paper. The main features of the study were then established precisely over them with black and red chalk, more watercolour and touches of pastel. The resulting details are extraordinarily refined: the embroidery on the woman's bodice, her earring which may be made of silver and amber, and the meticulous pleats in her hair are all delicately delineated.

What is striking about Liotard's Roman visit is that although he was only briefly in the city, he was employed by the highest echelons of Roman society and depicted figures at street level in his drawings – a pattern was therefore established which would serve him well later. Rome also proved to be a key setting for other encounters which were to propel Liotard's career. He is reputed to have visited a coffee house that was frequented by British Grand Tourists and while there overheard a conversation in which a copy he had made in Paris of the *Venus de' Medici* was praised. The discussion was led by the Hon. William Ponsonby, Viscount Duncannon, later 2nd Earl of Bessborough (1704–1793), and Liotard is supposed to have said: 'Eh! bien, Messieurs, je m'appelle Liotard et c'est moi qui l'ai peinte.' Ponsonby then invited him to join his party. The encounter sounds a little as though it is an exercise in self-mythologising on Liotard's part and the record of it is based on the account of his life he later dictated to his son, but it may well be true as visitors to Rome with cultural interests and ambitions tended to socialise together.

The connection with Lord Bessborough, as Ponsonby was known from 1739, was important to Liotard not only during his Mediterranean years, but also later. The two men met again during both of Liotard's trips to London (1753–4; 1771–4). Moreover, Bessborough was clearly a great enthusiast for Liotard's achievements, being recorded as having acquired in total seventy-two works by the artist. It is reasonably assumed that in view of this the two men must have corresponded quite frequently. However, a single later letter between them survives, signed 'Votre tres humble e tres obeisant Serviteur J.E. Liotard Gevene a 28 Juin 1763.' It is though a revealing one as it concerns a key technical aspect of the preservation of pastels. Liotard recommends in it the skills of a fellow artist from Geneva called M. Jurine (Sébastien Jurine 1722–1779) who was renowned for 'fixing' pastels – in other words providing a light, transparent preserving agent for them, that protected their surface and prevented losses. Liotard says in his letter that Jurine was as good at doing this as the Frenchman Antoine-Joseph Loriot (1716–1782), who was renowned as an inventor. Loriot devised a means of fixing pastels by sprinkling over their surface with a brush equal quantities of spirit of wine and fish glue. This is of interest in itself, but also seems to imply that Liotard sold portraits to clients unfixed and left them to make appropriate arrangements.

Bessborough was the son of the 1st Baron Ponsonby. In 1736, before travelling to Rome, he became a member of the Society of Dilettanti. This remarkable gentlemen's club was a significant cultural phenomenon in eighteenth-century London that linked British Grand Tourists, patrons, collectors, scholars and artists through a shared interest in the study of ancient Greek and Roman art and sociability. It was founded in 1734 and toasts at the Society's dinners were made to 'seria ludo' – to taking serious matters in a light-hearted spirit.

In 1739 Bessborough married Lady Caroline Cavendish, daughter of the 3rd Duke of Devonshire. He served as a member of Parliament from 1725 to 1758 and as a Trustee of the British Museum from 1768. Liotard remained on friendly terms with him for many years and Bessborough was not only a source of patronage but also proved to be an invaluable link between the artists and British aristocratic circles.

Bessborough's Italian journey can be plotted as follows: he arrived in Rome in December of 1736 and made visits to Florence and Venice in May of the following year. In February and March of 1738 he was then in Naples. The connection forged with him by Liotard was especially important for the artist not only because he had found an ally and patron in Italy, but also because the party of travellers he now formed part of wanted to undertake a journey to Constantinople and the artist was invited along. This adventure was made between April and October of 1738 and must have seemed especially exciting as it did not form part of a conventional Grand Tour, which would have been chiefly confined to Italy. The Constantinople visit was planned with three other British tourists, who would have provided Liotard with interesting company: Lord Sandwich, James Nelthorpe and John Mackye.

John Montagu, 4th Earl of Sandwich (1718–1792) had been educated at Eton and Trinity College, Cambridge. He became a Fellow of the Royal Society and the Society of Arts, but was chiefly later renowned as an army officer, being elevated to the rank of general in 1772. Before this he served as minister plenipotentiary at Breda, Aix-la-Chapelle and The Hague. His Italian tour at the beginning of his career had involved visits to Turin, Florence, Rome and Naples. He was apparently unsatisfied with 'the beauties he had met' in Italy and so was the chief instigator of the Constantinople journey, having 'bought a ship' and planned a Mediterranean voyage.

James Nelthorpe (d.1767) trained as a lawyer and like Bessborough became a member of the Society of Dilettanti. His Italian travels lasted from 1737 to 1739 and featured Leghorn, Rome and Naples as well as Florence and Venice. The last member of this party was John Mackye (1707–1797), who was born in Kirckudbright in Dumfries and Galloway, studied at Leiden University and also became a member of the Society of Dilettanti; he later served for over twenty-five years as a member of parliament.

Sandwich, Nelthorpe and Mackye were also linked by the fact that they became members of the short-lived Divan Club on returning to London. This was a dining club, founded by Sandwich and Sir Francis Dashwood (1708–1781), which was open to those who had visited the Ottoman Empire. The provocative toast given at club meetings was to 'The Harem.' The club only lasted for two years and was succeeded by the even more notorious Hellfire Club – renowned for the rakish and allegedly immoral behaviour of its members.

This curious group, now joined by Liotard, sailed in a boat called the *Cliston*. They left Naples in April 1738, visiting Sicily and Malta and then Greece and the Greek islands and finally reaching Constantinople. A stop was made at Athens where the Acropolis was inspected. Then Milos, Paros, Naxos, Delos and Lesbos were visited. Liotard made some fine drawings during this journey, which are primarily studies in red and black chalk of the ornate costumes of Maltese and Greek women, that show him formulating a record of local cultures, building on the Roman study of a woman he produced in 1737. His Maltese studies were used as the basis for at least one spectacular much later pastel, made in about 1745, now in the National Gallery of Art in Washington [FIG. 8].

This work is especially notable for the subtle way in which the clothing is depicted. The woman wears a bodice with dramatic winged cuffs and a matching damask skirt. Her overskirt of black taffeta and silk veil would have protected her from the sun. Details such as the blue velvet muff and sparkling bracelet and buttons demonstrate Liotard's unrelenting attention to detail; the points of light catching them and the pearl choker are established with drops of gouache (opaque white watercolour) overlaid on the pastel. The young woman wears ornate, probably kid-leather shoes with bows and buckles and stands on stone flags. Her clothes seem to be an especially refined version of the so-called 'faldetta', a form of women's shawl or cloak unique to Malta and the nearby island of Gozo and perhaps inspired by prototypes from Italy. Such clothes were conventionally made of cotton or silk and black in colour and were worn from the sixteenth century onwards.

Following the tour that Liotard's party made of Greek islands, they arrived at the ancient Greek city of Smyrna on the Aegean coast. Now called Izmir, this port was a very important trading centre for the Ottoman Empire. It was home to an international community of Turks, Greeks, Armenians and so-called 'Franks', a contemporary term used to describe expatriate French, Dutch and British traders. Liotard depicted some members of this cosmopolitan society, such as the French Consul, Gaspard de Péleran (1693–1747), his very fine drawing of whom is in the Musée du Louvre.

The next stop on the tour was Constantinople, where Liotard was to remain, while the British travellers he journeyed with returned to Italy. Undertaking a tour which extended beyond the well-worn routes of a conventional Grand Tour as they had done brought with it a pleasing degree of attention. In Turin in 1740 Sandwich was described by a fellow traveller as '... A man that has been all over Greece [and] at Constantinople ... and... talks... with a greater air than we little people can do that have only crawled about France and Italy.'

FIG. 8
Jean-Étienne Liotard
An Elegant Young Woman in Maltese Costume
c. 1744
Pastel with touches of white gouache on vellum, stretched on wood, 82.9 × 53.8 cm
Patrons' Permanent Fund,
National Gallery of Art, Washington
2002.121.1

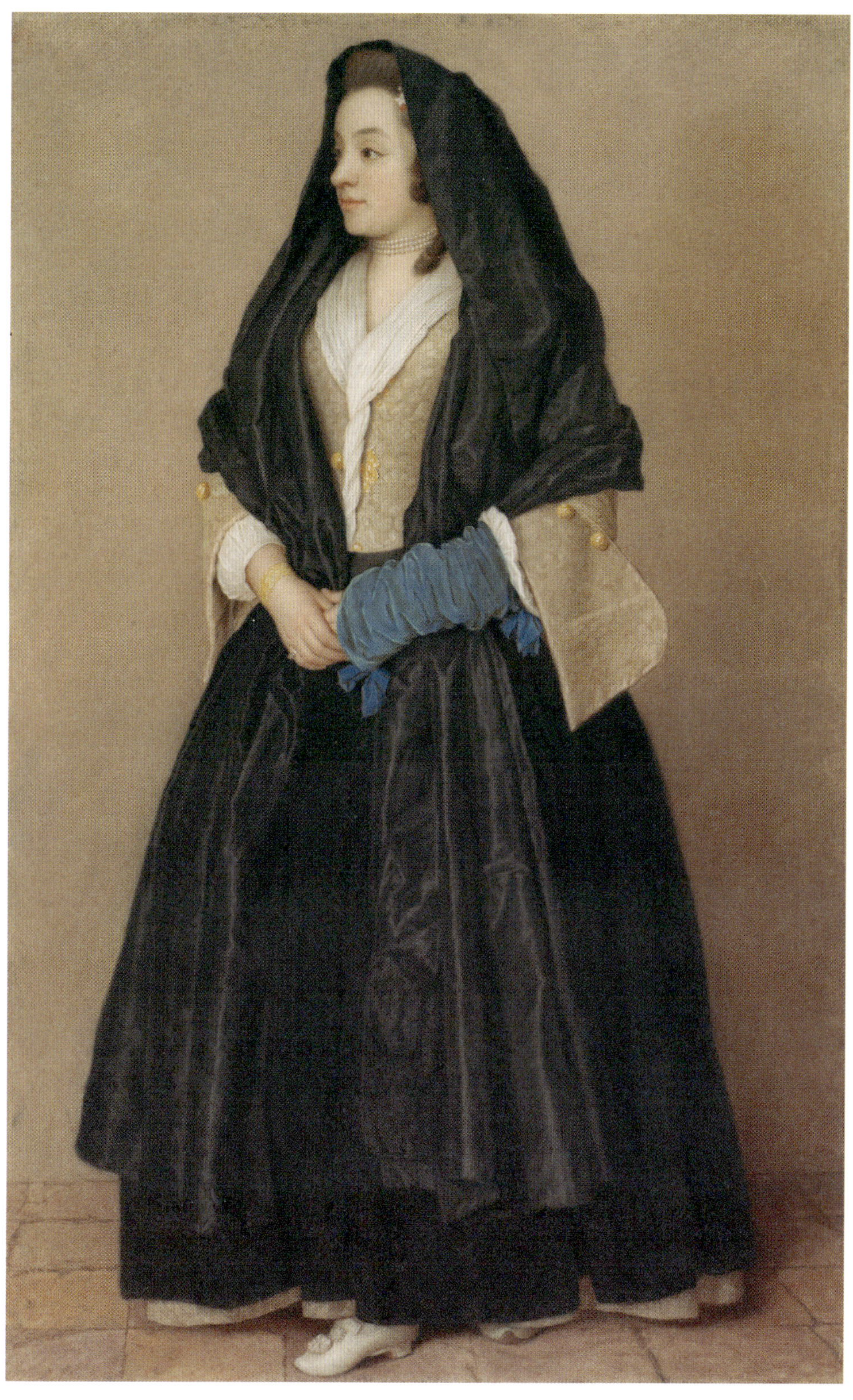

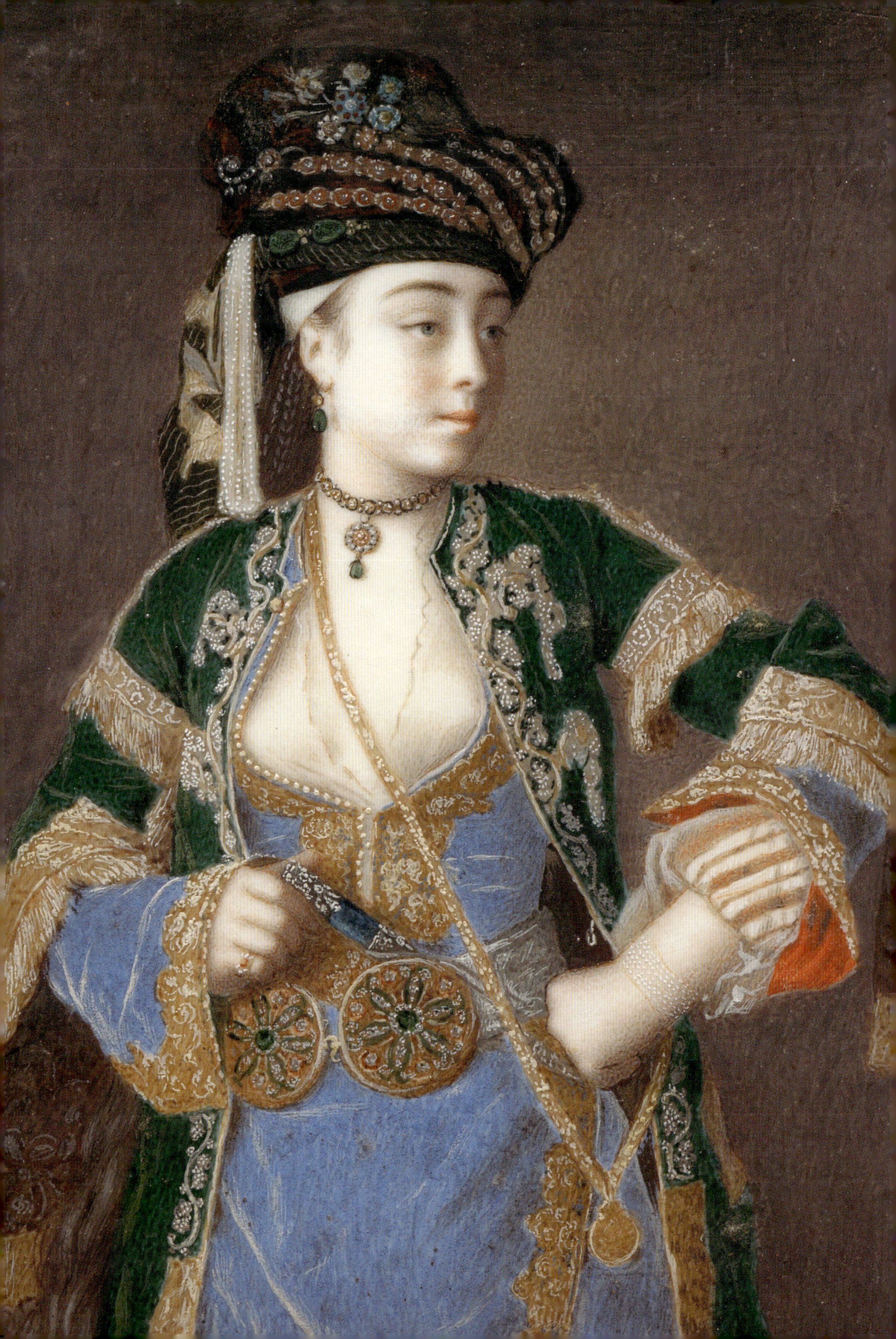

3 Adventures in Constantinople

... [Constantinople] far surpasses all ideas one may form to one's self of its grandeur and magnificence. From every part one meets with new objects of admiration. The diversity of colours that adorn the houses, the verdue of lofty cypresses, the towering height of the minarets... and the splendid domes of the royal mosques... far exceeds the most sanguine expectation...

This glowing and evocative description comes from a book published in 1799 that was based upon a journal kept by Liotard's travelling companion, the Earl of Sandwich. The experience of arriving in Constantinople evidently delighted the artist's party. As soon as they landed they sought out the British Ambassador, who provided them with lodgings. Sandwich's book, which was published a few years after his death by his chaplain, provides a detailed account of Ottoman history and the customs and culture that the tourists encountered. It also records that Liotard was instructed to:

draw the dresses of every country they should go into; to take prospects of all the remarkable places which had made a figure in history; and to preserve in their memories, by the help of painting those noble remains of antiquity which they went in quest of.

This suggests the initial planning of a more ambitious programme of artistic work and documentation than the surviving works by Liotard support. It also helps explain the splendid study of local costumes he had created in, for example, Rome and Malta. The drawings from life Liotard made in Constantinople, usually in red and black chalk, focused on fashions, customs and some details of interiors. There are though no known surviving studies of 'noble remains of antiquity' by him, although the appearance of Constantinople and the Bosphorus is glimpsed in one of the oil portraits that resulted from this period (see FIG. 12). Sandwich's curiosity about antiquities was presumably driven by his connections

Detail, FIG. 9

with fellow members of the Society of Dilettanti, for whom such interests were central to their ambitions.

The Ottoman Empire and its capital Constantinople, although not visited nearly as much as Italy, were an irresistible draw for European adventurers, diplomats, merchants and travellers in the eighteenth century. Ottoman embassies began to be sent across the continent in order to strengthen political ties during a period of relative peace, and one of the key consequences of the presence of splendidly attired representatives of the sultan arriving in Vienna or Paris was a heightened curiosity about Turkish culture and what were perceived as its alien and exotic and intriguing manifestations.

When Liotard was in the city (1738–42) it was ruled by Sultan Mahmud I (1696–1754). His reign was dominated by conflict with Persia and subsequent war with Russia in the 1730s, which was concluded in 1739. Daily administration of the state was conducted by Viziers, while Mahmud I was above all renowned for composing poetry. Liotard does not appear to have portrayed the Sultan himself, but he certainly had access to the higher and lower echelons of his court. He made for example drawings of Sadig Aga, who was Grand Treasurer of Mosques, and his brother Mehemet Aga. Both men were shown splendidly attired and seated on the ground, and their portraits were reproduced in fine engravings by the German printmaker Johann Christoph von Reinsperger (1711–1777). He also made a print after a Liotard drawing which depicted *The Dwarf Ibrahim* (Musée du Louvre) who was a member of the staff of the seraglio – the women's apartments in the Sultan's palace. Such dwarfs, along with mutes, were expected to entertain the Sultan's entourage; they held an exalted position in the complex hierarchy of the court and Liotard's study shows a mature man wearing very fine clothes.

This period of Ottoman life formed part of the so-called 'old regime' of the eighteenth century, characterised by a combination of some reforms and broader stagnation in political terms, which contrasted with the modernisation in the nineteenth century. The European embassies and trading houses and warehouses, where Liotard's stay must chiefly have been focused, were located on the slopes of Galata and Pera on the Golden Horn. The society encountered would have been similar to that seen at Smyrna – being both international and frequently changing. British merchants were active here, such as Francis Levett (1700–1764), whom Liotard depicted on a divan in Ottoman clothing and whose portrait was once again reproduced in a Reinsperger print. Levett's brother, Sir Richard, was Master of the Haberdasher's Company in London; together they established a formidable and lucrative trading network, that chiefly focused on the buying and selling of tobacco.

Other travellers from Europe to the Ottoman Empire were sometimes accompanied by artists, whose paintings and prints transmitted their encounters home and deepened further the fascination with what was perceived as an exotic and alien world. Liotard was not by any means the first painter and draughtsman to exploit such opportunites, but he made a significant and subtle contribution to this strand of escapist Euro-centric imagery. His most significant predecessor to undertake this type of work was the artist Jean Baptiste Vanmour (1671–1737), who, in 1699 accompanied the French ambassador to Constantinople and remained there for the rest of his life. Vanmour produced a long series of small oil paintings focusing on the citizens of Constantinople and notably documenting their dress. Engravings after these pictures were published in 1714 in France and became very popular and influential. Numerous editions in various languages, both official and pirated, were produced. It is highly likely that Liotard and his fellow travellers were all aware of such works, which informed a widespread taste for so-called 'Turquerie' – inventive, fantastic and sometimes crude designs in numerous media, from ceramics and snuff boxes to furniture and entire interiors. Liotard's contribution to this iconography covered some of the same ground as Vanmour, as he focused on interiors and dress and the seraglio (the apartments reserved for women in an Ottoman palace), but what is notable is the distinctive technical sophistication and careful characterisation that he brought to such work.

It is especially his black and red chalk drawings that illustrate these achievements. They include single figure studies of men and women, often with a strong focus on the details of their dress, some portraits of identifiable individuals, and a few sketched genre studies which record musicians and young and older women engaged in embroidery. Arguably the finest drawings are the more fully resolved genre scenes, such as Liotard's study of a *Maid Serving Tea* [FIG. 9]. Here a splendidly dressed woman reclines on a divan looking directly at the artist and us. The maid stands in attendance, in profile, in a pose which anticipates Liotard's

FIG. 9 (*overleaf*)
Jean-Étienne Liotard
Maid Serving Tea
c. 1740–42
Black and red chalk over pencil on two sheets of paper, 20.5 × 28.5 cm
Museum Oskar Reinhart, Winterthur
Inv. 528

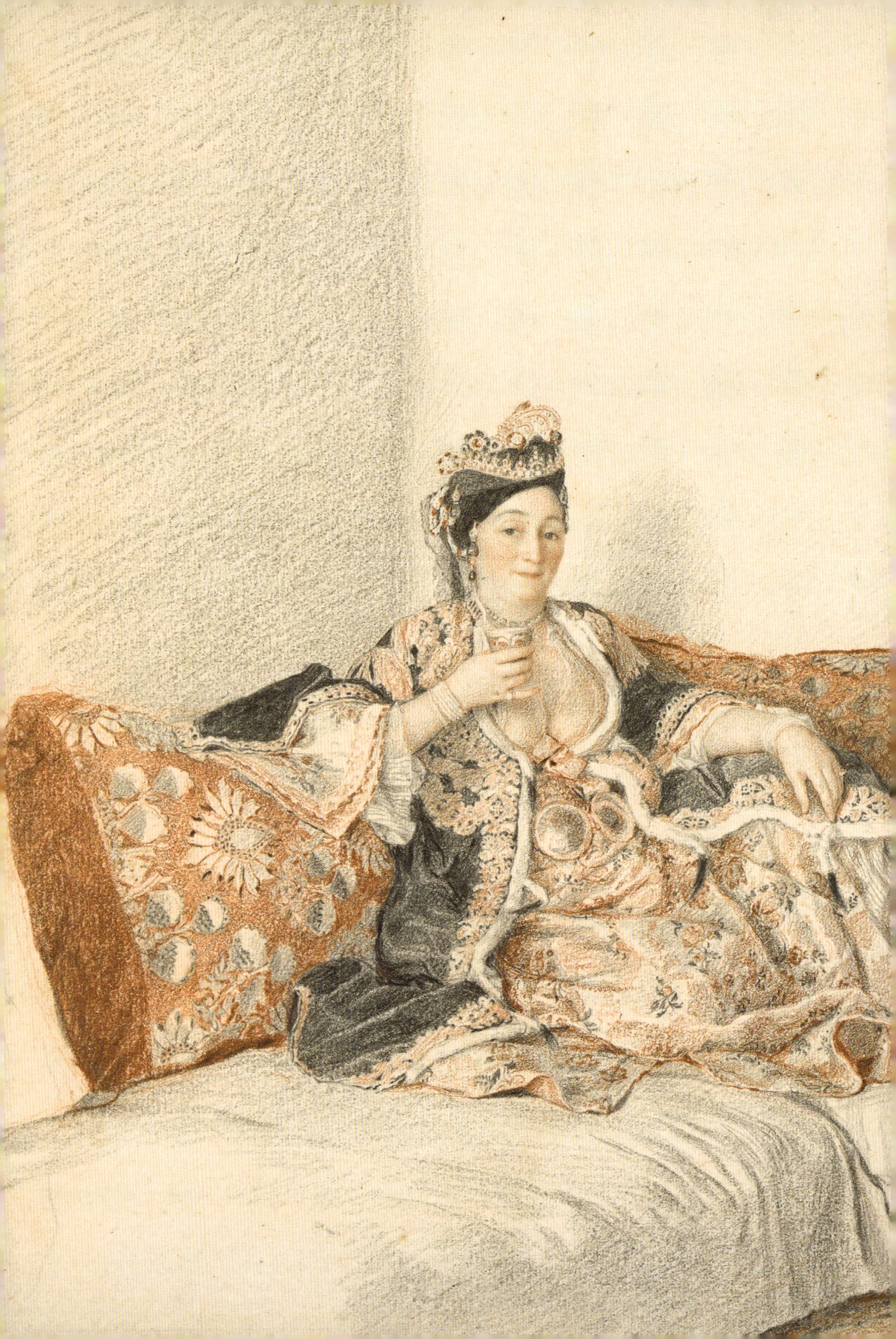

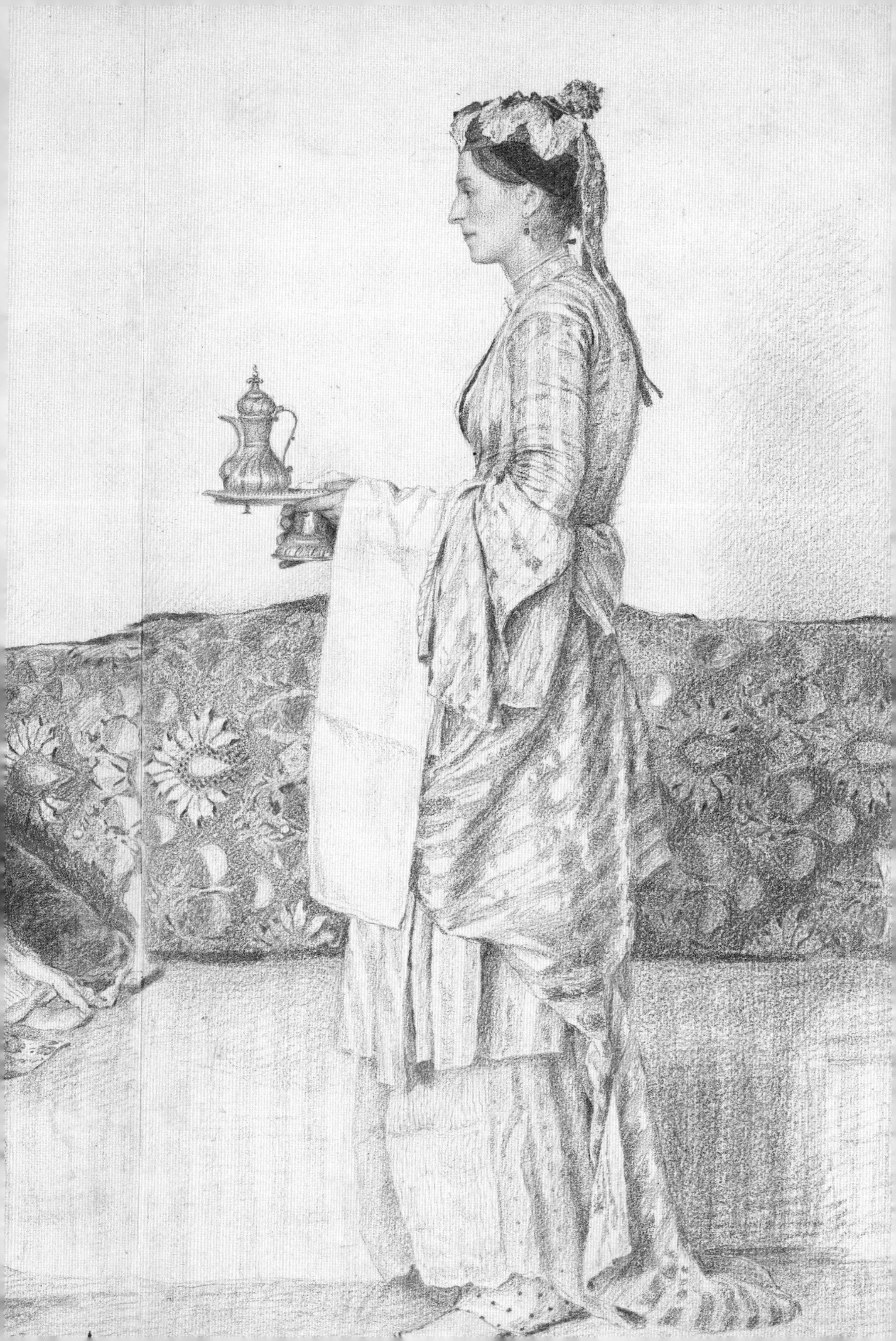

most famous pastel composition that was created about two years later – *The Chocolate Girl*. All the details of clothes, headdresses, jewels and sumptuously embroidered cushions are brilliantly evoked across two sheets of paper in red and black chalk, with the colour and tone of the paper when not drawn on acting as a foil, suggesting the texture of the walls and lighter elements of the fabrics. The drinking of tea was a ritualised domestic pastime in Ottoman households; the seated woman holds a porcelain cup of tulip design; the maid meanwhile carries a metal teapot called a *demlik* on a round tray, along with a container for sugar.

Almost all of the Constantinople drawings by Liotard depict figures in neutral settings, with plain walls, where the richness of elite life is evoked by details of fabric and dress, as is the case with *A Maid Serving Tea*. There is one surviving exception to this – a sketch which is more broadly drawn that may well be a study of Liotard's own lodgings in the city and is in the collection of the Musée d'Art et d'Histoire in Geneva. It is identified as such by an inscription by Liotard's son that describes it as his father's bedroom – presumably following a discussion the two men had some years later. What is striking is that the furnishings, with a simple divan, are altogether more humble than those in the other drawings of the period. When Liotard's party arrived in Constantinople, they are recorded as at least initially having lodged with the Ambassador. It might be imagined that the wealthy British travellers were offered grander apartments than the artist who accompanied them.

Literary as well as visual sources fed the European fascination with Ottoman life and customs. In about 1717 Vanmour painted Lady Mary Wortley Montagu (1689–1762) in Constantinople; she was the wife of Edward Wortley Montagu, the English Ambassador (1717–18). Lady Mary's observations about her experiences were committed to paper and shared in letters with friends. They were finally published in 1763 as her *Turkish Letters*, but widely circulated informally before then and recounted in detail the delights of visiting the public baths or the fascination of being invited to dine with the wife of the Grand Vizier, as well as scenes of 'indolent voluptuousness' experienced in private.

Jean Baptiste Vanmour and Lady Mary Wortley Montagu took to wearing versions of Turkish dress in Constantinople – a conceit adopted both by Liotard and his companions. The fashion for dressing 'à la turque' spread back to England and France and it was in this environment that Liotard continued later to wear his Turkish garb, thereby being both eye-catching and modish. Such cultural 'cross-dressing' as it has sometimes been called, also had a practical dimension in terms of comfort, as well as allowing for some degree of integration into local society. The cultural collision between European subjects and Ottoman settings and dress was explored in detail in some of Liotard's most ambitious works inspired by his Constantinople period. Among the most remarkable of these is a composition known in various versions that is perhaps most reliably given the rather innocuous title *Woman in Turkish Dress, Seated on a Sofa* [FIG. 10]. The fact that Liotard undertook to replicate it attests to the popularity of such a theme. He made a red and black chalk drawing of the subject while in Constantinople which was then used as the basis for later versions.

It seems most likely that the woman is not a local but a visitor to the city posing in Turkish clothes and surrounded by luxurious trappings. Liotard's composition has the air of a genre or everyday life scene, but a widely distributed and copied later print after the painting by Richard Houston (1721/22–1775) described it as a portrait of Mary Gunning, Countess of Coventry (1732–1760), one of the famous Irish Gunning sisters who was renowned for her beauty. This identification has been convincingly challenged, so we are left with something of a mystery about the precise identity of the young woman. It is possible Liotard was complicit in the confusion as he later mixed Turkish and European themes as a tactic to further his career and the association with a woman such as the Countess of Coventry who enjoyed something of a celebrity status in London would do him no harm.

What further complicates an already ambiguous situation is that another refined version of the composition (in the Musée d'Art et d'Histoire, Geneva) has an inscription by Liotard on the backing board of its frame that refers to two other women who in very different ways were to play significant roles in Liotard's life and career. The first is 'Mimica'. This is a Greek name, a diminutive of Dimitra. Mimica was reputed to be a young woman Liotard encountered in Constantinople, whom he hoped to marry, but whose mother prevented the match. This story comes from Liotard's biography later recorded by his son and is based on his reminiscences.

The other person noted on the inscription on the frame is Princess Caroline Louise of Hesse-Darmstadt (1723–1783). Later, between 1745 and 1746, Liotard gave her drawing lessons, and a splendid portrait of the princess at her easel by him is known in two versions. It may be the case that the frame of the *Woman in a Turkish Dress* was re-used for one of the princess's pastels and the reference to Mimica was simply a recollection of the artist's romantic encounter. A final complication to all this is provided by yet another version of the composition now in the Rijksmuseum in Amsterdam, in which the woman depicted has been identified as Marie Fargues, the artist's wife, whom he was to marry later in 1756. What all this means is that Liotard continued to use his Ottoman compositions long after his departure from Constantinople and was comfortable employing them with great flexibility to suit different sets of circumstances and keep alive all the reputational benefits he accrued from having made such a journey.

There can also be no doubt about Liotard's intentions to use this particular composition in order to explore and display a dazzling array of different materials and textures and his brilliant ability to replicate them in pastel: the silk and hand stitched flowers on the woman's dress, the dense pile of the carpet, the folded paper of the discarded letters, the leather book cover and the trimmings and mirror gathered up in the basket are all meticulously rendered. These details and the singing colours are given the quality of heightened reality as they contrast with a neutral backdrop. The contemplative pose, which draws on older images signifying introspection and sometimes melancholy, and the apparent abandoning of all the activities and distractions around the woman – writing, reading and needlework – may be intended to evoke the 'indolent voluptuousness' that was one of the derogatory tropes common in European views of Ottoman life to which Lady Mary Montagu had referred.

Perhaps one final observation about this resonant composition should be offered. Pastels allowed for the use of brilliant colours, but the fabrics seen in Constantinople made them a requirement – so there was a strong alignment between Liotard's favoured technique and the material world he entered in the Ottoman Empire. Related to this it's interesting to speculate about what degree of access he may have had there to Ottoman or perhaps Persian miniatures and manuscripts, in which jewel-like colours were expertly and brilliantly employed. Such works were often housed in *murakkas* – albums belonging to court officials. They could also be consulted in libraries and Liotard is known to have

FIG. 10
Jean-Étienne Liotard
Woman in Turkish Dress, Seated on a Sofa
c. 1752
Pastel over red chalk underdrawing on parchment, 58.4 × 47.3 cm
Bequest of Mrs Charles Wrightsman, 2019
The Metropolitan Museum of Art, New York
2019.141.16

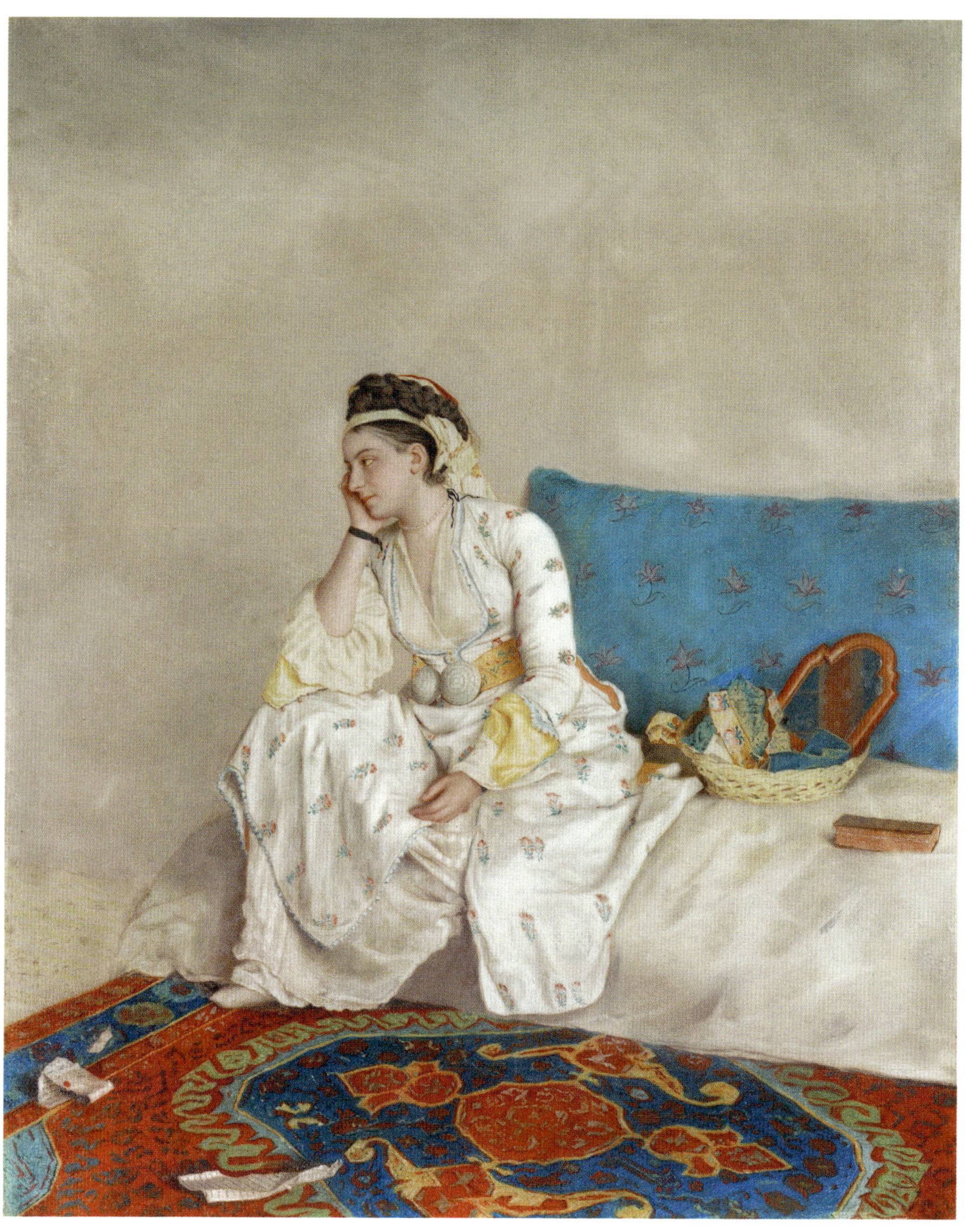

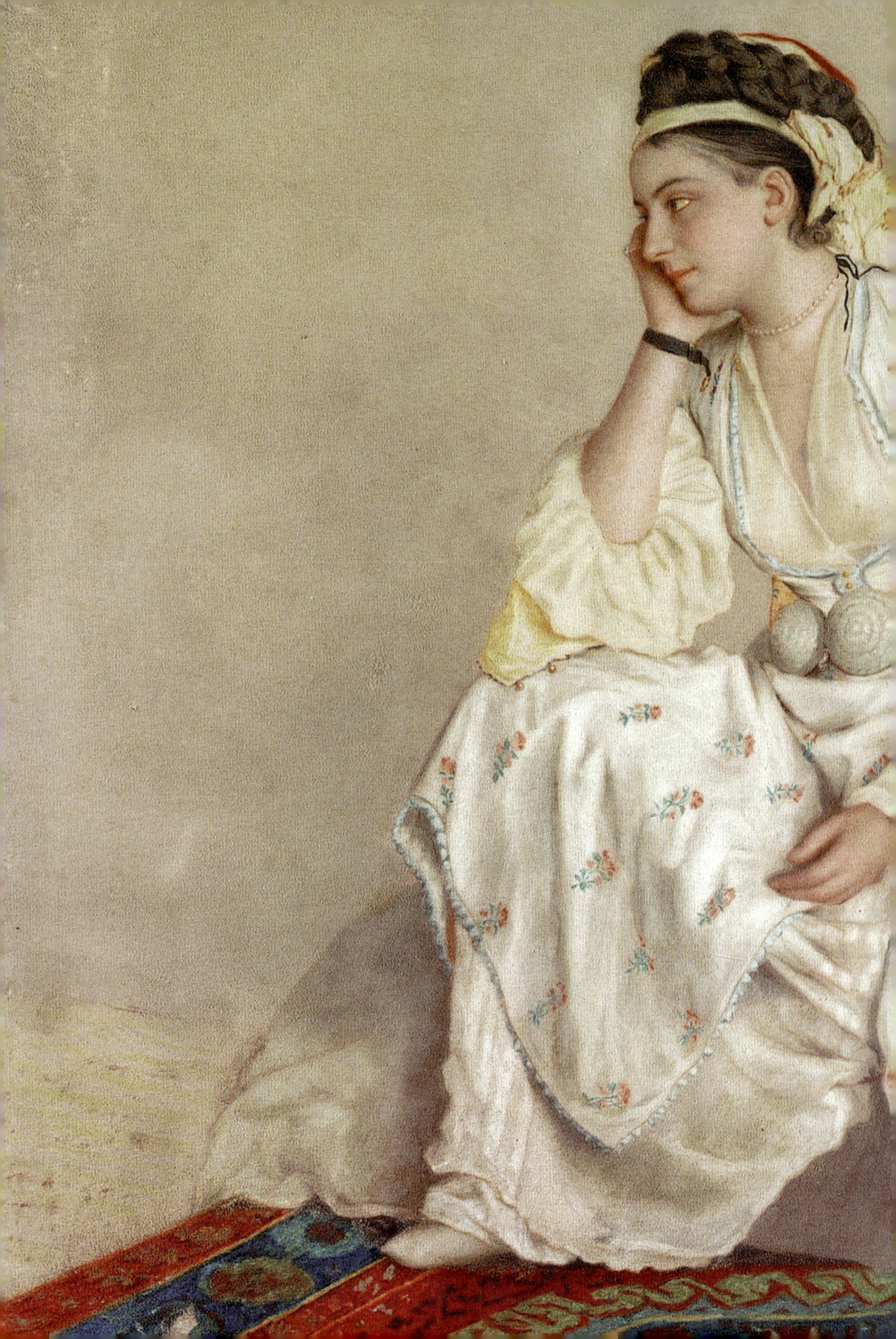

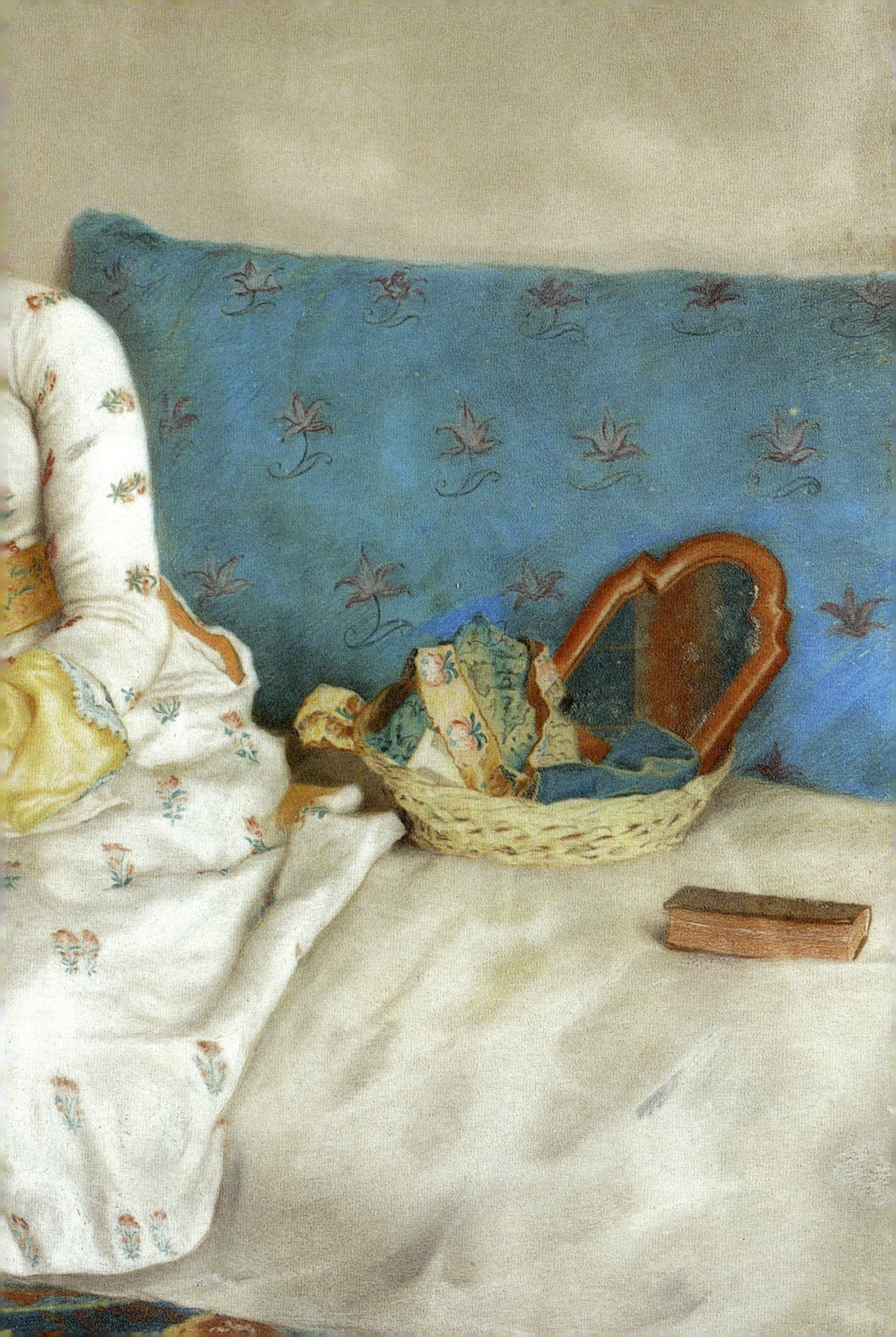

visited at least one library of this type in Constantinople – that formed by the Grand Vizier Damad Ibrahim Pasa. He made the visit along with the Venetian bailo (diplomat) Nicolò Erizzo (1722–1806).

Although he had such experiences Liotard's perception of Ottoman culture was inevitably an external one and limited in scope. He took some interest through his drawings in the material wealth of the new world he encountered – for example, as has been noted, by making sketches of a weaving loom and details of interiors. But most of his drawn and painted studies are figurative, carefully choreographed and focus on wealthy subjects. There are no street life or market scenes, of the type that so entranced nineteenth-century European visitors to Constantinople.

The main host of Liotard and his party when they arrived in the city was the British Ambassador, Sir Everard Fawkener (1694–1758) (see FIG. 24), who was to prove to be an important contact for Liotard, and future patron. In 1735 Fawkener was knighted by King George II and sent to be his representative in the Ottoman Empire. He arrived in Constantinople on 19 December and so had been there for three years before Liotard's arrival. Fawkener introduced Liotard to the British expatriate community and apparently persuaded the artist to remain after his travelling companions had departed.

Fawkener had pursued a commercial, diplomatic and administrative career and clearly had a capacity for sustaining friendships. He came from a family of silk merchants and his father was a leading figure in the Levant Company (which was granted its charter in 1592 by Elizabeth I and set out to regulate English trade with the Ottoman Empire; it remained in existence until 1825). He was paid in Constantinople by the Company; however, the expenses he had to incur because of his embassy led to some hardship and he asked to be recalled to Britain; this was agreed and he received permission to leave to return home on 8 November 1742. He was only supposed to take a short leave of absence but remained away because of the conflicts and chaos caused by the War of the Austrian Succession (1740–48). A new ambassador eventually arrived in 1747.

Earlier in his career in 1716 at the age of twenty-two Fawkener had been dispatched to Aleppo (now in Syria), where he traded with some success for nine years. On his way home to England in 1725 he stopped in Paris and met the great writer Voltaire; the two men became friends and correspondents. In 1726 Voltaire stayed in Fawkener's house in Wandsworth and in 1733 the writer dedicated his play *Zaïre* to Fawkener.

Zaïre or *The Tragedy of Zara* was a verse play in five acts, first performed in Paris in 1732, which proved a great success. It recounts a fictional tale of a Christian slave who was raised by the Sultan of Jerusalem, with whom she falls in love. Her father and brother are horrified that she will marry the Sultan and become a Muslim. She is made to promise to be baptised and to keep this plan a secret from him; the Sultan comes to believe, wrongly, that she is planning an assignation with another lover. He kills Zaïre with a dagger and then overwhelmed by remorse commits suicide. A tragedy of jealousy, intolerance and pathos, the play was translated into English and enjoyed a successful run at Drury Lane in 1736; it eventually became the most frequently staged adaptation of a Voltaire play in Britain. Its crude stereotypes convey an impression of the simplistic and negative views of Islamic culture widely held in Europe at the time of Fawkener's and Liotard's presence in Constantinople.

Liotard portrayed Fawkener in a red and black chalk drawing now in the collection of the Norwich Castle Museum and Art Gallery which encapsulates some of the peculiarities of the cultural collision that an embassy such as his signified, as Fawkener wears a silk dressing gown, presumably acquired locally, but sits on a chair that must have been shipped out from England; it is cane backed and decorated with a carved scallop shell. Such a piece of furniture is quite distinct from the divans that feature in most of Liotard's domestic drawings from his time in the Constantinople. Later Fawkener also became the subject of one of Liotard's fine enamel portraits (see FIG. 24) in which he is depicted in an entirely European mode.

On returning to London Fawkener was appointed Secretary to Prince William, Duke of Cumberland (1721–1765); in this role he witnessed the Battle of Fontenoy (1745) which was fought outside Tournai as part of the War of the Austrian Succession: it was a French triumph over forces led by Cumberland. Fawkener also accompanied the Duke to Scotland when he suppressed the Jacobite Rising of 1745 (whether Liotard had discussed with Fawkener his earlier encounter in the 1730s with Prince Charles Edward Stuart is unrecorded). That year Fawkener was appointed Postmaster General. His wide-ranging interests are further signified by the fact that in the early 1740s he was one of the financial backers who supported the founding of the Chelsea Porcelain Manufactory – the earliest such enterprise in England.

Although Fawkener was only drawn by Liotard during the Constantinople years, he proved to a be a key link with other commissions, such as a sensationally ornate watercolour study of the Austrian envoy to Constantinople (now in a private collection) and an oil study of the Englishman Francis Levett with the French Consul's daughter (Musée du Louvre). The artist's time in the Ottoman capital also resulted in the creation of some other particularly ambitious oil paintings. They are among his most spectacular works. The earliest is his 1738 three-quarter length painting of Bessborough (as Viscount Duncannon) [FIG. 11] who wears a Turkish costume featuring silk and fur and embroidery. It seems highly likely that he acquired these clothes in Constantinople and took them home to Britain as they reappear in paintings created for the Society of Dilettanti in London. A companion picture to the Liotard portrait was also created: a depiction of Bessborough's wife, Lady Caroline Cavendish (1719–1760), daughter of the Duke of Devonshire, whom he married in 1739. She wears an ornate, probably Italian costume and the dating of her portrait is a matter of debate.

More impressive still is Liotard's 1740 painting of Richard Pococke (1704–1765) [FIG. 12]. It depicts the sitter nearly life size and is Liotard's largest surviving work. The two men met in June of 1740 in the home of a Dutch Chaplain in Constantinople; they appear to have struck up a friendship as in July they travelled together for a short stay on an island called Büyükada a few miles south of the city; it is the largest of the so-called Princes' Islands in the Sea of Marmara. Pococke would have been very stimulating company as he was a formidable traveller and significant archaeologist and author; he also later became a Bishop in the Church of Ireland. Born in Southampton, Pococke toured England, Scotland and also became an Alpine explorer, but he was chiefly renowned for a four-year journey through Egypt and the Ottoman Empire during which he gathered information for his much celebrated *A Description of the East and Some Other Countries*, which was published in London (1743–45), three years after the encounter with Liotard. The book was especially admired for its insights into Egyptology produced many years before the more systematic archaeology of the Napoleonic era. It was illustrated with engravings based in some instances on drawings made by the author and was soon translated into German, French and Dutch.

Liotard's portrait shows his subject intensely staring at the horizon and wearing clothes he described in a letter he sent to his mother from Ephesus, in which Pococke noted 'As to my habit..., I have a blew linen garment lined with an ordinary fur & over that such a coarse great coat,

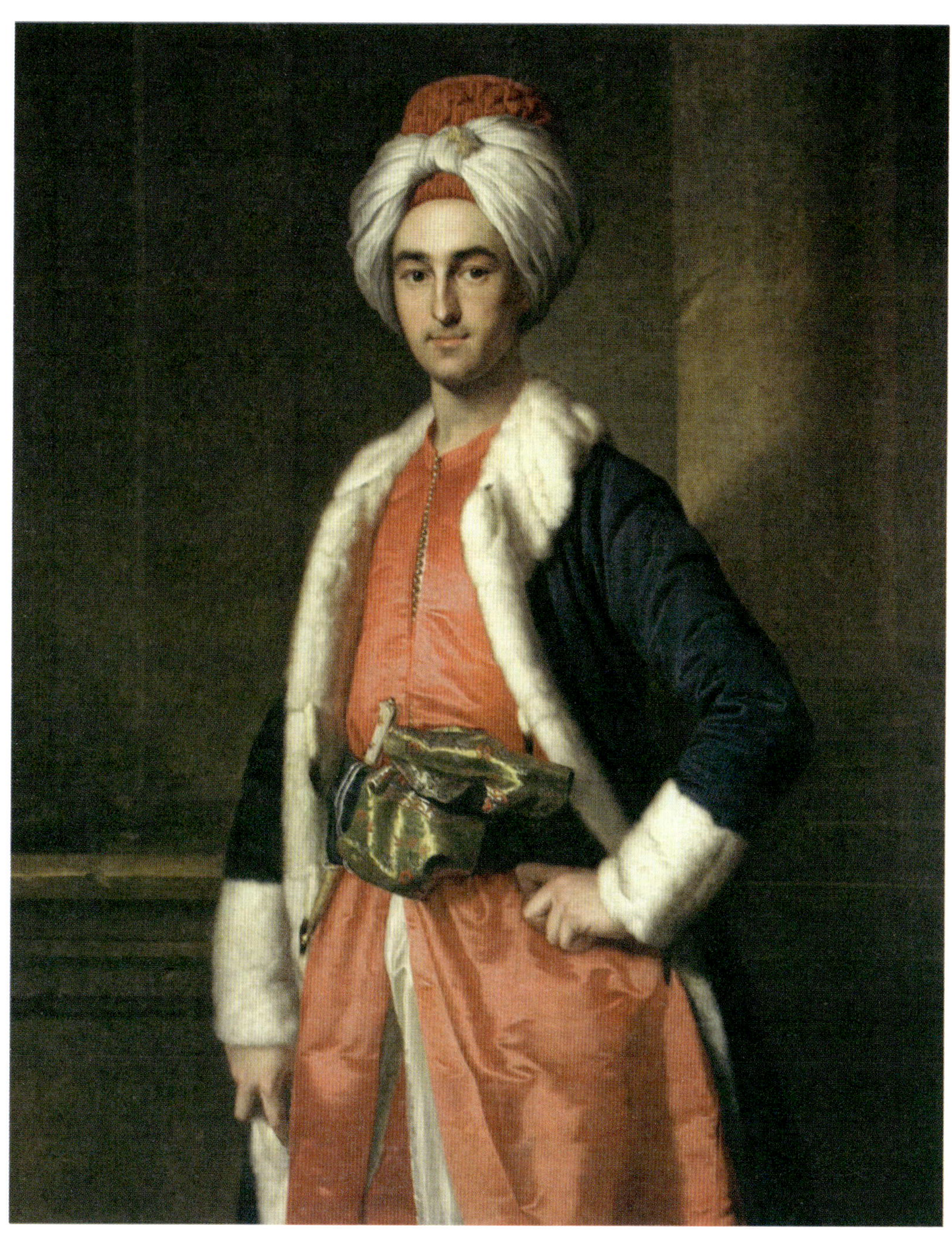

FIG. 11
Jean-Étienne Liotard
William Ponsonby, Viscount Duncannon
Oil on canvas, 124.5 × 99.7 cm
Trustees of the Stansted Park Foundation

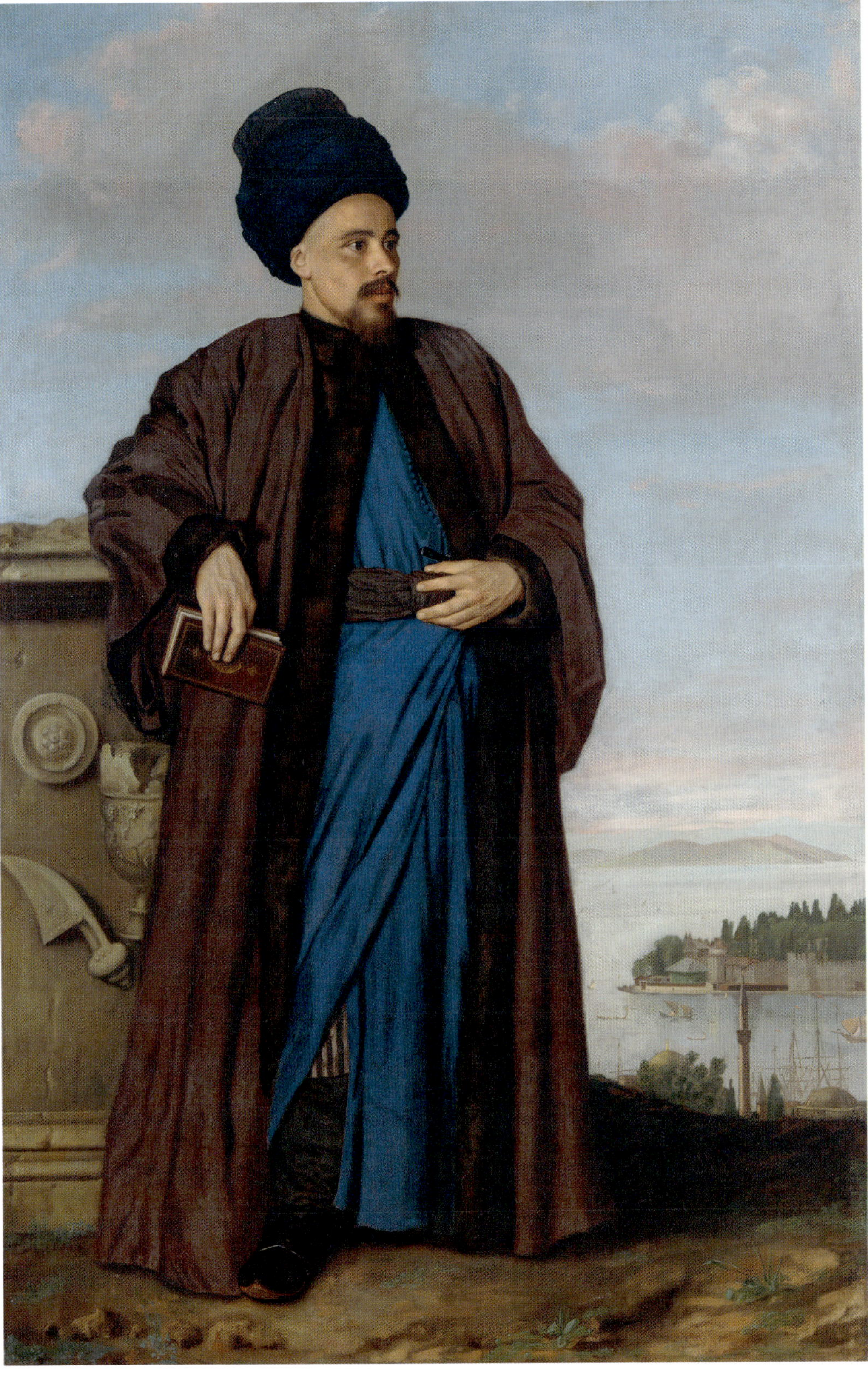

as the common people here wear, these girded about me.' He also wears a moustache and short beard, but his head is shaven and he sports a tall turban. Pococke is clearly depicted in Constantinople through the inclusion of the view of the Golden Horn at the right, where a minaret and shipping can be seen beneath a calm sky with pink-tinged clouds. He is also placed though resting nonchalantly on a sculpted plinth which is suggestive of the world of Ancient Rome rather than Ottoman culture. The form of the carvings ultimately recalls details found on classical buildings, such as the entablature of the Temple of Vespasian and Titus in the Forum. These types of objects (a dagger, jug and part of a shield) are connected with *bucrania*, forms of classical decoration associated with sacrificial oxen. The Roman entablature was well known, especially thanks to an engraving after it published in Paris in Antoine Babuty Desgodetz's (1653–1728) *Les Edifices antiques de Rome…* in 1682, which was reprinted in 1729 and 1779. Liotard did not follow the engraving precisely and may have used intermediary sources for his rather fanciful painted sculpture; the elements on it were also freely adapted by other, later artists. For example, they reappear in a different configuration in Hugh Douglas Hamilton's (1740–1808) Grand Tour pastel portrait of *The Honourable Frederick North* (National Gallery of Art, Washington). The carved objects in the Pococke painting perhaps also have another function as they might allude in broad terms to the eclectic collection he formed, which included antiquities, coins, medals and natural curiosities. His acquisitions were shipped to England to form a cabinet of curiosities and sold at auction after his death. Pococke's oil portrait was preceded by a drawing now in the Musée du Louvre, which established his pose, dress and the sculptural prop, and presumably pinned down the essential elements of the composition in a manner he approved of.

The connections between the Ottoman Empire and Western Europe, as well as resulting in portraits such as Pococke's, also resulted in memorable depictions of Ottoman travellers. Just two years after Liotard's work was made, a fine depiction of the Ottoman *Mehmed Said Efendi, Ambassador of the Sublime Porte* to France was painted in Paris by the artist Jacques Aved (1702–1766). Now in the collection of the Châteaux de Versailles, it illustrates the other facet of this period of rich cultural exchange.

FIG. 12
Jean-Étienne Liotard
Richard Pococke (1704–1765)
1740
Oil on canvas, 202.5 × 134 cm
Musée d'Art et d'Histoire, Geneva
Inv. 1984–22

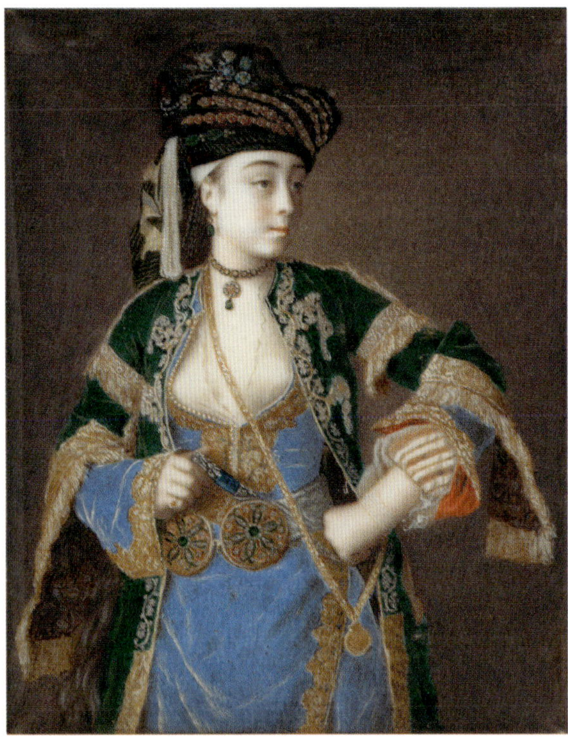

FIG. 13
Jean-Étienne Liotard
Laura Tarsi
c. 1741
Watercolour and bodycolour on ivory, 9.6 × 7.7 cm
The Syndics of the Fitzwilliam Museum, Cambridge
Inv. PD9–2006
ACTUAL SIZE

Probably a little after working on the grand Pococke portrait, Liotard created his smallest painting resulting from his Constantinople period – a miniature portrait in watercolour and gouache on ivory, which is just under ten centimetres high [FIG. 13]. The sudden shift in scale and medium we encounter here is typical of Liotard's ceaseless experimentation. The miniature's frame is inscribed 'Laura Tarsi, A Grecian Lady'. The subject was evidently among the artist's acquaintances in Constantinople, but whether she was indeed Greek remains unverified and further details about her life have so far proved elusive. Her three-quarter pose, similar in some respects to that of Pococke, allows above all a clear view of her splendid attire: her blue dress is trimmed with gold, while the green velvet gown features numerous seed pearls sewn into it. Pearls also adorn her wrist and hang from her ornate headdress, which includes embroidered flowers. A small knife rests in the sitter's belt and the overall effect has a slightly theatrical 'à la turque' quality. The miniature was brought back from Constantinople by John Manners, Marquess of Granby (1721–1770) in 1741. He was the son of the 3rd Duke of Rutland and after graduating from Cambridge undertook an Italian

Grand Tour, including a visit to Venice, as well as a journey to Constantinople, for which departed in April of 1740. He later became a member of the Society of Dilettanti, like the members of the party Liotard had travelled to Constantinople with, but was above all known as a soldier and the Commander-in-Chief of British forces. The composition of the miniature Granby acquired from Liotard was to prove useful to the artist as he created several other versions of it. These include one in the National Museum, Stockholm, in which the sitter's dress has been reworked in black and red. Liotard had landed on here another type of charming, exotic image he could freely adapt as an advertisement for his travels in order to meet the growing taste across Europe for *Turqueries*.

He continued to apply this tactic in the later 1740s, with works such as his oil painting of a *Woman on a Sofa Reading* [FIG. 14]. Although created in Paris it evokes Liotard's Turkish studies of dress and interiors and employs a model rather similar in appearance to the mysterious Laura Tarsi. The imposed European nature of the aesthetic and interpretation applied here is though clear when you look closely at the book being read and see that it is concerned with 'Virtue'. It is as though the artist formulated in this studious work a counterpoint to his *Woman in Turkish Dress, Seated on a Sofa* (FIG. 10) – which seems to focus on the results of a lack of attention and absence of virtue, as demonstrated by the abandoning of improving tasks. Liotard's *Woman on a Sofa Reading* also inspired some perhaps surprising echoes in later eighteenth-century British painting: its composition, with a reclining woman splendidly and exotically dressed, was re-used by Sir Joshua Reynolds (1723–1792) in his portrait from the 1770s of *Charlotte (Greville), Lady Williams-Wynn (1754–1830) and her Children*, in the National Museum of Wales. This seems to be an instance of an artistic adversary or competitor trying to outdo Liotard; it is indicative of the wide and enduring influence of his Turkish work.

Liotard remained in Constantinople for four years and must have created more paintings and drawings than those that survive, gradually refining further his impressive artistic skills. His presence in the city and growing artistic reputation provided the context for the next stage of his peripatetic career. In 1742 he accepted an invitation from Prince Constantine Mavrocordatos (1711–1769), a Greek nobleman who had been born in Constantinople. Mavrocordatos ruled over Moldavia under the Ottomans on four occasions from the early 1730s. Moldavia, north of Constantinople, was at this period a semi-independent principality chiefly considered a prosperous agricultural region and

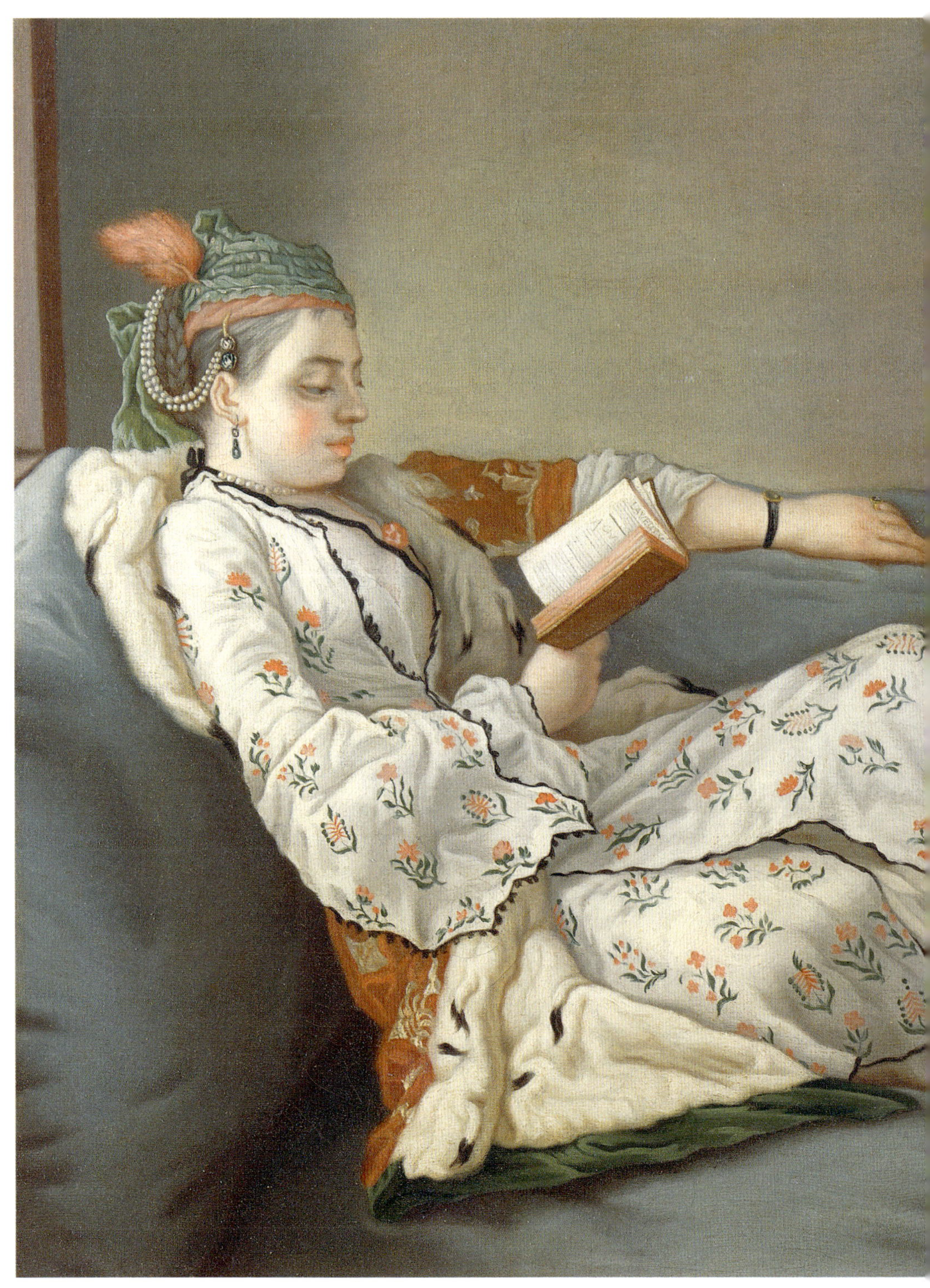

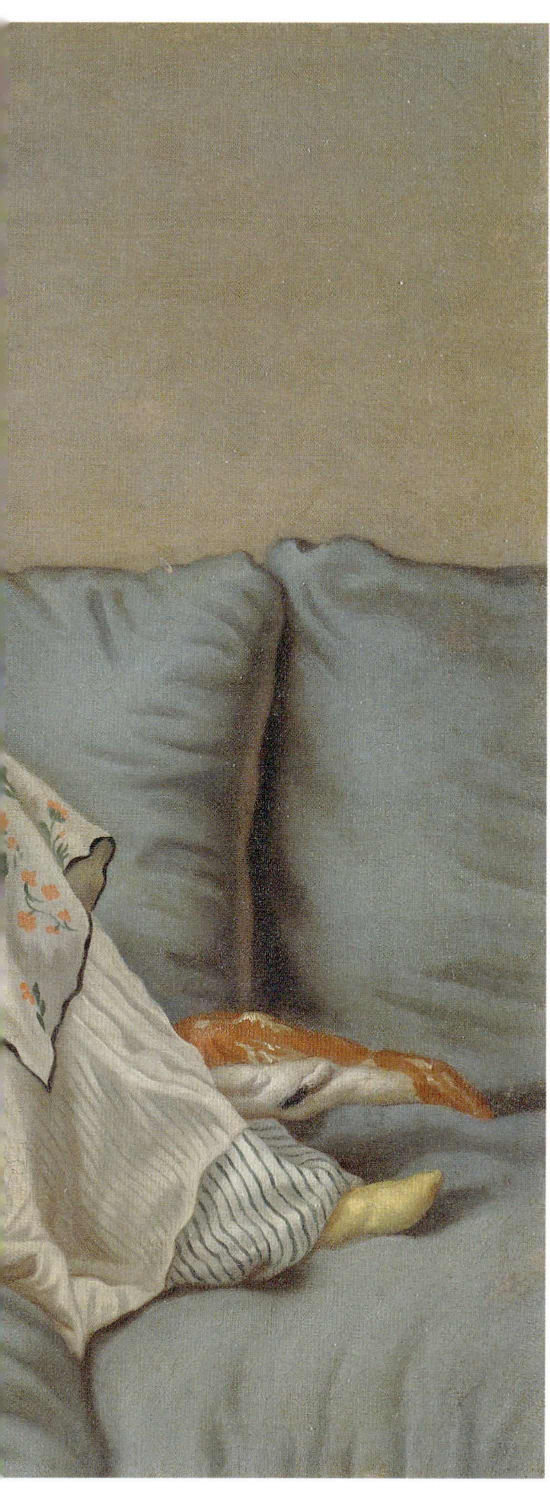

FIG. 14
Jean-Étienne Liotard
Woman on a Sofa Reading
1748–52
Oil on canvas, 50 × 60 cm
Galleria degli Uffizi, Florence

he was a reforming figure who sought to establish a fairer tax system and emancipate serfs. Mavrocordatos died after being taken as a prisoner in the Fifth Russo-Turkish War.

The capital of Moldavia was Iasi (Jassy), which is now in north-eastern Romania; the modern republic of Moldova borders Romania and extends across lands that were part of the principality of Moldavia. Liotard's journey north took three weeks and he spent ten months in Iasi depicting members of the prince's court. This was a daring and innovative assignment as no other Western European artists had visited the principality before him and an indication of his patron's liberal outlook. The drawings from this period once again include sensitive character studies, along with remarkably detailed depictions of the splendid clothes worn by Mavrocordatos's entourage, which illustrate the artist's enduring fascination with magnificent fashions. One example demonstrates this especially well: his portrait, now in Berlin, of the prince's wife, Ekaterina, (*c.* 1715–1775) [FIG. 15], whom he married in 1731. This refined drawing shows her enthroned, in her late twenties, wearing jewels at her neck and waist, as well as rings with diamonds and rubies. The layered and richly fur-lined gown, along with a fur hat all convey her status. Her static, perhaps resigned expression, was presumably considered decorous but may have reflected the length of time of the sittings. The artist took great pains over the portrait, intending no doubt to impress his new patrons, and, for example, reworking the area of the composition which included the princess's right arm, where a section of the paper was cut out and replaced. The result marks an interesting stage in the evolution of Liotard's royal portraiture, which had begun tentatively with the exiled Stuart court in Rome, here explored in particular symbols of almost Byzantine splendour, and was to move on, especially in London, to include works of remarkable informality. The Moldavian drawings are also very important from a documentary perspective as there are virtually no other surviving images of the court at this Ottoman outpost.

Liotard portrayed the Prince himself in a drawing that does not survive. It was used as the basis for an engraving produced in Paris by Georg Friedrich Schmidt (1712–1775). In it Mavrocordatos wears a fur hat and beard. As well as acquiring knowledge of a little-known region of the Ottoman Empire, Liotard at this period also added to his growing personal repertoire of exotic dress as he, like his patron, adopted the local Moldavian custom of growing a long beard and wearing a fur hat.

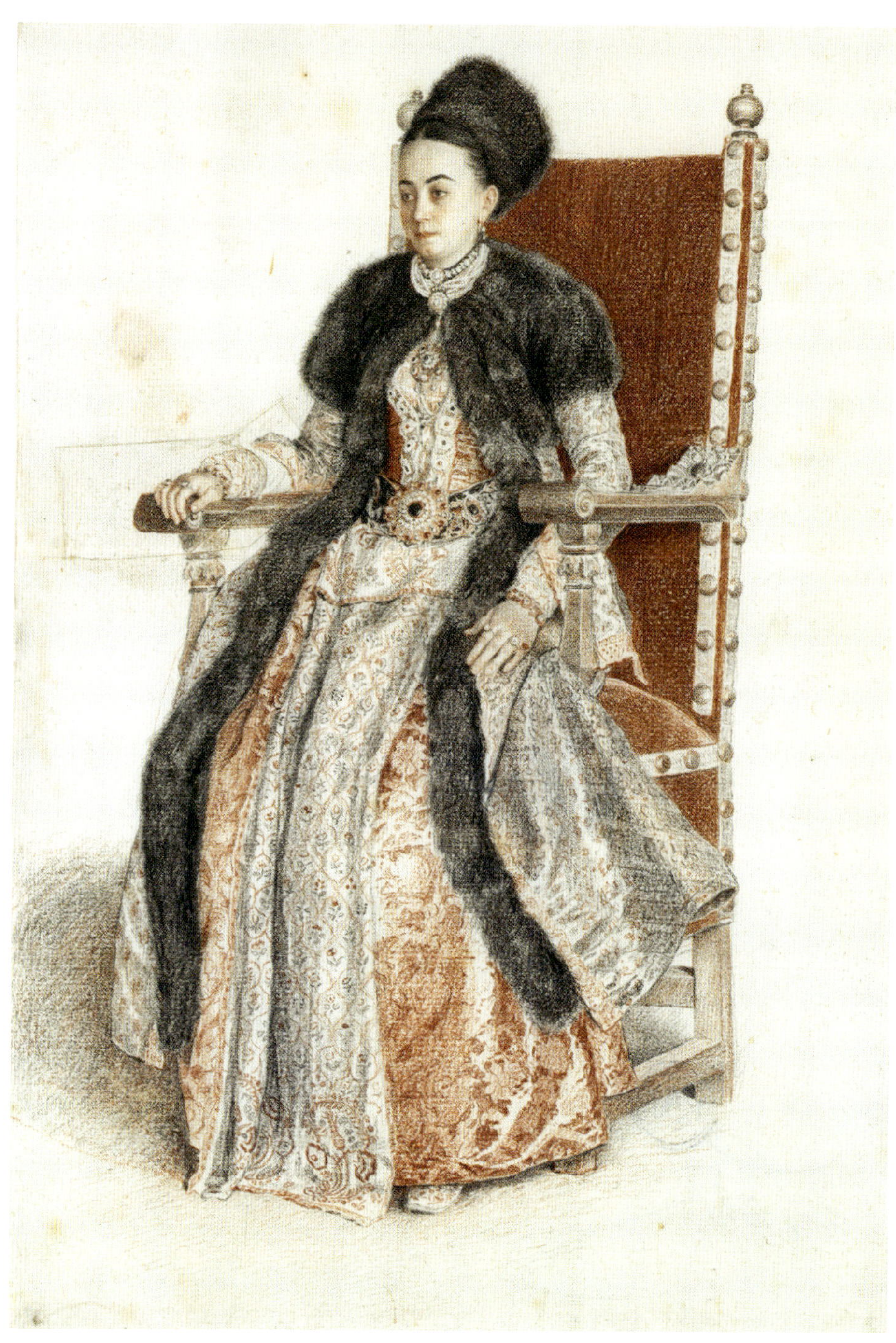

FIG. 15
Jean-Étienne Liotard
Ekaterina Mavrocordato (c. 1715–1775)
1742–3
Red and black chalk on paper, 21.7 × 15 cm
Kupferstichkabinett, Staatliche Museen zu Berlin
Inv. KDZ 1626

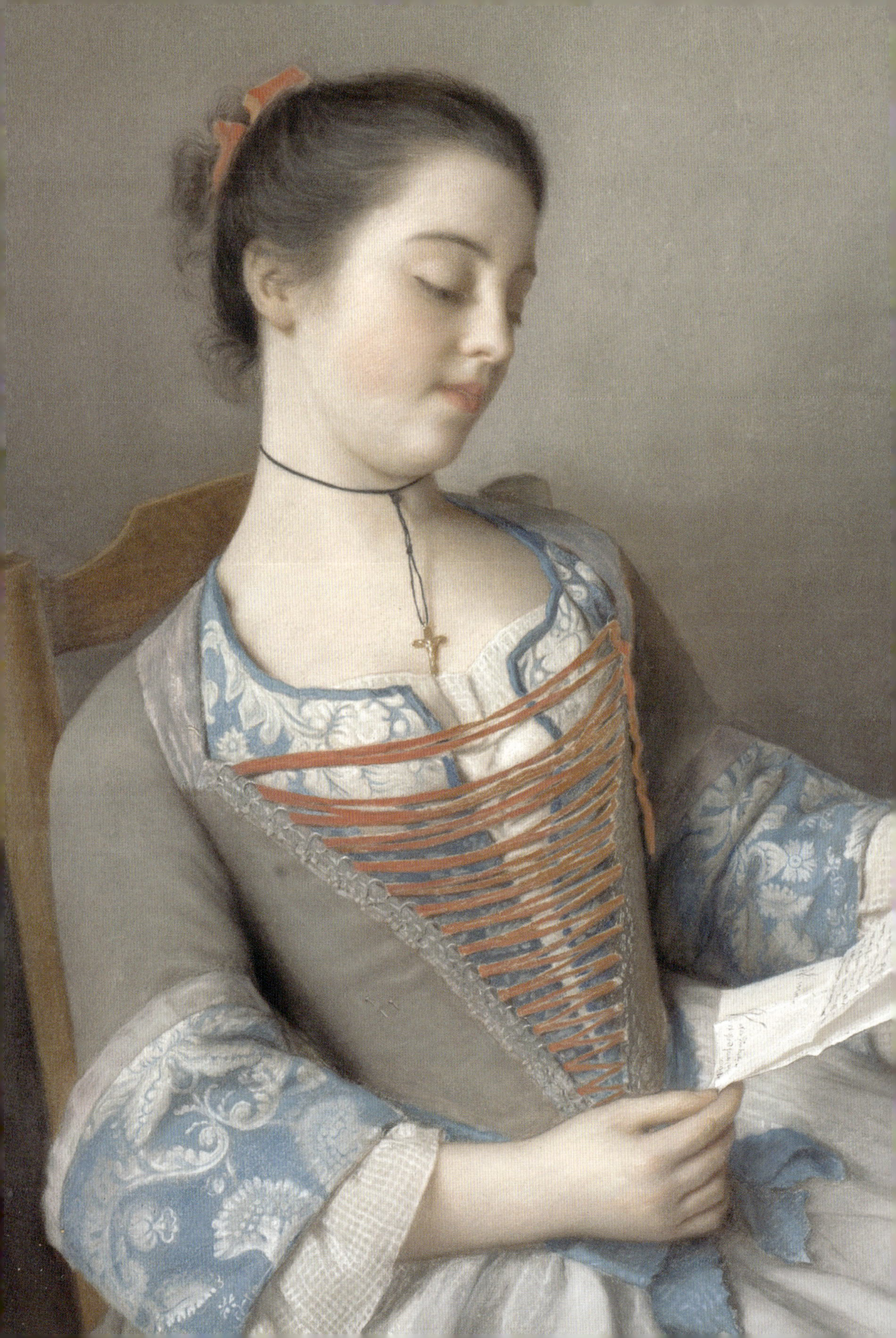

4 New Ambitions
Vienna, Venice and Paris

THE 1740S WAS A DECADE when Liotard established some of his most prestigious and inspirational connections with the courts and intelligentsia of Europe. They attest to an ambition and social deftness which few other artists of the era could match. He continued criss-crossing the continent in order to pursue opportunities for commissions and sales. He travelled from Moldavia through Transylvania and Hungary to Vienna, arriving in September of 1743. Liotard met with success quickly in the capital of the Hapsburg empire, where he stayed for about two years. His exotic garb and recent Ottoman experiences no doubt prompted curiosity about his life and skills; this cultural interest was though quite distinct from the perceptions of the Ottoman Empire which had been engendered in the previous century, as back in 1683 the Ottomans had overrun Hungary and laid siege to Vienna, so presenting an alarming military threat to its security.

Liotard soon portrayed Maria Theresa (1717–1780) and her husband Francis Stephen of Lorraine (1708–1765), the future Holy Roman Emperor. Maria Theresa had been ruler of the vast and disparate Hapsburg domains since 1740. They stretched from the Netherlands to Parma, Mantua and Milan, and across Austria, Hungary, Bohemia, Transylvania and Croatia. She gradually succeeded in unifying her lands and establishing her brand of absolutism through a fierce defence of Catholicism, centralising her civil service and military, and defining enemies of her state, most especially Prussia.

An interest in pastel portraiture in Vienna may have been established back in 1730 when Rosalba Carriera visited the city. Liotard's pastel portrait of Maria Theresa [FIG. 16] certainly proved to be especially well received. Her powdered face and hair are brightly illuminated before a dark backdrop; while the fur-trimmed gold dress, pearls at her elbow and diamond brooch all create an impression of great opulence and dignity.

Detail, FIG. 18

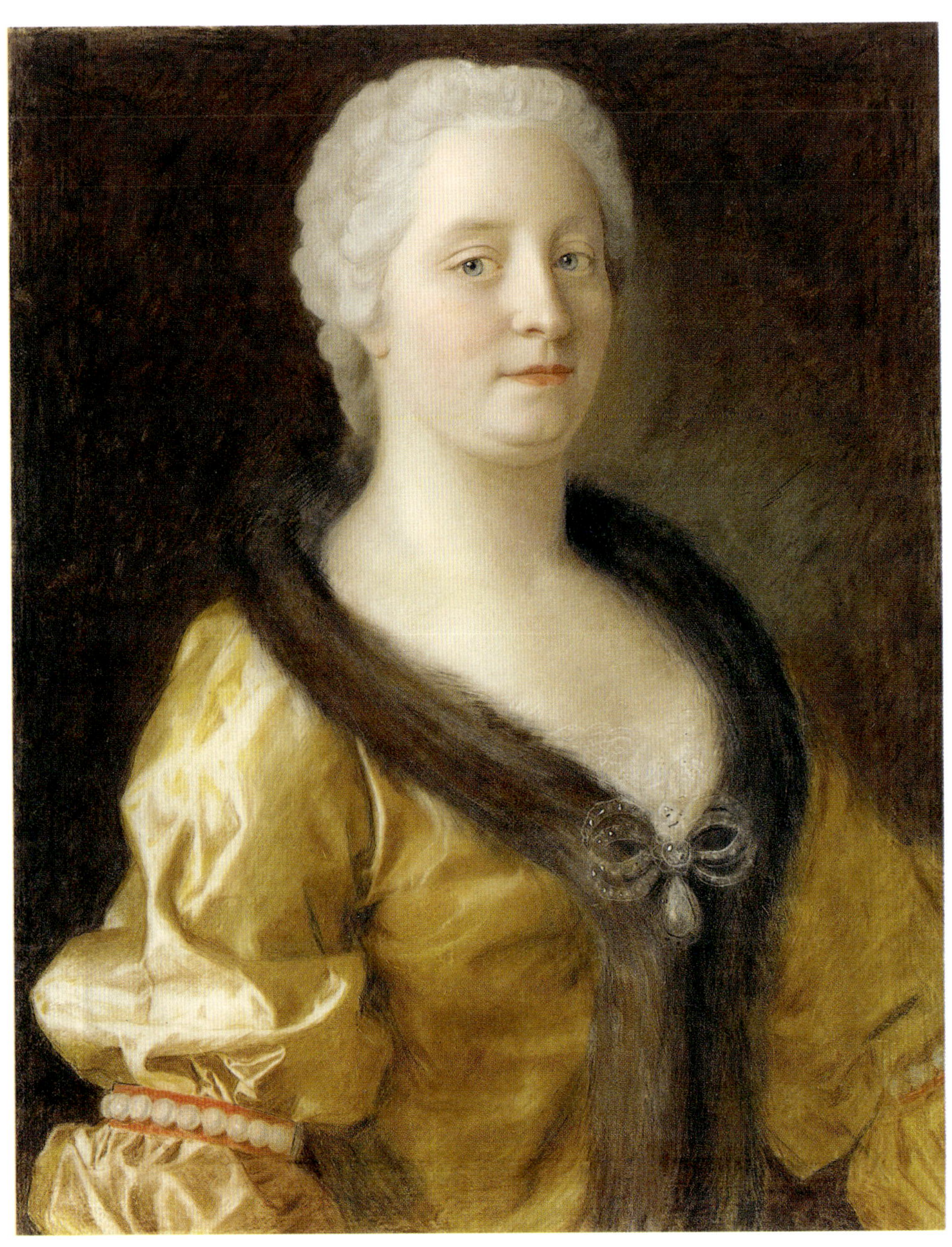

FIG. 16
Jean-Étienne Liotard
Maria Theresa (1717–1780) in a Fur-Trimmed Gown
1743
Pastel on vellum, 62 × 49.4 cm
Oesterreichische Nationalbank
Inv. No. 220002441

This portrait established a prototype that was widely reproduced in various media and as such played a role in conveying Maria Theresa's authority across her lands. Focusing on her face, it was a portrait in quite a different mode to the grandiloquent court portraiture with more florid and numerous attributes the Hapsburgs were accustomed to, which was chiefly inspired by French precedents. It marked the beginning of a fruitful relationship with her for Liotard which led to other commissions, acquisitions and her taking a close interest in his family. Her husband Francis Stephen who had been Grand Duke of Tuscany since 1737 also clearly had a high regard for Liotard's accomplishments and commissioned a self-portrait from the artist for the collection of such works in the Uffizi, Florence, which shows he continued to wear both the fur hat and beard in Vienna that he had adopted at the Moldavian court. It also has a large, bold inscription, which declares his name, Genevan origins and alter ego as 'Le Peintre Turc' – clearly Liotard wanted it to have an impact in the context of the famous collection of self-portraits in Florence. Much later in 1760 he was invited to provide some biographical information for an illustrated catalogue of the Uffizi self-portraits; he noted his chief works included such studies, as well as some of his great mature pastels that addressed genre subjects.

Portraiture remained the cornerstone of his practice, but Liotard's most famous work, which dates from the mid-1740s, was a remarkable genre scene. His *The Chocolate Girl* [FIG. 17], which is often described as *La Belle Chocolatière,* is tantalising, as it is untypical of the subjects he addressed as a pastellist up to this point, but also distils many of his most remarkable achievements in the medium. A beguilingly simple image, it depicts a young maid carrying a tray bearing drinking chocolate in a cup and a glass of water. She is not depicted in strict profile, as we can just see her right eye. The chocolate itself was a costly luxury, as was the oriental tray and the Meissen porcelain cup – and all allude to the presence of an unseen wealthy household with fashionable, international tastes.

Chambermaids in grand houses in Vienna had various duties which included making tea, coffee and chocolate, and the latter was usually consumed at breakfast, often while the maid's master or mistress was still in bed. Chocolate, like tea and coffee, had arrived in Europe in the sixteenth century as a colonial import; it was at first often considered a medicament and sometimes an aphrodisiac, and then gradually acquired the status of a more widely enjoyed luxury beverage, being especially prized in princely courts. It was valued particularly in France and

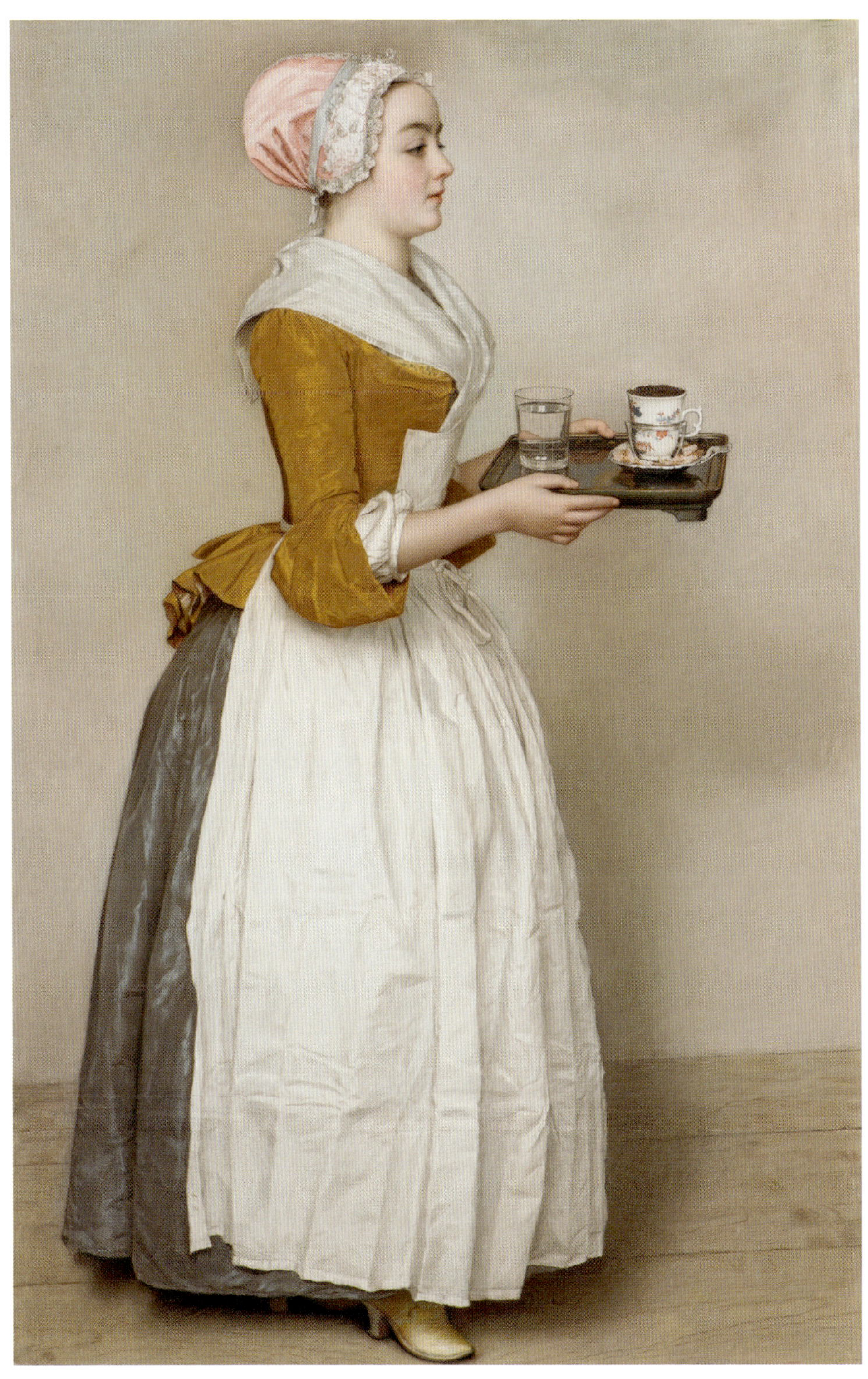

the vogue for it then reached Vienna in the early eighteenth century. The court poet there Pietro Metastasio (1698–1782) even wrote a canata called *La cioccolata*. Although the consumption of it had become such a fashionable pursuit with wider cultural resonances, not everyone shared an enthusiasm for chocolate – Maria Theresa apparently did not enjoy it, although her husband Francis Stephen did.

All these threads to the history of taste form a rich backdrop to Liotard's work. In addition, it is striking that the maid he concentrated on is modestly dressed and her station in life could not be more different from that of most of the artist's wealthy patrons. The pastel is though quite large (82.5 × 52.5 cm) and in effect what the artist did therefore was to ennoble his humble subject through the ambition of his composition and the precise care he expended on executing it. Details of lace, linen and pale skin with a delicate rosy complexion combine to create a serene, restrained masterpiece. Liotard's work also represents a novel contribution to the long tradition of depicting servants; in Dutch art of the seventeenth century, with which he would undoubtedly have been familiar, they were sometimes the subject of moralising narratives, being shown as unreliable and misbehaving. What we are presented with here is, however, a model of decorum and rectitude. Other eighteenth-century artists, such as Jean Siméon Chardin (1699–1779), depicted with dignity and grace the world below stairs on a number of occasions, but as this is a rarity in Liotard's career it is tempting to see it as an eye-catching, strategic statement on his part, intended to create a new sensation. If that was his intention then he certainly succeeded.

Between 1745 and 1746 Liotard travelled on to Venice, where his twin brother was living. He executed *The Chocolate Girl* in Vienna and took it to Italy perhaps as a *coup de théâtre* to advertise his skills for new admirers. Among them in Venice was Count Francesco Algarotti (1712–1764), who was a brilliant, mercurial polymath and a man engaged in collecting for himself and clients. On 3 February 1745 Algarotti purchased *The Chocolate Girl* from Liotard for the collection in Dresden of the Elector of Saxony

FIG. 17
Jean-Étienne Liotard
The Chocolate Girl
c. 1744
Pastel on vellum, 82.5 × 52.5 cm
Gemäldegalerie Alte Meister, Staatliche Kunstsammlungen, Dresden
Gal. no. P 161

and Polish King Augustus III (1696–1763), who was passionate about pastels. It formed one of the highlights of his magnificent Pastell-kabinett, in which numerous rococo works by Rosalba Carriera were displayed and it must have made an extraordinary impact as its restraint and subject matter was so distinct from them. The price was 120 zecchini – and the receipt survives in a private London collection. A zecchino was a small gold coin minted in Venice, which remained in use until the fall of the Republic in 1797.

In April 1746 the renowned Venetian artist Carriera, from whom Algarotti had bought many works, agreed with both the wisdom of his purchase and 'all the painters of Venice', in considering the picture 'the most beautiful pastel ever seen'. This was high praise from a distinguished fellow pastel specialist and it has remained a description associated with *The Chocolate Girl* which has undoubtedly contributed to its cult status. Liotard and Carriera must have met, as he acquired a depiction of the goddess Diana by her, which is recorded in the inventory of his collection; however, there seems to be no surviving record of what must have been a fascinating dialogue.

Later, in 1751, Algarotti expanded on Carriera's endorsement, writing to his friend, the collector and dealer Pierre-Jean Mariette (1694–1774), who is recorded as having a dim view of Liotard's achievements, about his stunning purchase:

> *I have bought a pastel picture about three feet high by the celebrated Liotard. It shows a young German chambermaid in profile, carrying a tray with a glass of water and a cup of chocolate. The picture is almost devoid of shadows, with a pale background, the light being furnished by two windows reflected in the glass. It is painted in half-tones with imperceptible graduations of light and with perfect modelling… and although it is a European picture it could appeal to the Chinese who, as you know, are sworn enemies of shadows. With regard to the perfection of the work, it is a Holbein in pastel.*

The Holbein comparison links the artist with an illustrious Renaissance predecessor and neatly pinpoints Liotard's realism and precision, as does the reference to the reflections. The latter are also of interest, as is the description of the shadows, because Algarotti had published in Naples in 1737 *Il Newtonianismo per le dame* (*Newtonianism for Ladies*), a popular exposition of Newtonian optics. However, the most intriguing reference in Algarotti's statement is to his perception of the taste of Chinese collectors. It may have been the case that this was a theme he discussed with Liotard; it re-emerges some years later in Liotard's own treatise on painting which he published in 1781. There he praised Chinese painting as pristine and unadulterated and consistent although considered it inferior to European artistic traditions.

As well as taking in an interest in aesthetic issues, Algarotti was a philosopher, poet and essayist who was knowledgeable about literary classics, architecture and opera. He could also count among his friends and correspondents a remarkable network, ranging from Frederick the Great to Voltaire and Pope Benedict XIV. The son of a wealthy Venetian merchant, Algarotti studied in Rome and Bologna and visited Paris, building a reputation for being urbane and knowledgeable and witty. In London he was made a Fellow of the Royal Society and became involved in a bi-sexual love triangle with the politician John Hervey (1696–1743) and Lady Mary Wortley Montagu (who had famously visited Constantinople before Liotard). He was undoubtedly one of the most remarkable members of Europe's intelligentsia collected by Liotard as a client. Liotard's surviving portraits of Algarotti (Kasteel Huis Doorn, Utrecht; Rijksmusuem, Amsterdam) are, however, it has to be admitted, relatively restrained; they depict him wearing a fur-lined blue velvet jacket but do not convey the breadth of knowledge or charisma of this extraordinary man. This may perhaps be explained by the brevity of their association.

After his Venetian triumph Liotard continued with his European travels. He returned to Vienna and then accompanied the Hapsburg court as it travelled to Frankfurt for the coronation of Francis I as Holy Roman Emperor. The coronation took place in St Bartholomew's Cathedral in the city and Francis succeeded Charles VII. Maria Theresa made him co-regent of her dominions while retaining political control over them; the process formed part of her campaign to strengthen her power. This experience also no doubt consolidated further Liotard's growing relationship with his Viennese patrons and allowed some connections to be forged with new possible subjects for portraits.

He then journeyed on to Bayreuth, where he portrayed Wilhelmina of Prussia, the Margravine of Brandenburg-Bayreuth (1709–1758), who was a lutenist and composer. Next Liotard stopped in Darmstadt, where he formed a connection with another new patron whom he had met in Frankfurt, Princess Caroline Louise of Hesse-Darmstadt (1723–1783). Liotard instructed her in drawing and the use of pastel over a six week

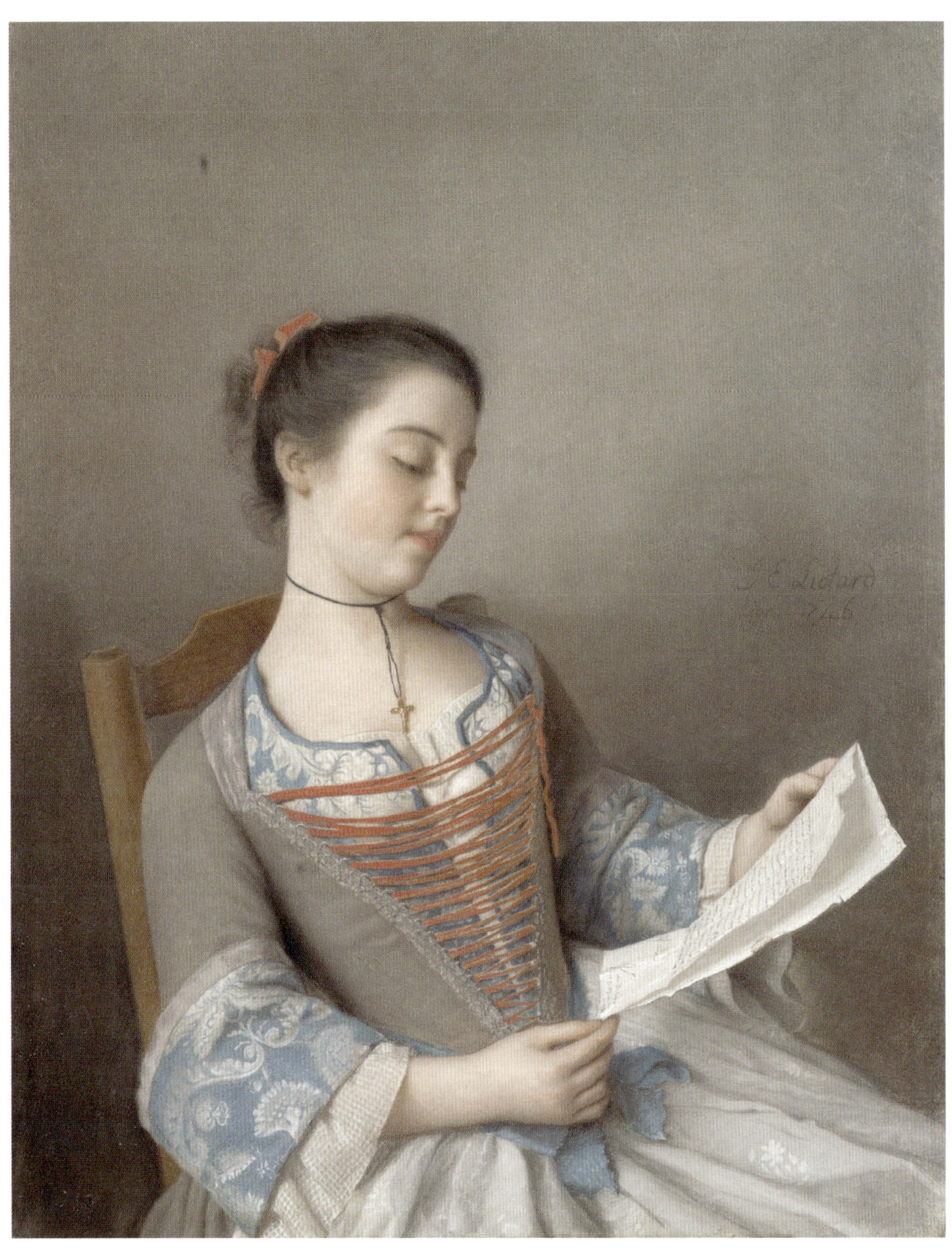

FIG. 18
Jean-Étienne Liotard
La Liseuse (The Reader)
1746
Pastel on vellum, 54.5 × 43 cm
Rijksmuseum, Amsterdam
Inv. SK-A-228

period; he also portrayed her at an easel using pastels. The princess was twenty-two at the time of their encounter and had a growing reputation for wide knowledge and curiosity about the arts. In 1751 she married then Margrave of Baden and she came to play a key role in establishing Karlsruhe as a great cultural centre, welcoming to the city distinguished German creative figures, such as Johann Gottfried Herder (1744–1803) and Johann Wolfgang von Goethe (1749–1832). As well as being a patron and an amateur artist, the princess was a collector of paintings, a linguist (who mastered five languages), a musician, and she took a serious interest in scientific disciplines such as botany. She proved that Paris did not have monopoly on sparkling salons and was a significant addition to the collection of polymaths Liotard encountered across his career.

Tours were then undertaken by the artist to Basel, Geneva and Lyons, where he stayed with his sister Sara, whose husband François Lavergne was a Genevan merchant based in the city. He made during this period a pastel which was to prove to be one his most popular creations. Called *La Liseuse* (*The Reader*) [FIG. 18], it depicts a young woman seated on a wooden chair, concentrating on a letter held up in her hands. The model was Liotard's thirteen-year-old niece Marianne Lavergne (1733–1809). Rather like *The Chocolate Girl* it is a work of disarming simplicity that succeeds as both a delicate character study and demonstration of the skills now very familiar in his finest pastels – a remarkable rendering of clothes and textures. These include the sitter's richly decorated sleeves, the red ribbons of her bodice, the crispness of the paper and the glint of the crucifix hanging at her neck. The text on the letter is not legible to us so it remains ambiguous what type of news she might be engaged with and her expression gives little away. The motif of a single figure reading in this manner was familiar from the work of a number of seventeenth-century paintings, most especially in the Netherlands, where it sometimes had romantic implications. It was though also found among the works of Liotard's contemporaries, such as the Veronese artist Pietro Rotari (1707–1762). The composition proved so appealing that Liotard made five versions of it – the finest arguably being the 1746 pastel in the Rijksmuseum reproduced here. Other artists also replicated it and prints were created after the pastels so spreading the reputation of a work that was sometimes styled *La Belle Lyonnaise*. The prints included engravings that Liotard had a role in marketing in Paris and London. In the 1750s he was to return to this winning formula of using relatives as models for use in genre scenes in some of the most ambitious of all his works.

Liotard next decided to return to Paris, still employing his striking long beard and Levantive garb to attract attention. His arrival in the city must have been a quite different experience to that during his period of training back in the 1720s. Over twenty years later the artist was now an established, if exotic figure, accomplished and trusted by the elite of European society. He lived in some comfort on the rue de la Corderie, in a wealthy neighbourhood, and as a clear indication of his status received a commission to depict the Marshal General of France, Maurice, Count of Saxony (1696–1750) [FIG. 19]. This portrait, executed in pastel on vellum, is somewhat unusual in Liotard's output, as a work clearly intended to compete with public propogandist portraiture in oil of the period; it is quite distinct from the more domestic and informal portrayals he had come to specialise in. The Count, known as Maurice de Saxe, was the illegitimate son of Augustus II of Saxony (1670–1733) (whose heir was Augustus III, the purchaser of the *The Chocolate Girl*). He pursued a military career from the age of twelve, at first in the Imperial army, and then from 1720 serving France. He became famous for his exploits in the 1740s at the Battles of Fontenoy, Rocourt and Lawfeld, and Liotard includes a cavalry skirmish in the background at the right. In 1747, the year before he sat for his portrait, Maurice de Saxe was appointed Marshal General of the armies of the King, hence the prominence of the splendid baton prominently held in his left hand. He also became related to the French crown at this moment, as his niece, Maria Josepha of Saxony (1731–1767) married Louis, Dauphin of France (1729–1765).

All this achievement and these connections served Liotard well, as the Count introduced the artist to the French court and this resulted in agreement via a special licence that he could portray the royal family. The resulting portraits are rather formal and this is perhaps explained in part by the rigidity of protocols at Versailles, but also by the fact that they were to be exhibited in public. They were not shown in the prestigious Salons in the Musée du Louvre, as Liotard was not a member of the Académie royale, but rather at the Académie de Saint-Luc, the older trade guild for artists in Paris. This was though an important moment in terms of the visibility of Liotard's works both as a pastellist and a draughtsman: in the 1751, 1752 and 1753 exhibitions at the Académie de Saint-Luc the public would have had access for the first time to not only examples of his royal portraiture but also some drawings he had made in Constantinople which were also put on display. He also showed in this context a wider selection of works to give a flavour of the range of his

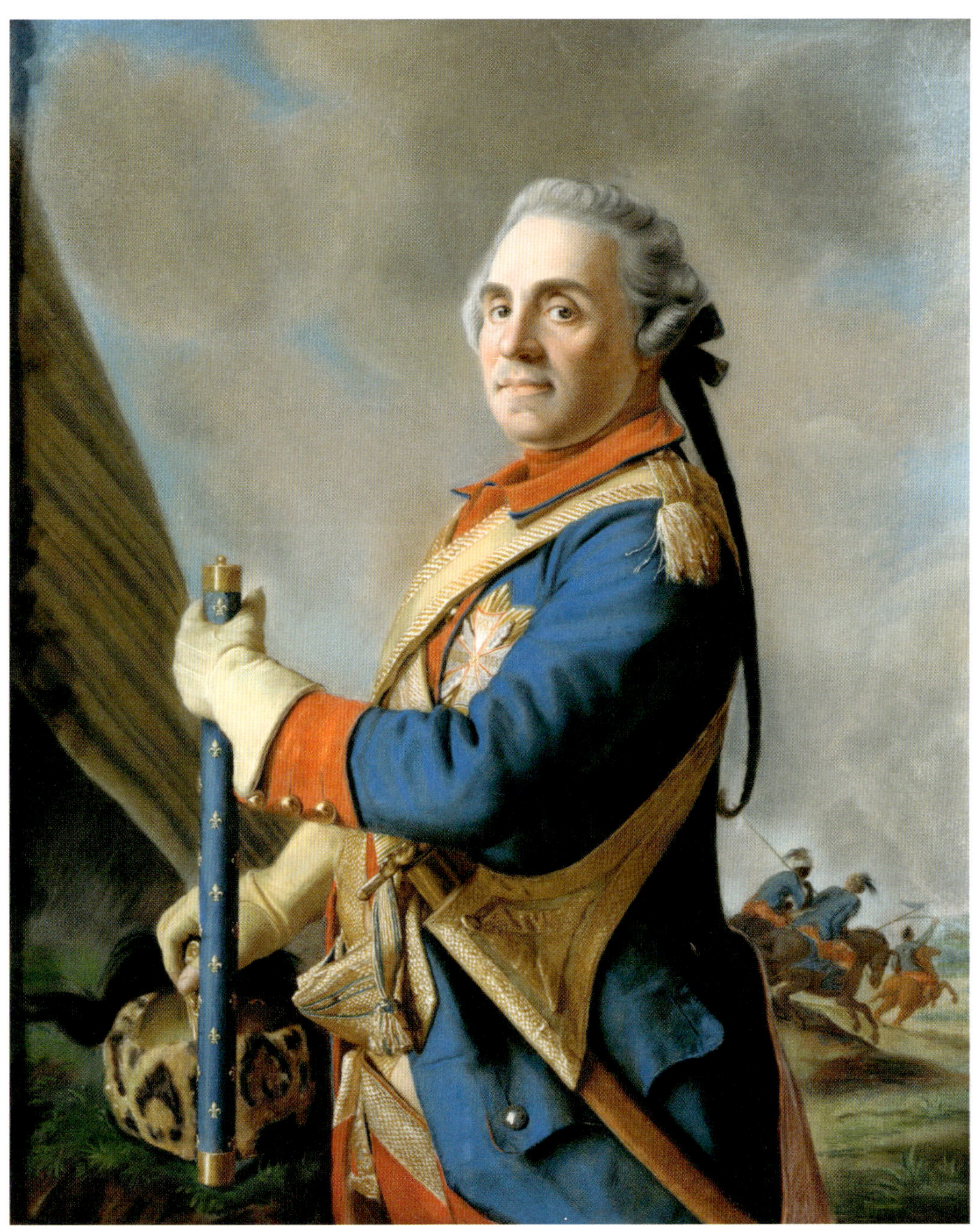

FIG. 19
Jean-Étienne Liotard
Marshal General of France, Maurice, Count of Saxony (1696–1750)
1748
Pastel on parchment, 64 × 53 cm
Gemäldegalerie Alte Meister, Staatliche Kunstsammlungen, Dresden
Gal. no. P 160

achievements, including miniatures and pastels such as *La Liseuse.* In the catalogues to the exhibitions he was described as 'peintre du roi' (painter to the king), so making the most of his new status. The exhibitions did attract some complimentary interest, along with comments about the extravagant prices Liotard expected.

The set of Bourbon portraits eventually included ten works – depicting eight princesses, the Dauphin and the King himself, Louis XV. The pastel of Louis, Dauphin of France can stand to illustrate the qualities of the series [FIG. 20]. The monarch's only son is shown in a manner that makes no concession to hide his considerable physique or jowly features, but his splendid coat with gold trimmings signifies his status. The wide blue sash of watered silk that dominates the composition denotes his membership of the illustrious chivalric Order of the Holy Spirit, which had been founded in the sixteenth century. Louis died from consumption fifteen years later and so never became King, although three of his sons were destined to be rulers of France. Unlike his unpopular father, he was renowned as a well-educated, devout and cultivated figure. With Maria Josepha of Saxony he had thirteen children.

English visitors to Paris were also depicted during this period by Liotard. Philip Yorke (later Lord Royston and then 2nd Earl of Hardwicke) (1720–1790) sat for a now lost pastel portrait in 1749. It is worth noting as it elicited some interesting gossip about Liotard's relationships with his clients: in a letter to his wife, Lady Jemima Campbell, Yorke stated:

> *He tells me I have a difficult face to hit, & I will not answer that He will succeed better than others, but It shall not be my fault if He does not. He is a very odd Fellow, & always wears the Turkish Dress with a long Beard wch reaches down to his middle. He has lately drawn a very good Picture of Ml Saxe, & is now painting all the Mesdames, but He tells me, the Lady is not his Friend.*

The 'Mesdames' were the Bourbon princesses and 'the Lady' was probably the Dauphine. He may not have forged a positive relationship with her; however, Liotard maximised the benefits of his new connections with the French court, producing replicas of his Bourbon portraits, some in pastel and others as miniatures, which spread awareness of a prestigious episode in his career, albeit one that had resulted in restrained and rather rigid works.

It is interesting to consider again at this point how his court portraiture followed a complex and richly varied trajectory. It had started with the

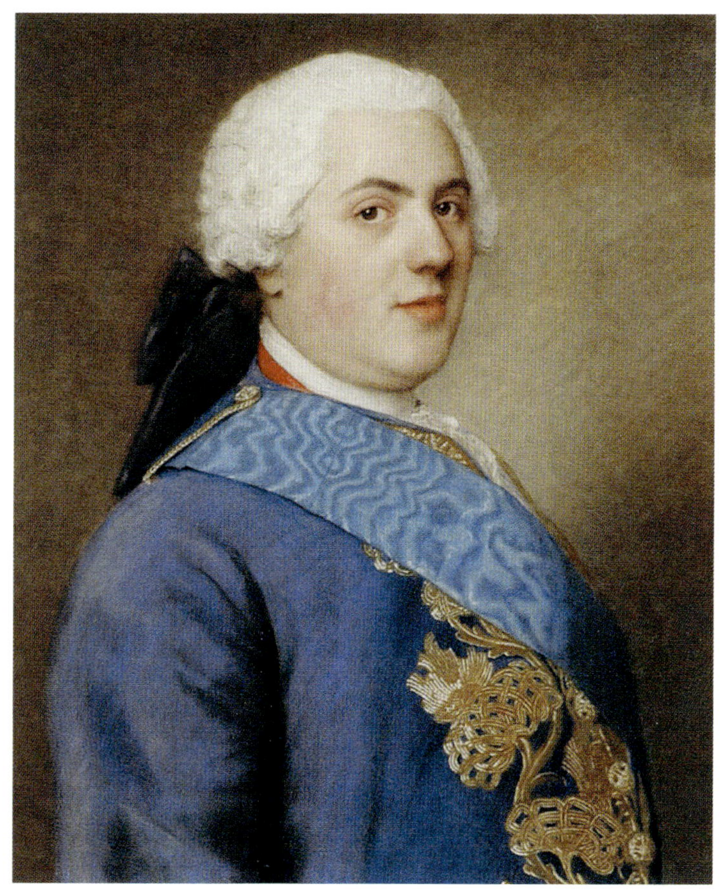

FIG. 20
Jean-Étienne Liotard
Louis, Dauphin of France
1749–50
Pastel on vellum, heightened with gouache, 59 × 49 cm
Fondazione Ordine Mauriziano, Stupinigi, Turin

exiled Stuarts in Rome (1730s) and included a fascinating interlude in Moldovia (1742), before reaching the informal depictions of the Princess of Hesse-Darmstadt in the role of an artist (1746). The far more formal Bourbon project in Paris followed (late 1740s). What was to come were intensely private and candid portraits of the Hanoverians in London (1750s) and the Austrian Imperial Family in Vienna (1760s). These were to show Liotard learning from the informality of his non-royal portraits and taking the trend that has been described as the domestication of monarchy much further.

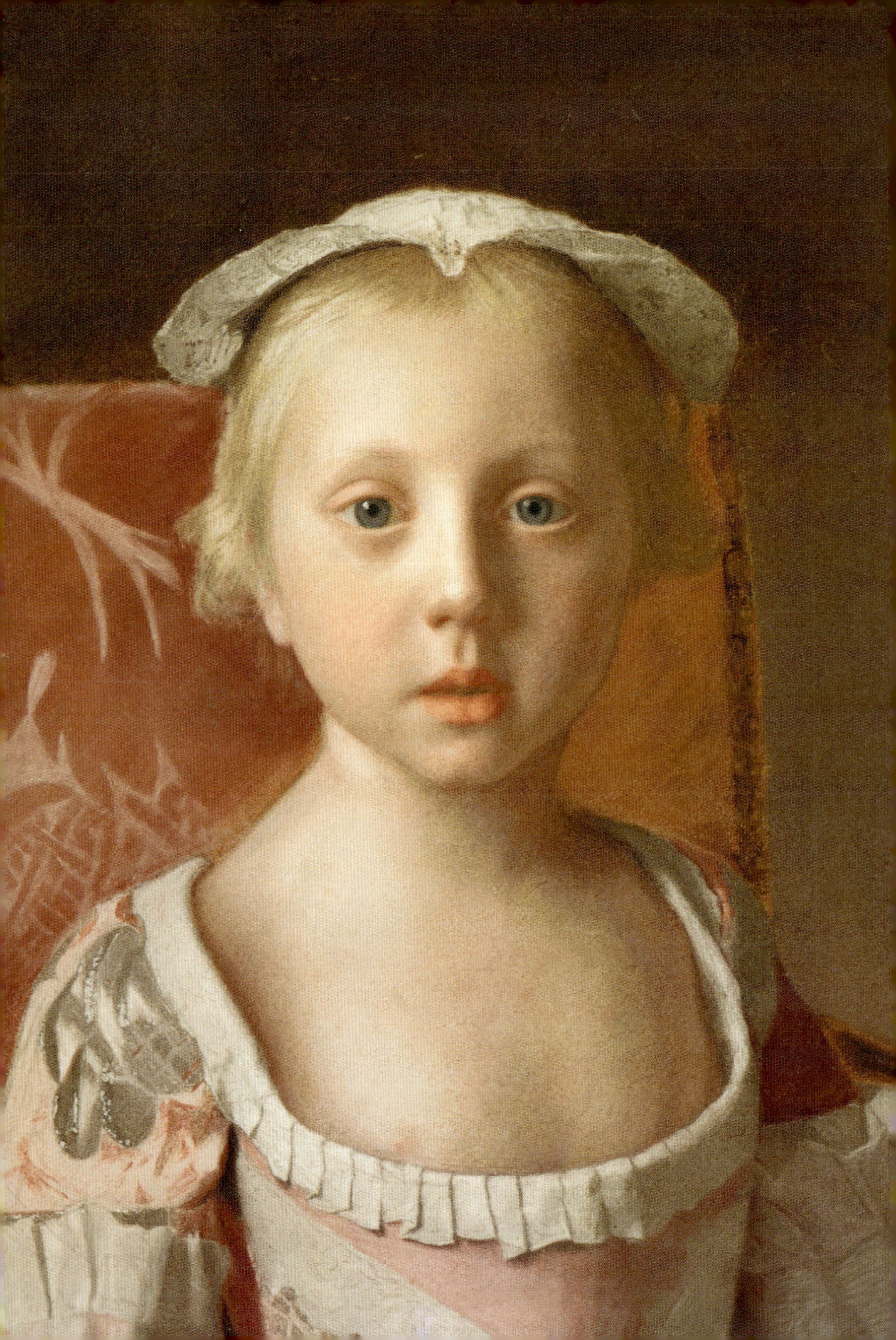

5 Sensations in London and Lyons

LIOTARD PROVED TO BE A NEW STAR in the cultural life of mid-eighteenth-century London. He travelled there from Paris and once again sought to make the most of his exotic credentials and appearance in order to maximise the impact of his arrival. In March 1753, it was reported in *Old England's Journal* that 'This Week a Turkish Gentleman arrived here, who is very eminent in Portrait Painting… [He] is dressed in the Habit of his country, and remarkable by his Beard being long, curiously shaped and curled.' The confusion over his nationality was presumably not a problem for the artist himself, as it generated a great deal of interest. It was by no means the first time that such curiosity had been aroused; when King George I (1660–1727) arrived in in England in 1714 his entourage had included two turbaned Turkish valets.

However, as is often the case when fresh talent lands unexpectedly not everyone approved. No less a figure than the painter Joshua Reynolds, the future President of the Royal Academy, took a dim view of both Liotard's skills and his curious demeanour. Reynolds commented that there was 'something of the Quack' about Liotard, that his behaviour was the 'very essence of Imposture' and, most damning of all, that 'his pictures are just what ladies do when they paint for amusement.' As well as a condescending sniff of disapproval, perhaps what we hear here is some concern about competition, as Liotard was an accomplished portraitist who could command significant prices and so was treading on Reynold's territory as an artist. The most interesting element in his condemnation, however, concerns the status of pastels: Reynolds dismisses them to the realm of domestic life, the female sphere of amateur art, and by implication also damns a medium that had come to be especially associated with continental practice through figures such as Rosalba Carriera.

Detail, FIG. 23

At the moment of Liotard's arrival, London was becoming a global metropolis; the largest city in Europe, it offered splendour and squalor and a population drawn from all across Britain and the continent. Creating institutions to promote the arts was underway: in 1711 the St Martin's Lane Academy had been formed and the first meeting of The Society of Arts was held in 1754 when Liotard was in the city; it would not be until 1768, however, that the Royal Academy of Arts was founded. Creative figures active in the city at this period included painters such as William Hogarth (1697–1764), who effectively exploited suspicions about European culture in his more bombastic and nationalistic paintings and prints.

Liotard's presence in London prompted suspicion but also gossip that served him well and was widely dispersed. In 1755 Lord Chesterfield, in an attempt to denounce the quantity of cosmetics worn by women at the time, spread the rumour that '... Mr Liotard... refused a fine woman [who was presumably wearing a great deal of makeup] to draw her picture, alleging that he never copied anybody's works but his own and God Almighty's.' This piquant anecdote which further enhanced his reputation for depicting the 'truth' did Liotard no harm; it was repeated in the British press and even reported in a newspaper in Maryland in America.

When Liotard was in the city there were other pastellists working there, notably Francis Cotes (1726–1770), who in 1768 became, along with Reynolds, a founding member of the Royal Academy. The medium was though not one that excited many patrons and it was perhaps most effectively used by British artists a generation later, particularly through the work of John Russell (1745–1806) who enjoyed a highly successful career. Russell exhibited extensively at the Academy and in the 1780s and 90s, becoming 'Crayon Painter' to the Prince of Wales and the King. In the 1750s, however, a pastellist needed strong advocates, which Liotard had in men such as Fawkener and Bessborough, and to be attention-grabbing, as he undoubtedly was through his continental reputation and appearance.

Probably because of the considerable curiosity he generated and the fact that he had portrayed the French royal family, Liotard secured British royal sales and commissions, the results of which are some of the most refined portraits of the period. His extraordinarily accomplished and detailed self-portrait in the Royal Collection [FIG. 21] gives us a clear impression of how Liotard presented himself at court and why the contemporary press was so intrigued. It is a miniature enamel, arguably

FIG. 21
Jean-Étienne Liotard
Self-portrait in Profile
1753
Enamel, 6.1 × 4.6 cm
Royal Collection Trust
RCIN 421436
ACTUAL SIZE

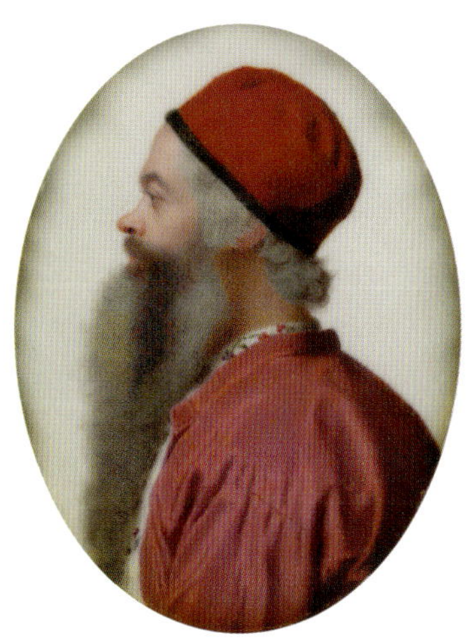

his finest work in this medium, now housed in a later frame, in which he depicted himself in strict profile. The 'turkish' hat, gown and embroidered shirt, along with his luxuriant Moldavian beard appear especially brilliant as they are set off by a plain white backdrop. An inscription on the reverse dates the enamel to 1753. In the same year Horace Walpole described Liotard in a letter to the diplomat Horace Mann (1706–1786) as wearing 'a Turkish habit and a beard down to his girdle'. Walpole considered it a form of self-advertisement and a strategy 'to draw customers' – which is a fair estimation. He also shared, however, some of Reynolds's disapproval of Liotard, describing him as 'avaricious beyond imagination'. Walpole may have held this negative estimation of the artist but nonetheless arranged to have the self-portrait engraved and it became perhaps the best-known image of Liotard in England. It was used as the frontispiece of the volume of Walpole's *Anecdotes of Painting* in which an account of the artist appeared. The *Anecdotes* were largely based on notes compiled by the antiquary and engraver George Vertue (1684–1756).

The enamel self-portrait was probably one of a group of miniatures bought two years later by Augusta, Princess of Wales (1719–1772). The Princess is also recorded as having made two payments 'to fetch a Large Picter from Mr Leotarld [sic]... to send it to Kew'. This remains mysterious, however, as the works she is known to have acquired from him are all small in scale. Most importantly they include a remarkable sequence of pastel portraits by her new exotic visitor. The Princess's husband, Frederick Prince of Wales (1707–1751), the eldest son of King George II

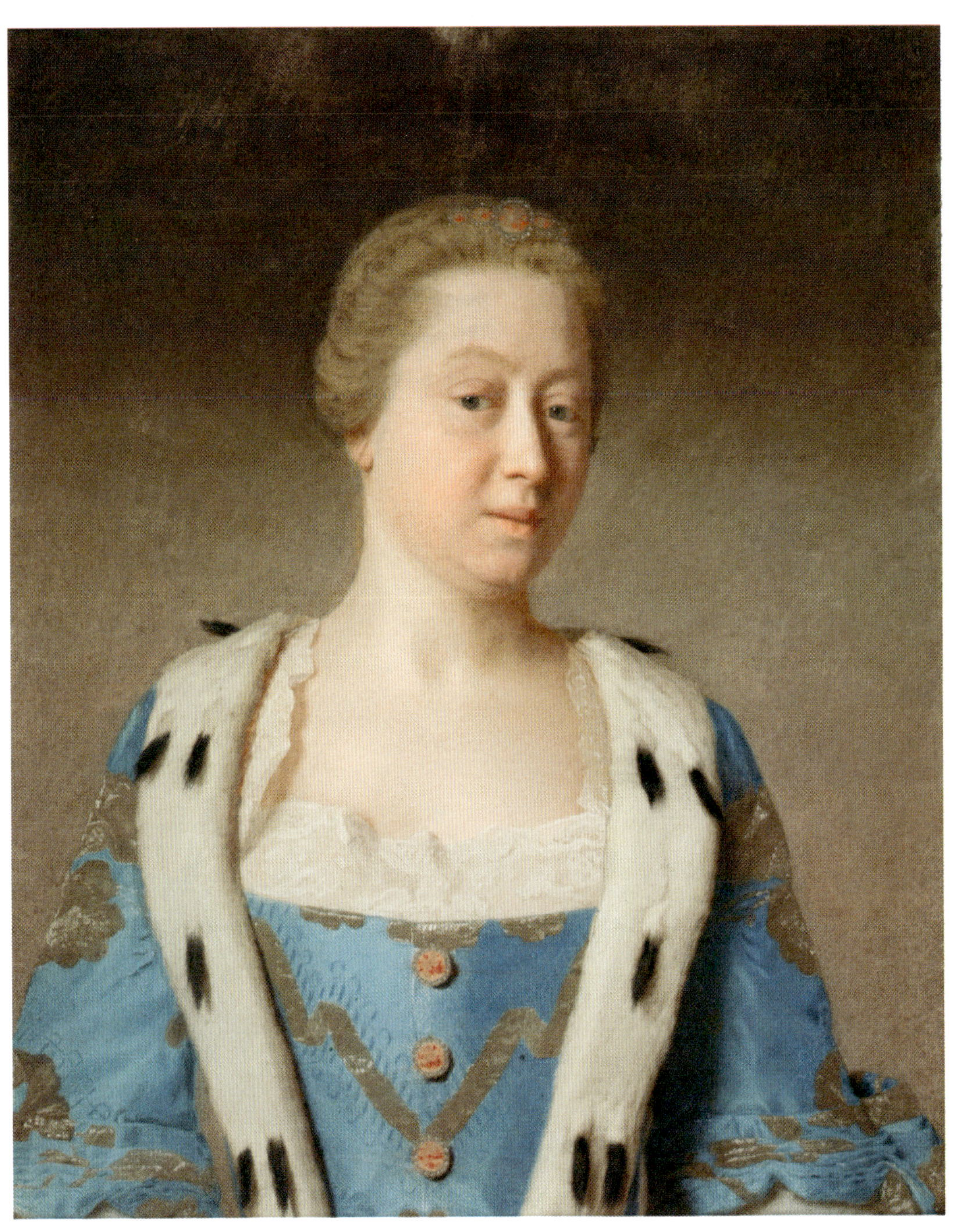

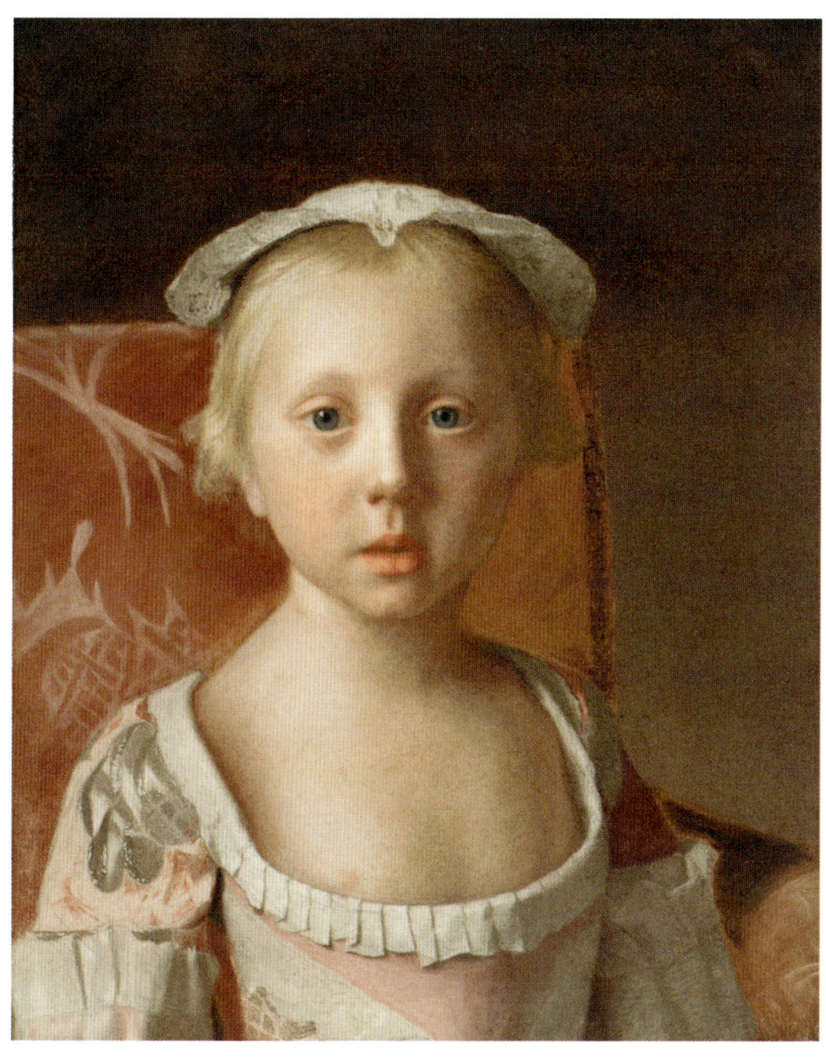

FIG. 22
Jean-Étienne Liotard
Augusta, Princess of Wales (1719–1772)
1754
Pastel on paper, 64.8 × 51.4 cm
Royal Collection Trust
RCIN 400892

FIG. 23
Jean-Étienne Liotard
Princess Louisa Anne
1754
Pastel on vellum, 40 × 30.5 cm
Royal Collection Trust
RCIN 400900

(1683–1760), had died before Liotard's arrival in London and so the commission was carried out for the recently widowed Augusta. It includes a portrait of her [FIG. 22] as well as separate studies of nine of her children. Her late husband was also depicted by Liotard posthumously, in order to complete the family set, probably using a portrait of the Prince from the 1740s as the basis for his work. This is a very rare instance where the 'truth' of direct observation had to be set aside; the compromise of being reliant on another artist's work was presumably considered by Liotard a price worth paying to secure the rest of the commission.

The Augusta series all survive in their original frames and the Princess is shown without a wig, facing the artist, with her head slightly turned to the right and an expression of mild curiosity on her face. The blue silk, silver thread, lace and ermine of her court dress dominate the composition. The red and silver buttons form part of a suite matched by the jewel in her hair. These details allude to her status, but overall the effect is remarkable for its relatively intimate and unceremonious qualities. Among the studies of her children Liotard's depiction of Princess Louisa Anne (1749–1768) [FIG. 23] especially stands out because of its sensitivity. She is a little girl in an adult world; the chair she sits on seems too large for her and her stiff, formal dress is ill-fitting; it has slipped and her breast is just visible. It is the direct eye contact with the artist and us that is most memorable and anticipates some of the artist's studies of his own children. She was presumably startled by Liotard's appearance at this period – which we know from his miniature enamel self-portrait. An artist styled as a wizard is scrutinising the Princess and no doubt recording her appearance at some speed. His ability to retain her attention may have been helped by an opportunity for her to attempt drawing. It seems highly likely that Liotard encouraged some of the royal children to draw in order to ensure they enjoyed the encounter with him and sat still; there is a red chalk child's sketch on the reverse of Liotard's portrait of Edward Augustus, Duke of York (1739–1767) which formed part of the Augusta series.

Such works represent a startling innovation in the context of British court portraiture of the mid-eighteenth century. Princess Augusta had previously been depicted by the Frenchman Jean Baptiste Van Loo (1684–1745) and the English artist George Knapton (1698–1778) who offered a proficient service for public imagery in oil paint. Liotard's naturalistic and richly coloured pastels were though primarily for the

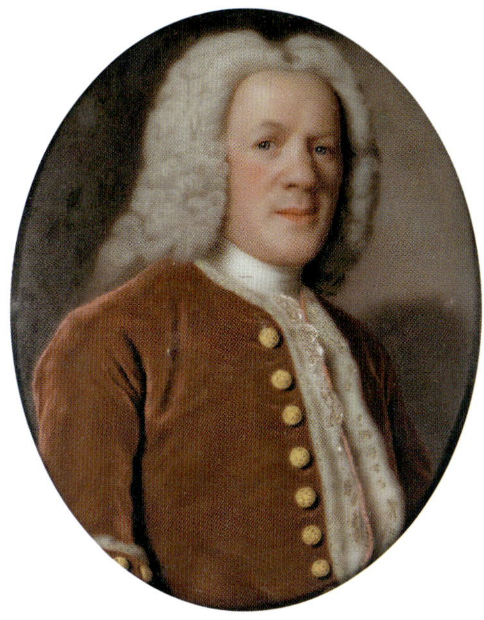

FIG. 24
Jean-Étienne Liotard
Sir Everard Fawkener
1754
Enamel on copper, 8 × 6.6 cm
Ashmolean Museum, Oxford
Inv. WA 2001.276
ACTUAL SIZE

family circle. There are various figures who might have acted as an intermediary between the artist and his new patron; however, the most compelling candidate is Sir Everard Fawkener, Liotard's most important patron in Constantinople. When Fawkener returned to Britain, following his diplomatic service, as has been noted, he was appointed Secretary to Prince William Augustus, Duke of Cumberland, who was the brother-in-law of Princess Augusta; so he was perfectly placed to offer recommendations. A miniature enamel portrait of Fawkener by Liotard dating from 1754, the year after the royal commission, is now in the collection of the Ashmolean Museum [FIG. 24]. It's a very refined, quizzical image, which suggests artist and sitter are in conversation; the textures of Fawkener's wig and brown velvet coat are brilliantly evoked. In spite of success in his professional life, sadly Fawkener fell from prominence because of his addiction to gambling and died at Bath in poverty just a few years after Liotard's London visit. His collection was sold in 1759 by the auctioneer James Ford and included, as well as 'several large portraits of English gentlemen by Liotard', antique bronzes, vases, books and 'two curious Egyptian mummies of a woman and a child'.

There are interesting points of comparison between the portrait of Princess Augusta and other British commissions executed at the same moment, such as Liotard's portrait of the Charlotte, Marchioness of Hartington (1731–1754) [FIG. 25] at Chatsworth. She was the daughter of Richard Boyle, the Earl of Burlington. Extraordinarily wealthy, she was to marry the 4th Duke of Devonshire; they had four children and Liotard depicted her in the year of her premature death at the age of twenty-three. Just like Augusta, before meeting Liotard her iconography had chiefly been formulated by George Knapton; by contrast the pastellist offered a more liberating and candid form of portraiture. The light falling on her face, turn of her head and eye contact mean her interrogation of us is as unmediated as Liotard's of her. Both Augusta and Charlotte adopted similar poses and wear magnificent fur-trimmed blue silk gowns.

As almost all royal portraiture has an underlying agenda about the continuance of the family line, arguably the most important of the pastels of Augusta's children, was the depiction of the heir, George, Prince of Wales (1738–1820). However, it is striking that it was not the portrait from the series that Liotard chose to reproduce as a print; instead he selected two works to reproduce that were compositionally more innovative: the portrait of Princess Louisa Anne, which has a wonderful quality of immediacy and engagement, and the portrait of Henry Frederick, Duke of Cumberland (1745–1790), which shows the boy building a house of playing cards in a manner inspired by the works of Chardin. Following the death of her husband Augusta was accused of bringing up her children in a manner that was too closeted, away from the court and wider scrutiny; these prints provided, however, a glimpse for some of their circumscribed life. As well as having this immediate function, the Augusta pastels also established a fascinating prototype for the sequence of oil portraits Thomas Gainsborough (1727–1788) made about thirty years later of George III, Queen Charlotte (1744–1814), and their thirteen children which date from the early 1780s. Unlike Liotard's works, however, these became visible in the wider world as they were exhibited at the Royal Academy.

It is especially remarkable that Liotard was awarded this important commission as his first royal project had been to depict the enemies of the Hanoverians – the exiled Stuarts in Rome; presumably this was glossed over or not mentioned at all during any conversations that occurred during the sittings. They must have been conducted with strict protocols adhered to and in a deferential manner; we know, for example, that Augusta was accompanied by one of her daughters when she was being depicted.

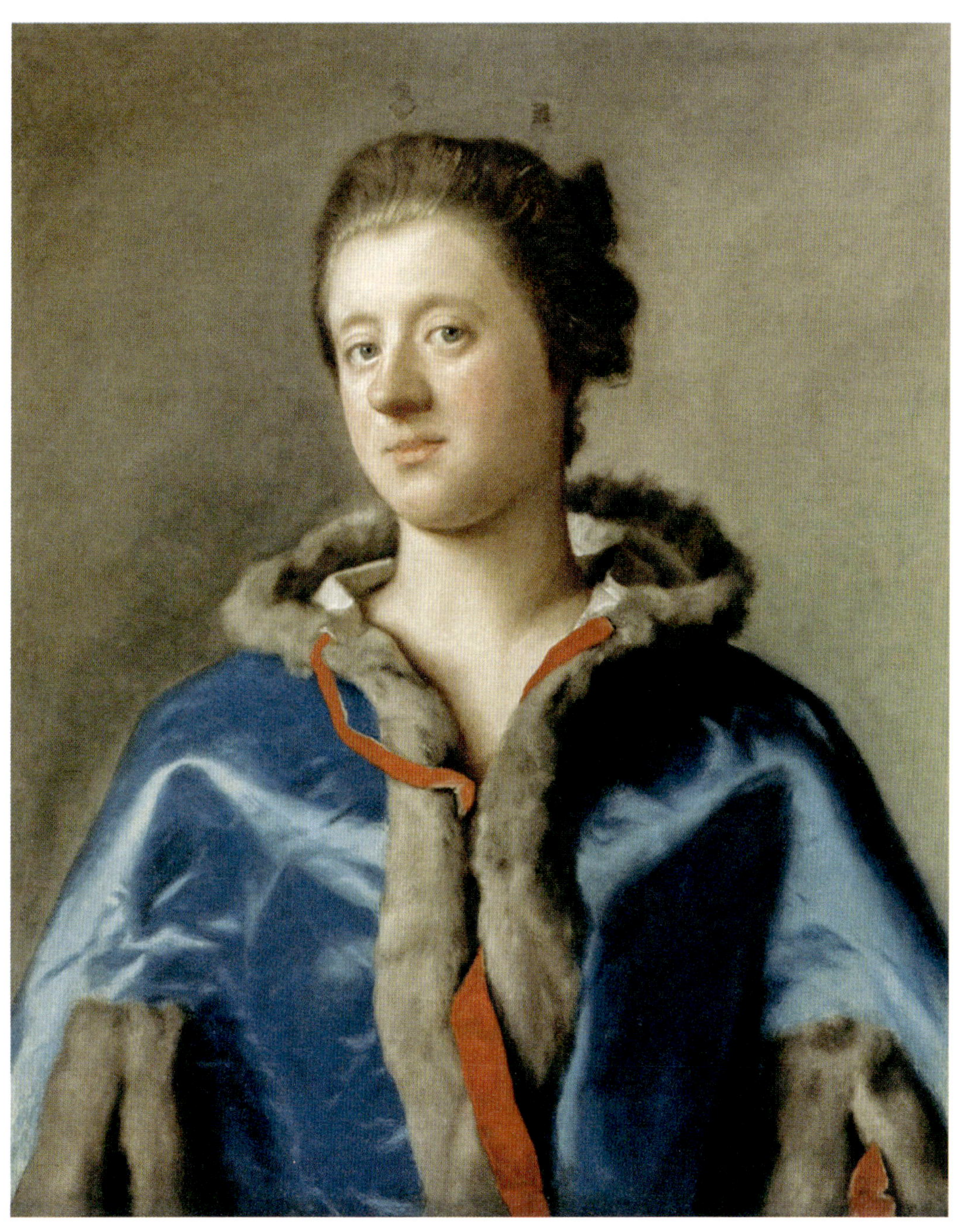

FIG. 25
Jean-Étienne Liotard
Charlotte Boyle, Marchioness of Hartington
1754
Pastel on paper, 57.6 × 48 cm
The Trustees of the Chatsworth Settlement,
Chatsworth House, Derbyshire

The British royal portraits were not intended for public display, as the earlier Bourbon sequence had been, hence their intimacy, but the prints after them could be shown to other clients by the artist. This was perhaps irresistible as it provided a means of sharing and showing off yet another prestigious commission which was something of a coup. In order to promote his range of skills and patronage Liotard is also recorded as promoting exhibitions of works in London in 1753 and 1754. They were shown in premises adjacent to his lodgings in Golden Square, Soho. According to the *Public Advertiser* you had to pay two shillings to view the exhibition although 'Friends are welcome to see the Paintings gratis.' Whether you paid or not the displays were designed to entice and exploit the celebrity status of the artist and his clients. They featured, as well as 'Drawings… all done from the Life at Constantinople…' 'A Collection of PORTRAITS in crayons, most of them Originals'. These included '… an original Picture of the Czar Peter the Great, done from the life… a Picture of the Empress Queen on Horseback… [and] an Original Drawing of the last Pope'. None of these are now known. Liotard also displayed for 'the Curious in Painting' works such as his 'The Three Graces, drawn at Rome', a pastel which survives in the collection of the Rijksmuseum in Amsterdam; it was based on the marble group in the Villa Borghese, but 'coloured here after Life'.

The London commissions Liotard fulfilled beyond his royal commitments included some of the artist's finest mature works. Especially refined among them is the pastel portrait of Eva Maria Garrick née Veigel (1724–1822) [FIG. 26]. Her husband, the renowned actor, David Garrick (1717–1779), who was like Liotard a Huguenot, had been depicted by him in Paris in 1751 and the opportunity to create a companion portrait for that work was taken up across the Channel. Eva Maria was a distinguished performer: she was a dancer from Vienna who arrived in London in the mid-1740s. She also represents a fascinating point of intersection between different circles in which Liotard moved. It was suggested that her stage name 'Violette' was given to her by Maria Theresa, with whom Liotard forged a close alliance. Moreover, her patron in London was Dorothy Boyle, Countess of Burlington (1699–1758), the wife of the 3rd Earl, who was related to some of the most important of Liotard's British aristocratic sitters. Eva Maria renounced her dancing in order to support her husband's career when they were married in 1749. As she was Catholic and he was Protestant they went through two ceremonies. Liotard's portrait of Garrick which was quite freely executed by Liotard in an

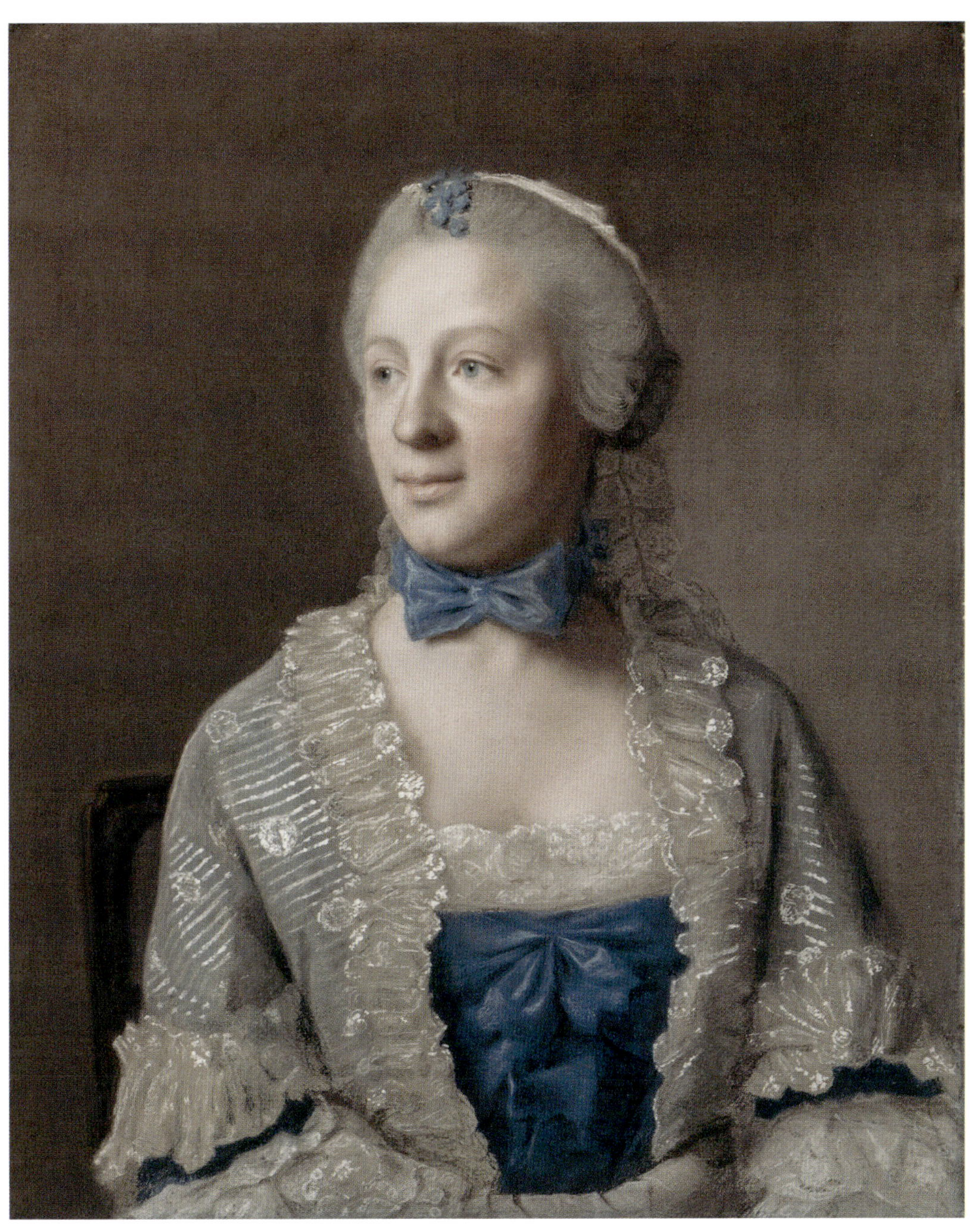

FIG. 26
Jean-Étienne Liotard
Eva Maria Garrick nee Veigel (1724–1822)
c. 1754
Pastel on paper, heightened with gouache,
57.6 × 47 cm
The Trustees of the Chatsworth Settlement,
Chatsworth House, Derbyshire

uncharacteristic loose style, shows the actor turning and gesturing with raised eyebrows, as though in the process of performing a role; his portrait of Eva Maria is by contrast quieter and more serene. A slight indication of a smile steals across her face, while the highlights on the transparent gauze on her dress catch the light and were achieved with touches of gouache (opaque watercolour), applied over the pastel.

Liotard created at the same period a wonderfully subtle portrait of Harriet Churchill, Lady Fawkener (*c.* 1726–1777) [FIG. 27]. This is a more intimate work, not least because of the knowing relationship set up through eye contact with us, the viewer, and the artist. It may be the case that such a connection was permissable because Liotard had a sustained association with Lady Fawkener's husband, Sir Everard, whom he had met in Constantinople, and knew and depicted in England (see Fig. 24). She is portrayed with her work box and a thread in her hand; the sittings could have taken place at Liotard's lodgings in London, or on a visit to the Fawkeners' country home, Westhorpe House near Little Marlow in Buckinghamshire. Harriet wears relatively modest clothes for a Liotard portrait, with a white dress, black shawl and so-called 'bergère' (shepherdess-style) hat. What is remarkable, however, is the way in which the artist has, for example, depicted the black lace in such a manner that the white cotton can be seen beneath it.

Lady Fawkener was the daughter of Lieutenant-General Charles Churchill (1679–1745), who was a member of parliament and nephew of the 1st Duke of Marlborough (1650–1722); her mother was unknown, but her illegitimate status did not result in any prejudice; in fact she was admired by contemporaries for being elegant and amiable company. She married Fawkener in 1748 when she was half his age, six years before she sat for the portrait. The couple had three children: their sons were William Augustus Fawkener (*c.* 1750–1811), who became a diplomat and civil servant, and Everard Fawkener, who pursued a military career. Their daughter, also called Harriet (1750–1831) was renowned as a society hostess, became a companion to Georgiana, Duchess of Devonshire (1757–1806) and was a supporter of the abolition of slavery.

During the first half of the 1750s, as well as working on single figure portraits such as the study of Lady Fawkener, Liotard amplified his ambition not only for his own practice, but for the art of using pastels in a much wider sense, by creating extraordinarily ambitious and large works that combine portraiture and genre elements with exquisite still lifes. They were created during what was clearly a very productive and

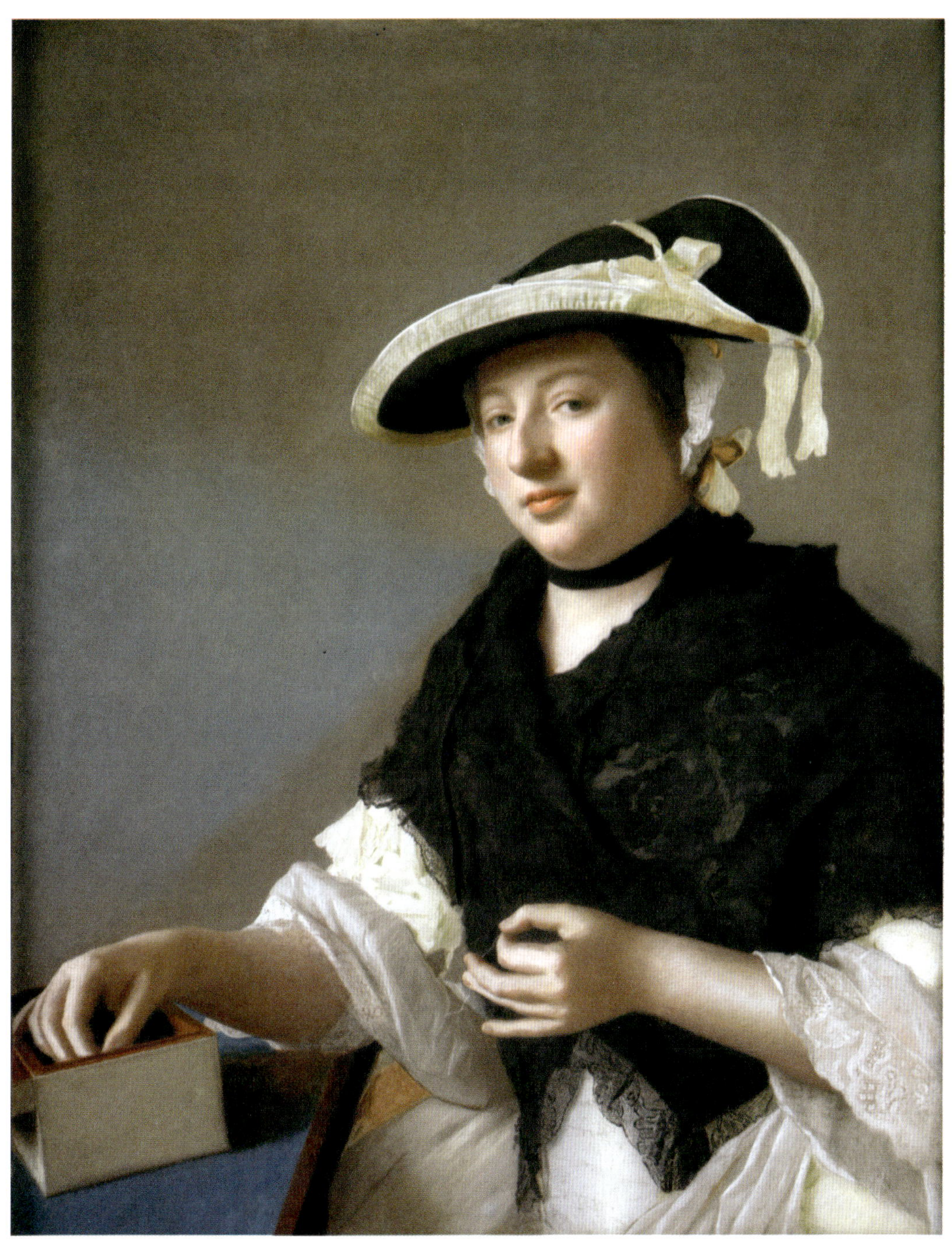

FIG. 27
Jean-Étienne Liotard
Harriet Churchill, Lady Fawkener
1754
Pastel on vellum, 73.6 × 58.5 cm
Compton Verney, Warwickshire
CVCSC:0288.B

happy visit undertaken to relatives in Lyons. The first, called *L'Ecriture* (*The Writer*), dates from 1752 [FIG. 28]. It was executed on six sheets of joined blue paper and is over a metre wide. The models for the figures are two members of Liotard's extended family: the young man seated at the desk is his nephew, Jacques-Antoine Lavergne (1724–1781), and the boy standing at the right may be a nephew of Jacques-Antoine's or a young manservant ('un laquais'). Although these identifications are possible, essentially what we are shown here is a very subtle glimpse of everyday bourgeois life, which focuses on the pleasures and virtues of writing. The man is soberly dressed but has a diamond ring twinkling on his finger and rests his elbow on a splendid piece of folded cloth: this inclusion is probably no accident as Lyons was renowned as a centre for the production of luxury silk. He has paused from his writing with a quill pen and is attended by the boy who holds a candle – presumably brought to facilitate the melting of sealing wax. In a passage of extraordinary virtuosity Liotard depicted the boy's hand in such a way that the light from the flame of the candle shines through its flesh. He seems to be concentrating hard, keeping the flame burning and looking at the seal and stick of wax. A book protrudes from beneath the slope on which the writing has been taking place; it is inscribed 'L'art d'aimer et de plaire' which is the subtitle of a play called *Zélide* by Jean-Julien-Constant Rénout (1725–1780) that was published a year after the pastel was made. It has been speculated that this might be an advanced copy of the script belonging to a younger brother of Jacques-Antoine's, who was an amateur actor.

Whatever the role of this literary source may be, the visual precedents for the pastel are clear. Liotard was competing with works from the 1730s painted in oil in Paris by Jean-Siméon Chardin which he probably saw in the city. These featured genre scenes in which identifiable models were employed, delighted in the rendering of still life details, and included the motif of objects protruding from partially opened draws or apertures in furniture in the foreground (as the book does in Liotard's work): such devices make a subtle if compelling link between the space in the scene and the viewer's. Particularly close to *L'Ecriture* in all these respects is Chardin's *Child with a Top* in the Musée du Louvre of 1737–8. Its model was a nine-year-old boy called Auguste-Gabriel Godefroy (1728–1813) who eventually became controller-general of the French navy and a significant collector. He stands by a desk with books, ink, a quill and paper, watching a spinning top. A porte-crayon with a piece of pastel in it protrudes from a drawer in the foreground. Liotard may have known the work itself, or an engraving after it created in 1742 by Bernard Lepicié which reverses the composition and is even closer to his pastel.

Two years later Liotard revisited these themes and created a magnificent work which complements *L'Ecriture*, called *The Lavergne Family Breakfast* [FIG. 29]. This pastel has recently been acquired by the National Gallery in London and is now undoubtedly the most ambitious of Liotard's works in a British public collection. Here we see a female genre scene which broadly mirrors the composition of *L'Ecriture* and depicts a young woman serving hot milky coffee to a little girl. It was executed on nine pieces of joined paper and is signed and dated ('Liotard / a lion [Lyon] / 1754') on the sheet of music which protrudes from the drawer in the left foreground. It was sold in London by Liotard for 200 guineas to the Earl of Bessborough; this price is especially significant as it appears to be the highest that the artist ever achieved during his life for a single work, and is a measure of the contemporary acclaim the pastel received.

The *Public Advertiser* noted that Liotard had returned to London in the summer of 1754 from France and '… brought over a couple of large Conversation Pieces in Crayons of his highest finishing'. The terminology here is revealing – clearly the 'highest finishing' description refers to the level of detail and resolution in *The Lavergne Family Breakfast* as well as perhaps some pride in the achievement it represents. A 'Conversation Piece' was a term widely used from the late seventeenth century in England to refer to a painting of a convivial figurative group, usually in a private domestic setting or landscape, sometimes inspired by Dutch or French precedents: conversing within it was implied as was the fact that it might engage and stimulate a conversation among viewers.

Once again in thematic terms Chardin genre scenes in oil come to mind as possible sources, such as his *The Diligent Mother* and *Saying Grace* (both 1740, Musée du Louvre), but they do not provide a precise model. Liotard appears to have invented his composition, ensuring the type of detail he excelled at defining was fully apparent. The clothing and the still life are meticulous and invite close looking and admiration. The child dunks a biscuit into her coffee which reaches the top of the cup and almost spills over. The porcelain and silver items on the table are gently reflected in its lacquered top; their arrangement and the care with which they are depicted anticipate the still lifes Liotard was to produce from the 1770s. Meanwhile, while the woman is dressed and ready to face the day the little girl's hair has been prepared with paper curlers, which are yet to be removed. They were called 'papilottes' or butterfly curls and

FIG. 28
Jean-Étienne Liotard
L'Ecriture (The Writer)
1752
Pastel on six sheets of blue paper, 81 × 107 cm
Schönbrunn Palace, Vienna,

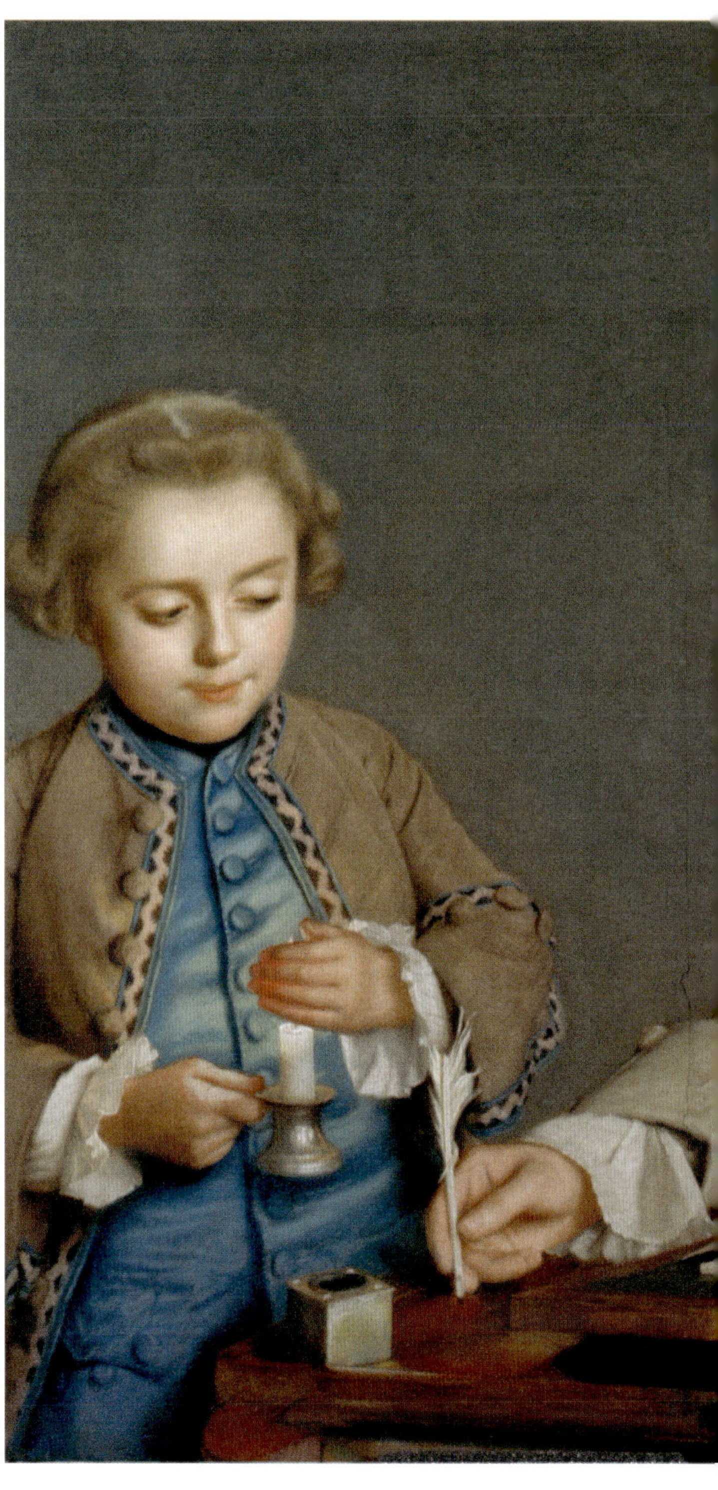

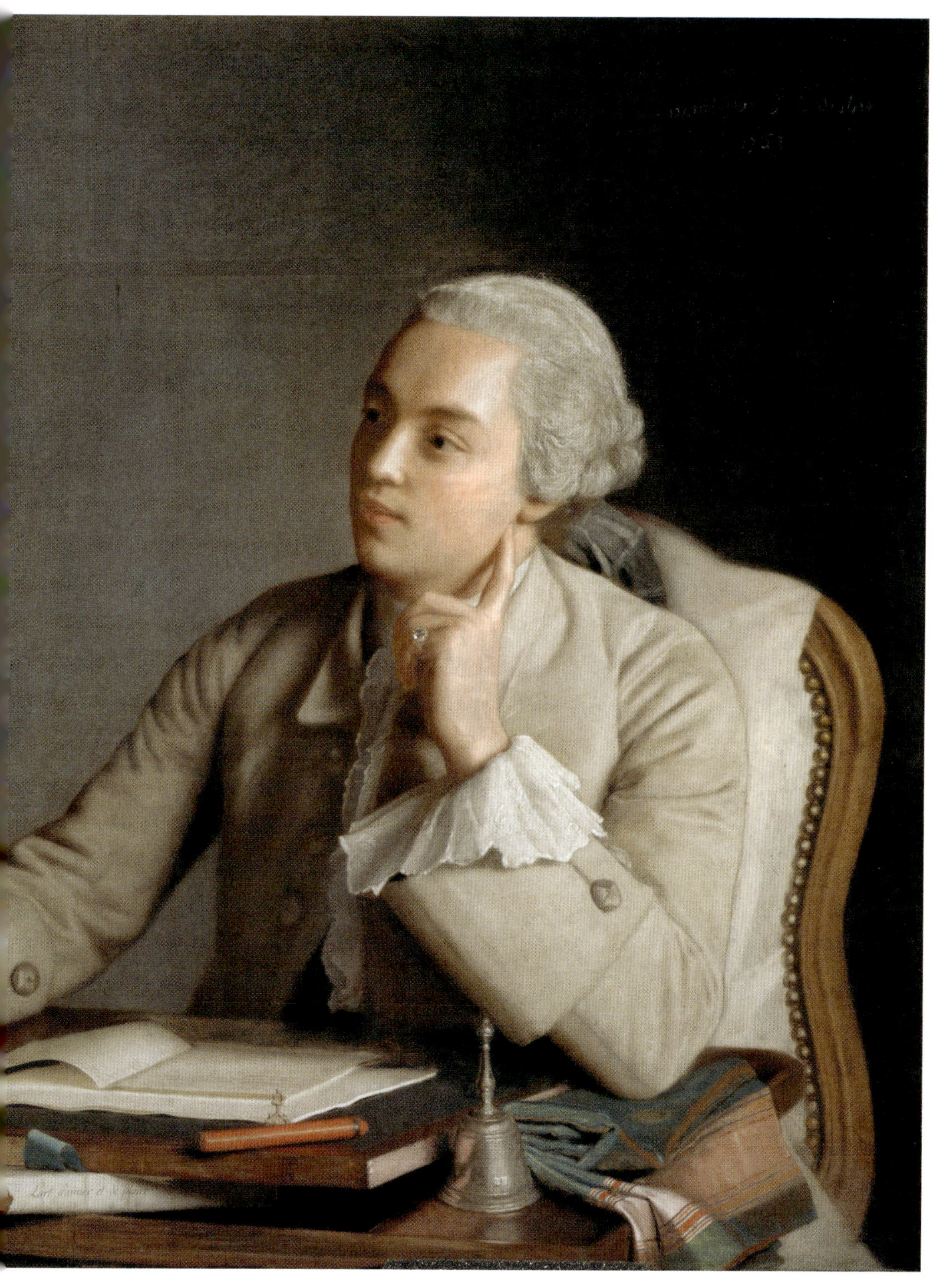

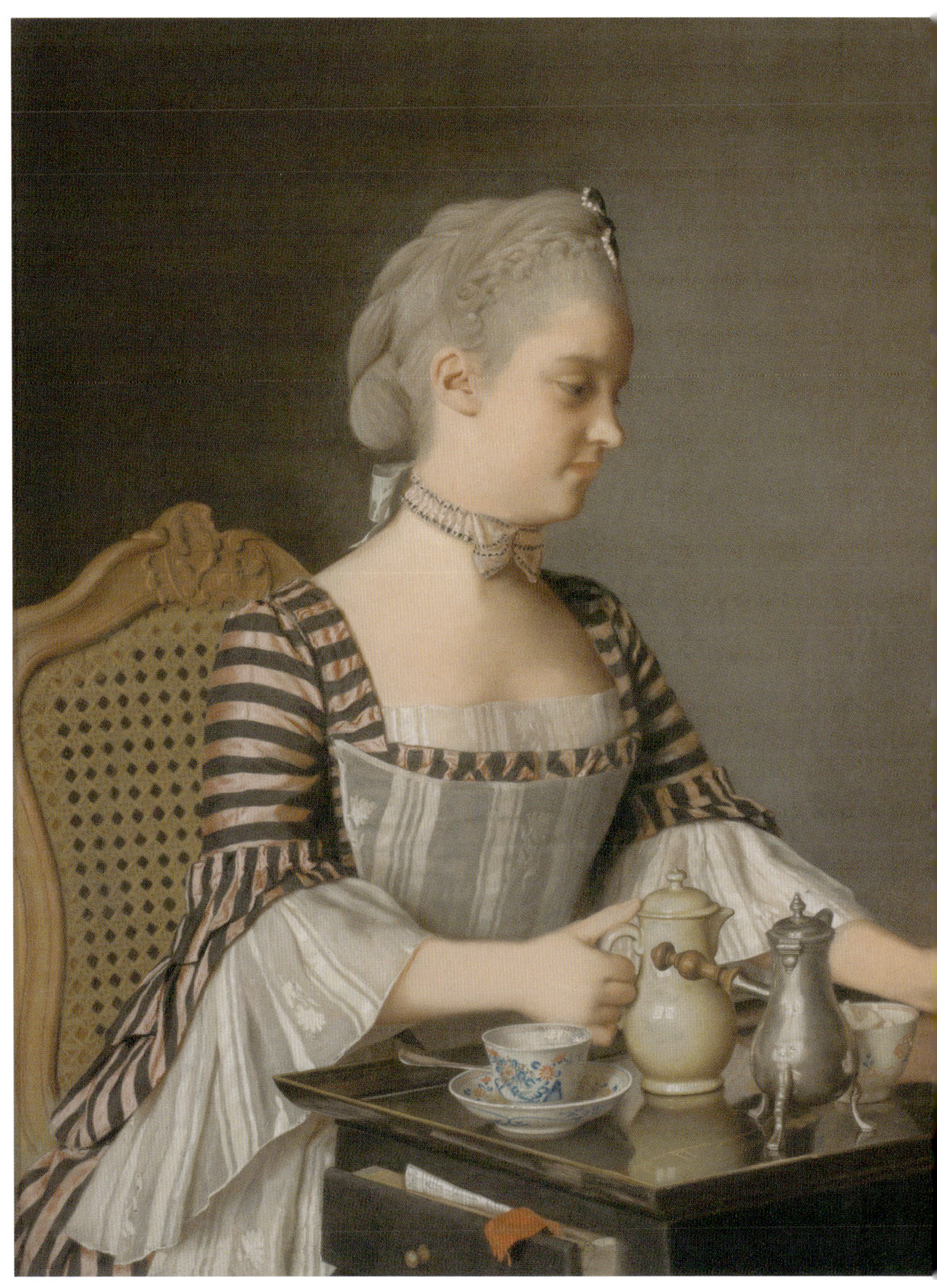

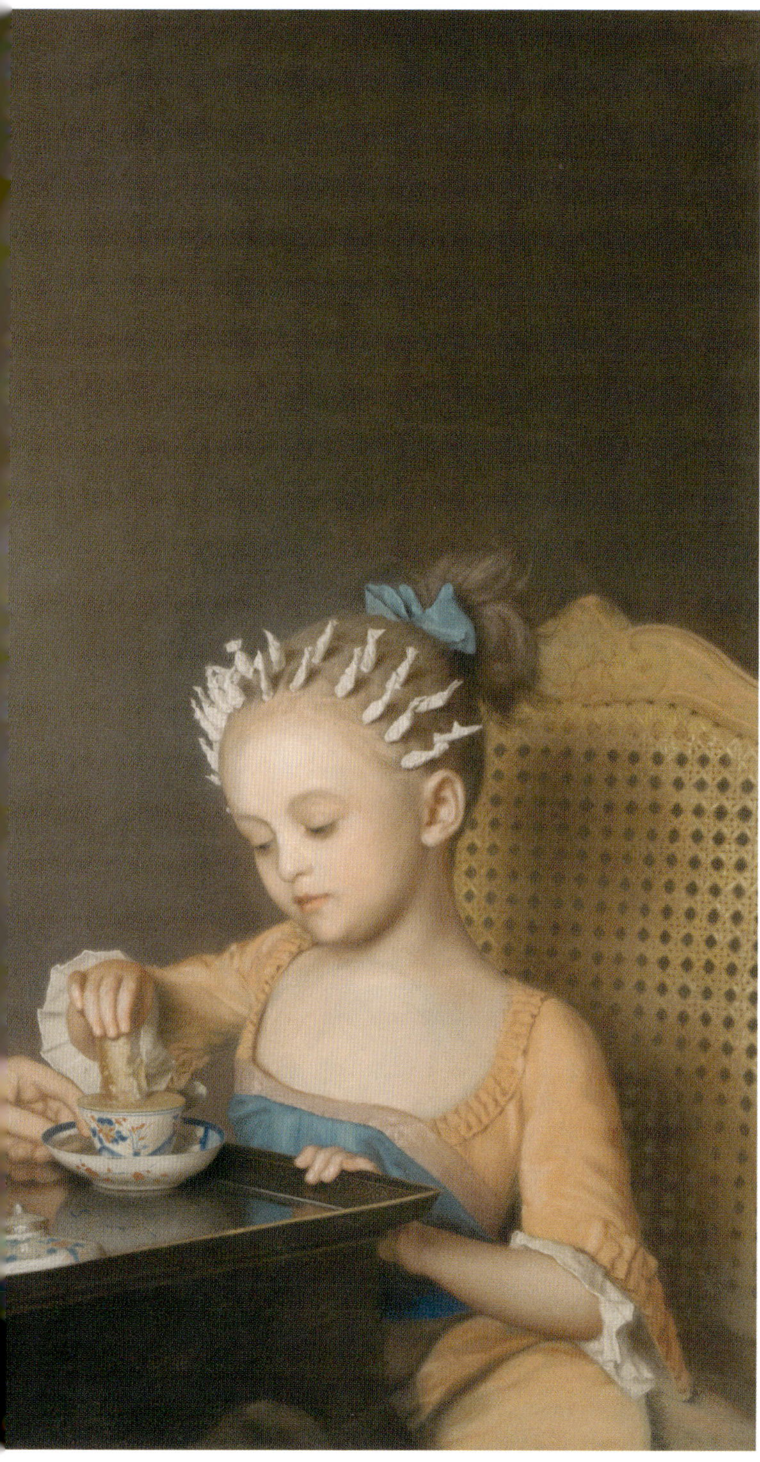

FIG. 29
Jean-Étienne Liotard
The Lavergne Family Breakfast
1754
Pastel on paper stuck down on canvas, 80 × 106 cm
National Gallery, London
NG6685

were made of triangular sheets of paper; the curlers would be pressed with a heated pinching iron before being removed. By contrast the woman has an especially complex coiffure already in place. Overall the palette adopted by Liotard is warm, being dominated by browns and delicate pink pastels; the blues of the girl's dress, ribbon and the floral designs on the oriental porcelain subtly complement it. This is a breakfast of luxury and refinement in polite society and is underpinned by themes of adult responsibility, manners and quiet affection.

There is an obvious although important distinction between these two great pastels which relate to mid-eighteenth-century social conventions: the man and boy in *L'Ecriture* are perhaps depicted as engaged with commerce or at least worldly pursuits; whereas the woman and girl in *The Lavergne Family Breakfast* are confined to the domestic sphere, albeit one of great comfort and pleasure. Both works are also gentle reminders of how instruction between generations underpinned civilised discourse and life.

It would be unwise to suggest that Liotard was making some sort of very overt didactic statement about how children might be brought up but nonetheless it is interesting to consider his pastel conversation pieces in the wider context of debates around the definition and qualities of childhood. It was eight years later in 1762 that the Genevan philosopher Jean-Jacques Rousseau published his treatise *Emilie, or On Education* in which he described a fictitious pupil who was born with innate goodness, entitled to happiness and vulnerable. This sensitive evocation of the state of childhood, which was to have far- reaching consequences, was highly controversial at the time and at odds with the views of, for example, the Catholic Church or an earlier writer like Thomas Hobbes (1588–1679), according to whom children needed rigid discipline to rescue them from their sinful state. In the domestic sphere Liotard conjures up for us the children are all charm and tentatively learning about what society expects of them: they seem embodiments of Rousseau's sympathetic and appealing vision.

The sitters have long been associated with the Lavergne family, Liotard's Lyons relatives, whom he also depicted in *L'Ecriture*. His elder sister Sara (1692–1757) married François Lavergne (1678–1752) and they settled in Lyons in the early 1730s. The precise identity of the woman and little girl has been debated. Recent research has proposed that the woman is either Catherine, Marguerite or Andrienne Lavergne and the girl their niece, Anne Delessert (1749–1802). She would therefore be five years of age. Although it would be pleasing to pin this down, it is not vital for an appreciation of the pastel which is not in any formal sense a portrait and has so many other pleasures to offer the viewer. It is interesting though that the most likely relationship seen here is one of a niece and niece, as that neatly mirrors the nephew and nephew relationship in *L'Ecriture.*

In 1773 when returning to Britain Liotard took the opportunity to make a copy in oil of his remarkable pastel breakfast scene (private collection), no doubt aware of its special status in his career and wanting to retain for himself an aide memoire of it. The oil version has a darker tonality and makes use especially of cast shadows to create a sense of spatial recession. He also made a point of referring to it in his later *Traité des principes et des règles de la peinture* (1781).

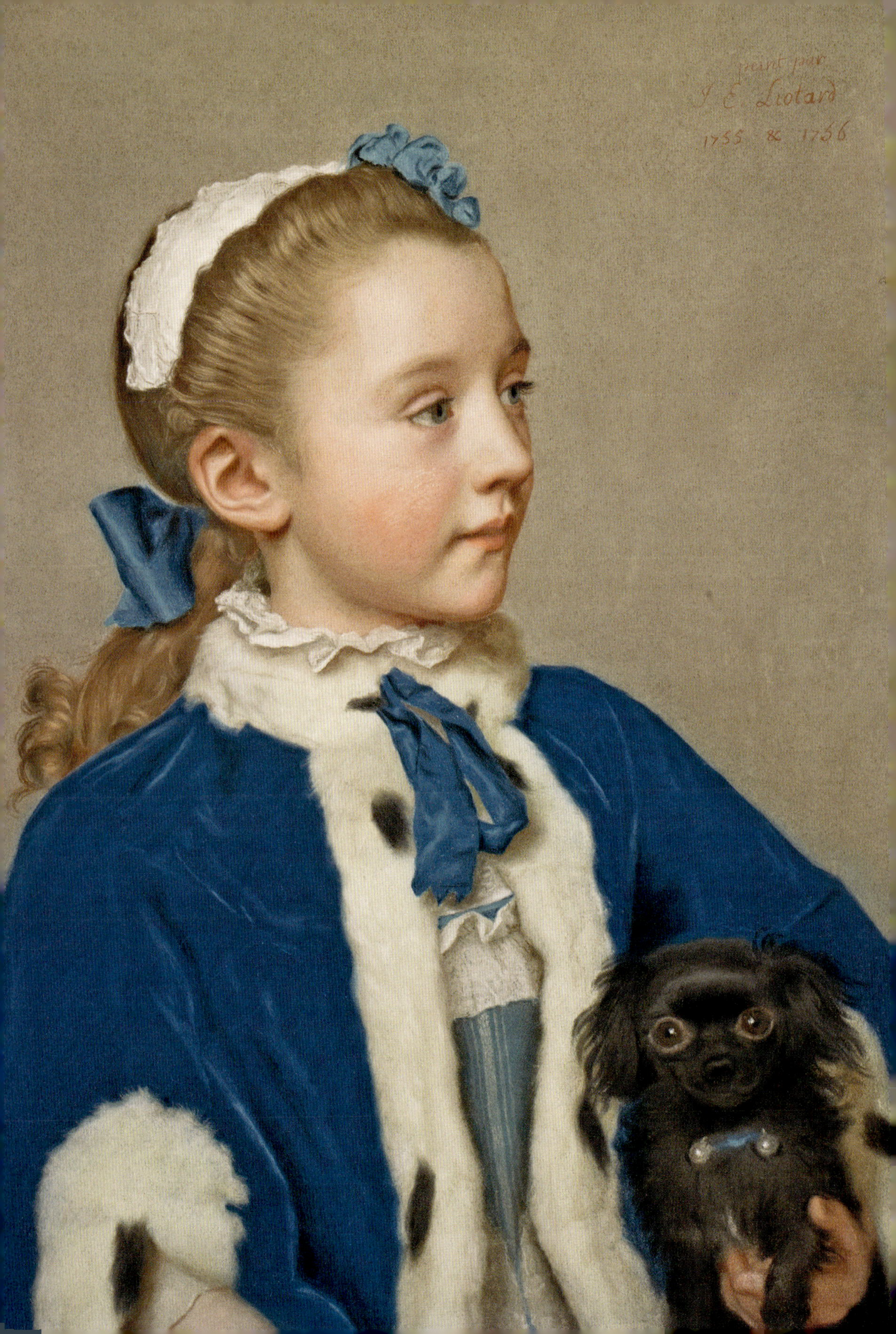
peint par
J. E. Liotard
1755 & 1756

6 The Netherlands and Returning to Geneva

FOLLOWING MANY YEARS OF travelling and the professional success Liotard enjoyed in London, he turned his attention, when in his fifties, to establishing a home life and his extended family connections helped with this. He left England and arrived in Holland in August of 1755, staying in Delft with his nephew, Jean-Louis Maizonnet. A visit was also undertaken to The Hague, where Liotard became a member of the *Confrerie Pictura* – an academic association of local artists which had been founded in the middle of the seventeenth century. Liotard's Dutch period was characterised by constant work as he created some fifty portraits during his two year stay in the Netherlands. He also worked on an oil painting that was profoundly influenced by seventeenth-century local art; called *A Dutch Girl at Breakfast* and showing a scene of domestic calm, it was recently acquired for the collection of the Rijksmuseum in Amsterdam.

It seems highly likely that it was his nephew who introduced Liotard to the woman who was to become his wife – Marie Fargues (1728–1782). Their wedding took place in Amsterdam on 13 August 1756. According to a number of accounts, in order to proceed with the marriage it was agreed that Liotard would sacrifice his by now famous beard, which reached his waist. It was apparently shaved off and ceremonially placed in a special box! Quite what the fate of this peculiar relic was is not recorded.

Liotard's talent did not diminish after he shaved and his marriage was appropriate for various reasons as Marie came from a merchant and Huguenot family, just like her husband. She was considerably younger than him, being twenty-eight at the time they met. Marie and the children she was to have over the next few years became the subjects of some especially sensitive and affectionate pastel portraits, drawings and prints. His first portrait of Marie herself, a rather austere pastel, is dated

Detail, FIG. 33

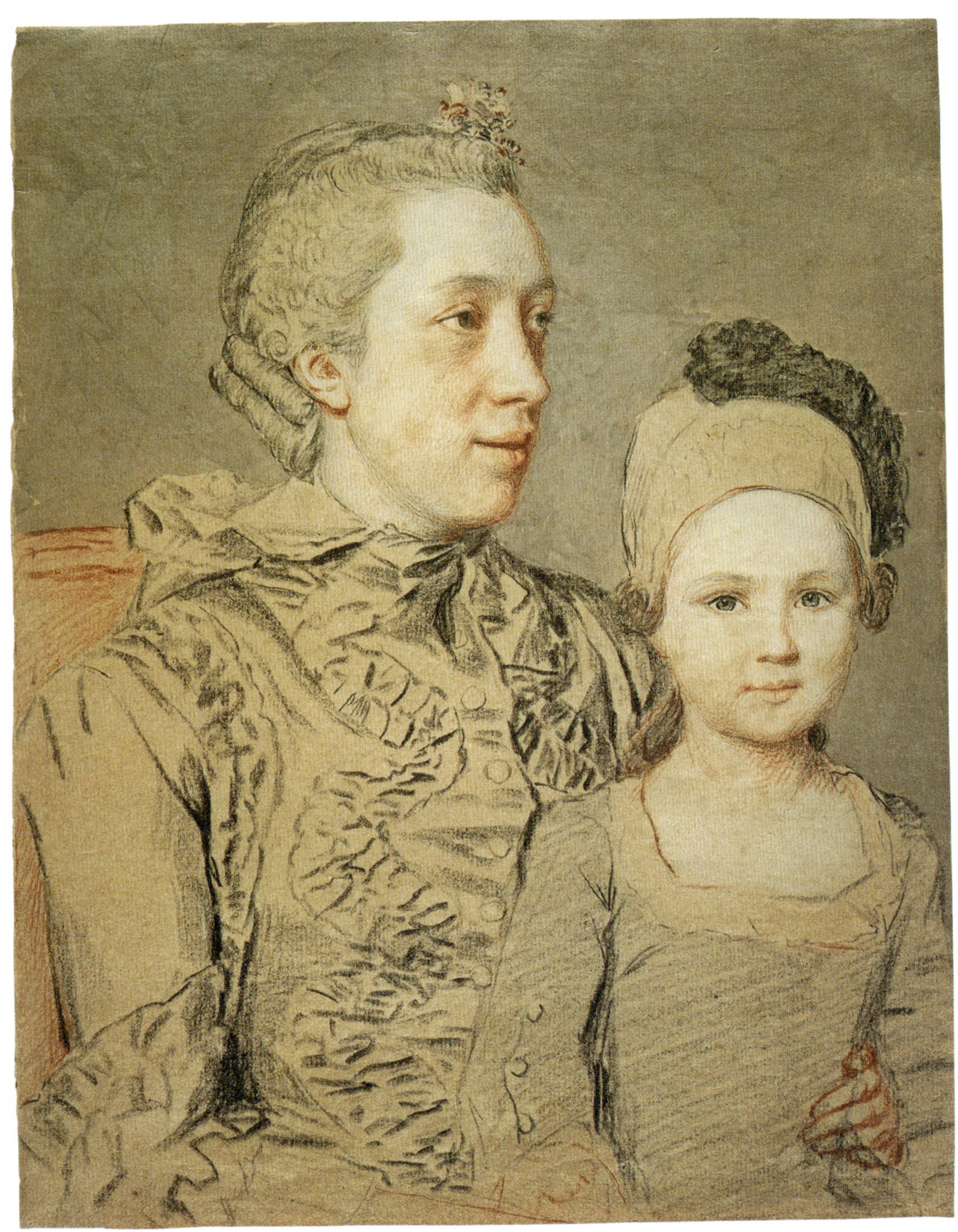

FIG. 30
Jean-Étienne Liotard
Marie Liotard-Fargues with Her Eldest Son Jean-Étienne Liotard
1761–62
Black and red chalk, with watercolour washes on the verso, 24.5 × 19.6 cm
Musée d'Art et d'Histoire, Geneva.
Gift of the Société auxiliaire du Musée
Inv. 1934–32

1757 and is thought to have been made as a gift for her unmarried sister, Jeanne Fargues, before the couple left for Geneva. Marie never returned to the Netherlands.

Liotard and Marie had six children in Geneva, two boys and four girls. One of the girls, Marie-Antoinette (1760–1761) did not survive beyond infancy. All the other children reached adulthood, however, with four of them living on into the nineteenth century: Jean-Étienne (1758–1822), Marie-Jeanne, called Mariette (1761–1813), Marie-Thérèse (1763–1793), Jean Daniel (1764–1821/8) and Marie-Anne-Françoise, known as Marianne (1767–1830).

Reflecting parental pride, Marie and the couple's eldest son Jean-Étienne became the subject of an especially fine drawing by Liotard, which is thought to date between 1761 and 1762 [FIG. 30]. Liotard's three-year-old son stares directly at his father in this intimate study, in a manner similar to the way in which Princess Louisa Anne had done about seven years earlier in London. He sits on his mother's lap, while she maintains a three-quarter pose, looking to the right. Their clothes are freely drawn in a schematic manner, while their faces are more precisely defined. The drawing was executed in black and red chalk with watercolour washes, especially used across the clothes and in the background. The white of the paper gives the impression of the hue and pallor of their skin. This makes it look as though drawing was created in the so-called 'trois crayon' technique, in other words using black, red and white chalk – a method mastered many years earlier by Watteau and others, which Liotard could employ to great effect.

Among the more fully resolved portraits Liotard made of his family, his much later pastel portrait of Marie-Thérèse aged six has a special place because of its animation and intense charm [FIG. 31]. It shows the little girl grasping a painted wooden doll, the colour of whose fine clothes complement her own, and gesturing with her index finger. In a diary kept by one of her siblings this action was neatly explained as she is apparently telling us to keep silent as the doll is asleep. The composition has been compared with a print of the 1730s after a lost painting by Chardin which shows a little girl holding a doll that is dressed as a nun, but the theme of silence is absent from it and the attached poem. Perhaps more relevant are older religious and mythic works which Liotard may well have been familiar with through prints, such as Annibale Carracci's (1560–1609) much reproduced *Il Silenzio* of 1599–1600, a painting that was bought by George III in 1766 and remains in the

FIG. 31
Jean-Étienne Liotard
Marie-Thérèse Liotard Holding a Doll
c. 1775
Pastel on parchment, 45 × 50 cm
Schönbrunn Palace, Vienna

FIG. 32
Jean-Étienne Liotard
Marie-Thérèse Liotard
1780
Mezzotint on paper, 44.2 × 38.6 cm
Collection Jean Bonna

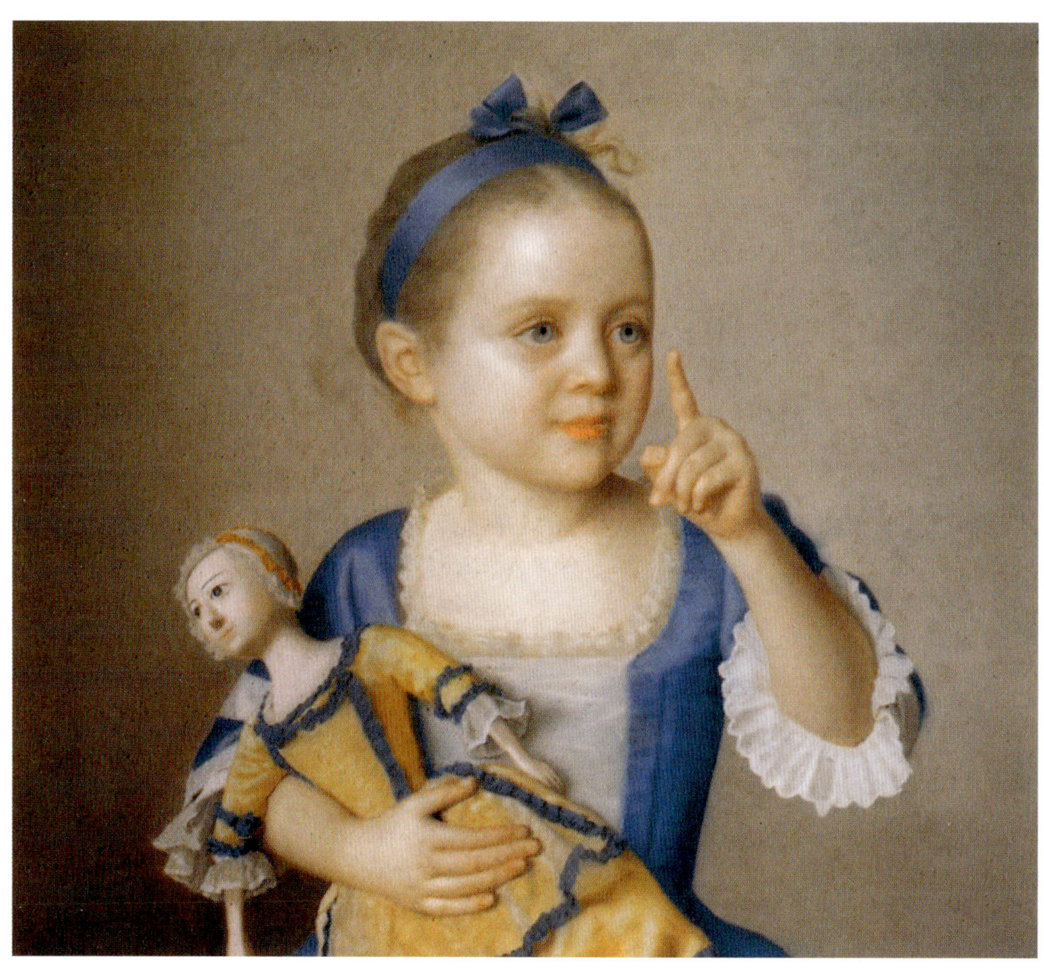

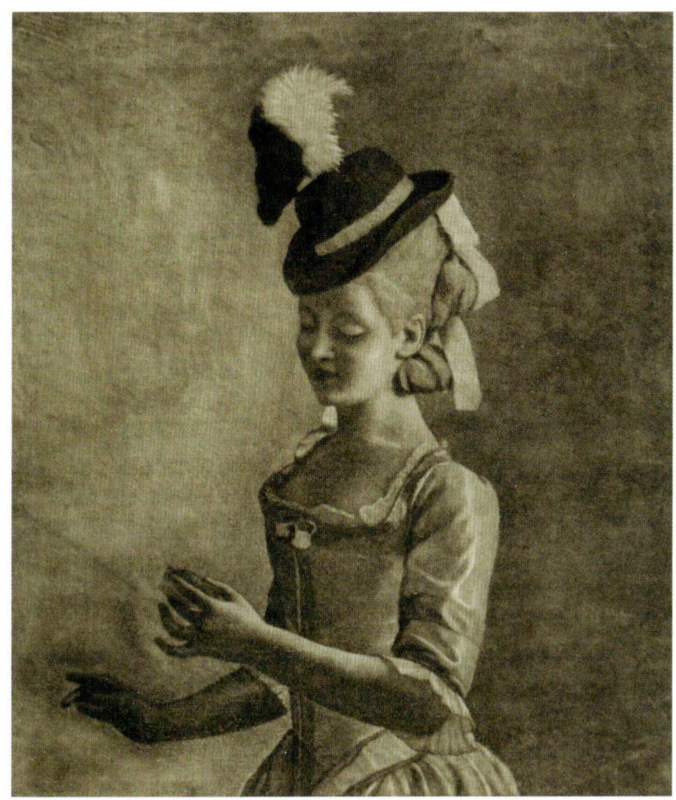

British Royal Collection; it shows the Virgin gesturing for silence as the Christ Child sleeps. An interesting, secular point of comparison is also provided by a renowned French sculpture from the decade before Liotard was creating his pastel: Étienne-Maurice Falconet's (1716–1791) *L'Amour Menaçant (Menacing Love)* of 1757 in the Rijksmuseum, Amsterdam, in which a cupid exhorts the onlooker to silence and secrecy.

Liotard's delightful pastel of his daughter Marie-Thérèse entered the collection of her godmother Empress Maria Theresa – and it is reasonable to suppose he expended such care on it with this end in mind. Marie-Thérèse also became the subject of one of her father's finest prints [FIG. 32]. This mezzotint depicts her at sixteen and once again combines portraiture with an element of genre – as she holds and admires a miniature portrait, which we can safely assume is one of her father's. It is an image of great elegance and poise that was created as one of six prints Liotard created to complement and illustrate his *Traité des principes et de règles de la peinture*, which was printed in Lyons

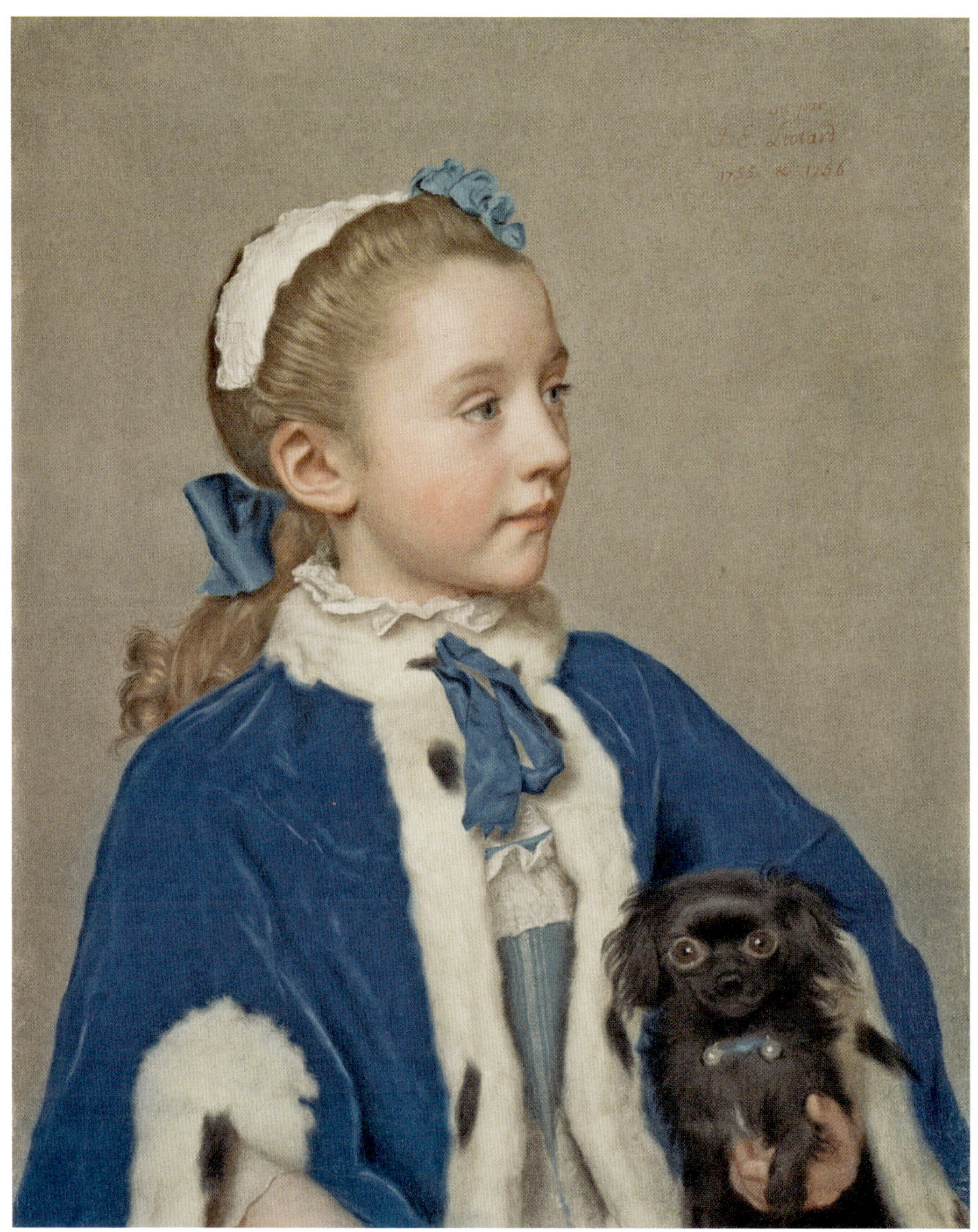

FIG. 33
Jean-Étienne Liotard
Portrait of Maria Frederike van Reede-Athlone at Seven Years of Age
1755–56
Pastel on vellum, 54.9 × 44.8 cm
The J. Paul Getty Museum, Los Angeles
No. 83.PC. 273

in 1781. The series also included a fine mezzotinted self-portrait. The artist's experimentation with printing techniques in old age after a long interval from such work must have been chiefly because of his work on the treatise, but it also formed part of a wider campaign of exploring different subject matter as well as techniques – as it was in the 1770s and early 1780s that he tested his skills with genre scenes and still lifes.

During the years when Liotard's family was growing up he did not remain in Geneva but continued to fulfil commissions elsewhere and began to assemble a collection of old master paintings, chiefly of Dutch seventeenth-century works; these were a desirable enrichment to any home but were also an asset that might be sold on later. He combined collecting opportunities with creating portraits and enchanting works dating from this period include his tender depiction of Maria Frederike van Reede-Athlone [FIG. 33], who came from an aristocratic Dutch family. Her most renowned relative was Godard van Reede, 1st Earl of Athlone, Baron van Reede (1644–1703), who became a general; he fought in the Franco-Dutch War and in Ireland and travelled to England in 1688 with William, Prince of Orange, who became William III. Liotard's connection with the family was established through Willem Bentinck van Rhoon (1704–1774), the son of the 1st Earl of Portland, who had settled as a diplomat in Holland.

The portrait of Maria Frederike was commissioned by her widowed mother whose late husband had been the 4th Earl of Athlone. It depicts her at the age of seven, although the execution of the pastel was spread across two years, as Liotard's red chalk inscription at the upper right testifies. The brilliant blue velvet and ermine of her luxurious shawl and it's unruly bow, which was perhaps inspired by French fashions, dominates the composition and contrasts with the more subtle blue-grey of the dress beneath – the colours of which match the collar of her startled lapdog, who confronts us and the artist directly, while the sitter looks with curiosity to the right. Light catches the girl's well brushed light brown hair and intensifies the hypnotic stare of her pet, who's breed is a matter of debate – he might be a type of so-called Japanese Chin or Japanese Spaniel or a Phalene. This is the only instance when Liotard depicted such an animal; all his other child portraits feature inanimate attributes. There are in fact very few studies of animals by him – cattle do though appear in copies he made in pastel of seventeenth-century Dutch paintings.

The mid-1750s, as well as being marked by such outstanding child portraiture, was also notable for portraits of remarkable creative figures. On a brief return to Paris in 1757 Liotard made wonderfully thoughtful and engaging portraits of Charles-Simon Favart (1710–1792) [FIG. 34] and his wife. Favart, whose father was a pastry cook, excelled as a dramatist, librettist of comic operas and theatrical impresario. He was a friend of the painter François Boucher (1703–1770) who depicted bucolic pastoral scenes from his plays. Favart became director of the Opéra-Comique, writing about one hundred and fifty works, renowned for their wit, humour and fluency. One of his plays, *Les Amours de Bastien et Bastienne*, was used as the inspiration for an early and little-known opera by Mozart, composed in 1768 when he was twelve. Favart also maintained a correspondence with Count Giacomo Durazzo (1717–1794), a Genoese diplomat and theatre director in Vienna, that provides insights to the theatrical world of the *ancien régime*. Maurice de Saxe, whom Liotard had portrayed back in 1748, paid unwanted attentions to Favart's wife Marie-Justine-Benoîte Favart (1727–1772), making her his mistress and virtually imprisoning her. She was renowned at the time she sat for Liotard as a highly celebrated dancer, singer and writer.

In the same year, 1757, back in Geneva, Liotard created one of his most intriguing portraits of a polymath – François Tronchin (1704–1798) [FIG. 35]. Tronchin, like Pococke (FIG. 12) and Algarotti, was one of the remarkable intellectuals that Liotard encountered. He was a distinguished financier, civic leader in Geneva, writer, collector and patron of the arts. Tronchin was friendly with Voltaire, delivered lectures on paintings, funded artists' travels and was especially enthusiastic about the merits of seventeenth-century Dutch and Flemish art, an enthusiasm shared by Liotard. His fine collection included Rembrandt's *A Woman in Bed* (now in the Scottish National Gallery in Edinburgh), with which he chose to be depicted. It is easy to imagine a discussion between Liotard and Tronchin about this decision, not least because Liotard is later recorded as owning a painting which he thought was a Rembrandt self-portrait. Tronchin's Rembrandt, which was painted in 1647, is a complex and ambiguous work of considerable sensuality, which probably employed a woman in the artist's intimate circle as model for the Old Testament figure Sarah, Tobias's wife. According to the Apocryphal Book of Tobit, Tobias, assisted by the archangel Raphael, defeated the devil Asmodeus who had killed Sarah's seven previous

FIG. 34
Jean-Étienne Liotard
Charles-Simon Favart (1710–1792)
1757
Pastel on vellum, 70 × 55 cm
Private collection

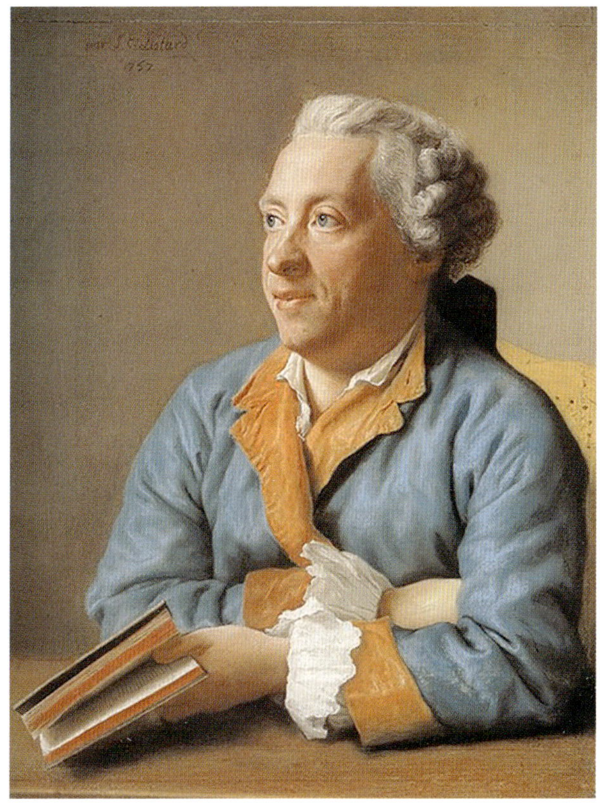

husbands on their wedding nights. She rises from her bed looking on encouragingly at the latest conflict.

The painting is displayed beside Tronchin unframed on a spindly easel, and with a gentle smile and eloquent gestures he appears to be engaged in expounding on its merits. He has another unidentifiable picture behind him and on the table lie an architectural plan, a musical score and a book, so subtly demonstrating the breadth of his knowledge and interests. Tronchin's collection also included Italian paintings; ninety-five pictures from it were sold in 1770 to Catherine the Great of Russia (1729–1786) and are now in the Hermitage Museum, St Petersburg. Diderot acted as the agent for the sale. It did not mark the end of Tronchin's collecting; during the following decades he set about forming a second collection, which came to include a further two hundred and fifty paintings.

FIG. 35
Jean-Étienne Liotard
François Tronchin (1704–1798)
1757
Pastel on vellum, 38 × 46.3 cm
The Cleveland Museum of Art,
John L. Severance Fund
Inv. 1978.54

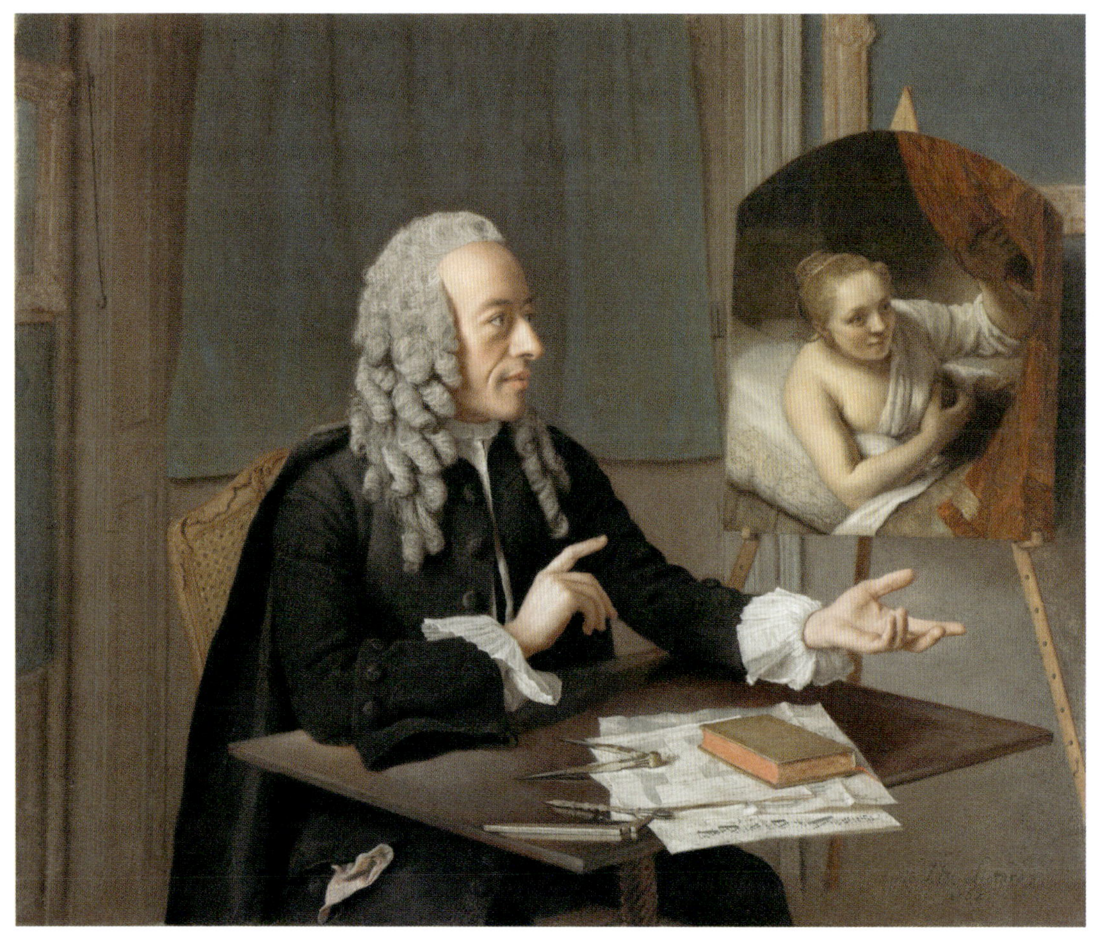

Liotard depicted other members of Tronchin's family in drawings and pastel, although none were as ambitious as this work, which makes an animated and idiosyncratic addition to the tradition of portraits of collectors and connoisseurs. Liotard may well have expended such care over it because of personal connections between the artist and sitter: Tronchin was the godfather of Liotard's daughter, Marianne. In addition, his cousin was a highly regarded physician, whose patients sometimes made good use of their time in the city by arranging for Liotard to portray them.

Important works such as the Tronchin portrait were created in Geneva, which essentially remained the centre of Liotard's career for the rest of his life, but he still continued undertaking journeys during the 1760s and 1770s, revisiting now familiar cities to seek and fulfil commissions. These trips included return visits to Vienna in 1762, the Netherlands from 1771 to 1773, and London from 1772 to 1774. Although Liotard was turning seventy by the time of this London visit he still had the energy to maintain his international reputation and practice.

It was though through the 1760s that numerous portrait commissions were secured from prominent families in Geneva, some of which must be counted as being his greatest triumphs. They include single works and pendant pictures, among which, because of the infectious sense of pleasure and companionship they convey, his portraits of the Thellussons should be highlighted [FIGS 36 and 37]. There was a long tradition of creating complementary paired portraits to commemorate marriages, to which these subtle and joyous works make a memorable contribution. The sitters seem to convey genuine affection, deftly pinpointed in the dialogue of glances by Liotard. All of the elements of the pastels are enhanced by their brilliant colours and pristine condition. Isaac-Louis de Thellusson (1727–1790) was from a family of bankers and politicians and later was elected mayor of Geneva. He wears a magnificent silk robe embroidered with flowers and leans back nonchalantly, looking across at his new – and second – wife. Julie de Thellusson, née Ployard (1740–1820), brought wealth to the alliance as her father was a successful merchant. They married in September 1760 at Jussy outside Geneva. The blue and white and lace of her ornate gown complements the colours of her husband's clothing; the couple are also unified by the presence of miniatures of each other: hers is worn on her wrist and framed with diamonds and his is set into a ring on his little finger. The presence of these miniature portraits underlines one of the key

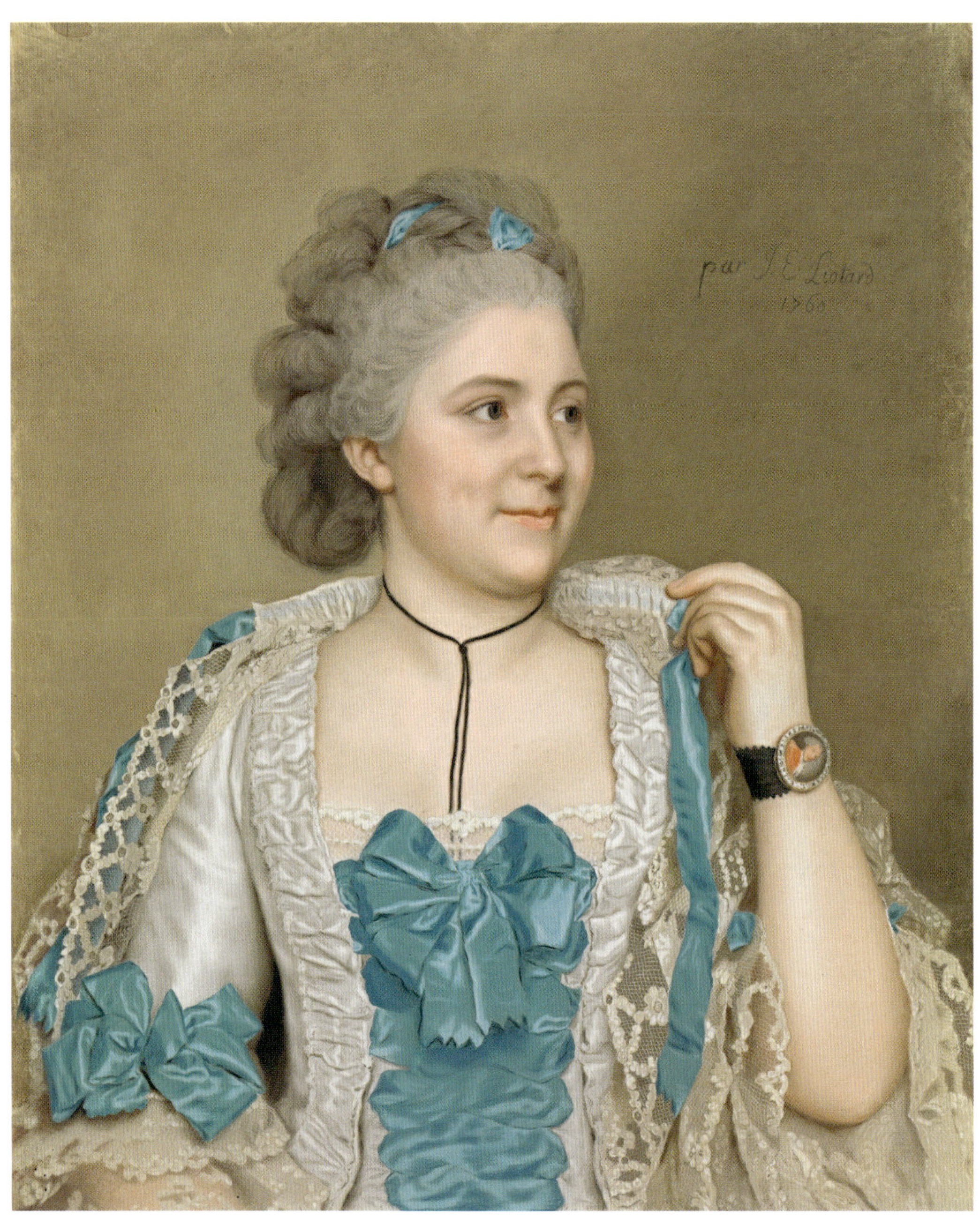

FIG. 36
Jean-Étienne Liotard
Julie de Thellusson-Ployard
1760
Pastel on vellum, 70 × 58 cm
Museum Oskar Reinhart, Winterthur
Inv. 278

FIG. 37
Jean-Étienne Liotard
Isaac-Louis de Thellusson
1760
Pastel on vellum, 70 × 58 cm
Museum Oskar Reinhart, Winterthur
Inv. 277

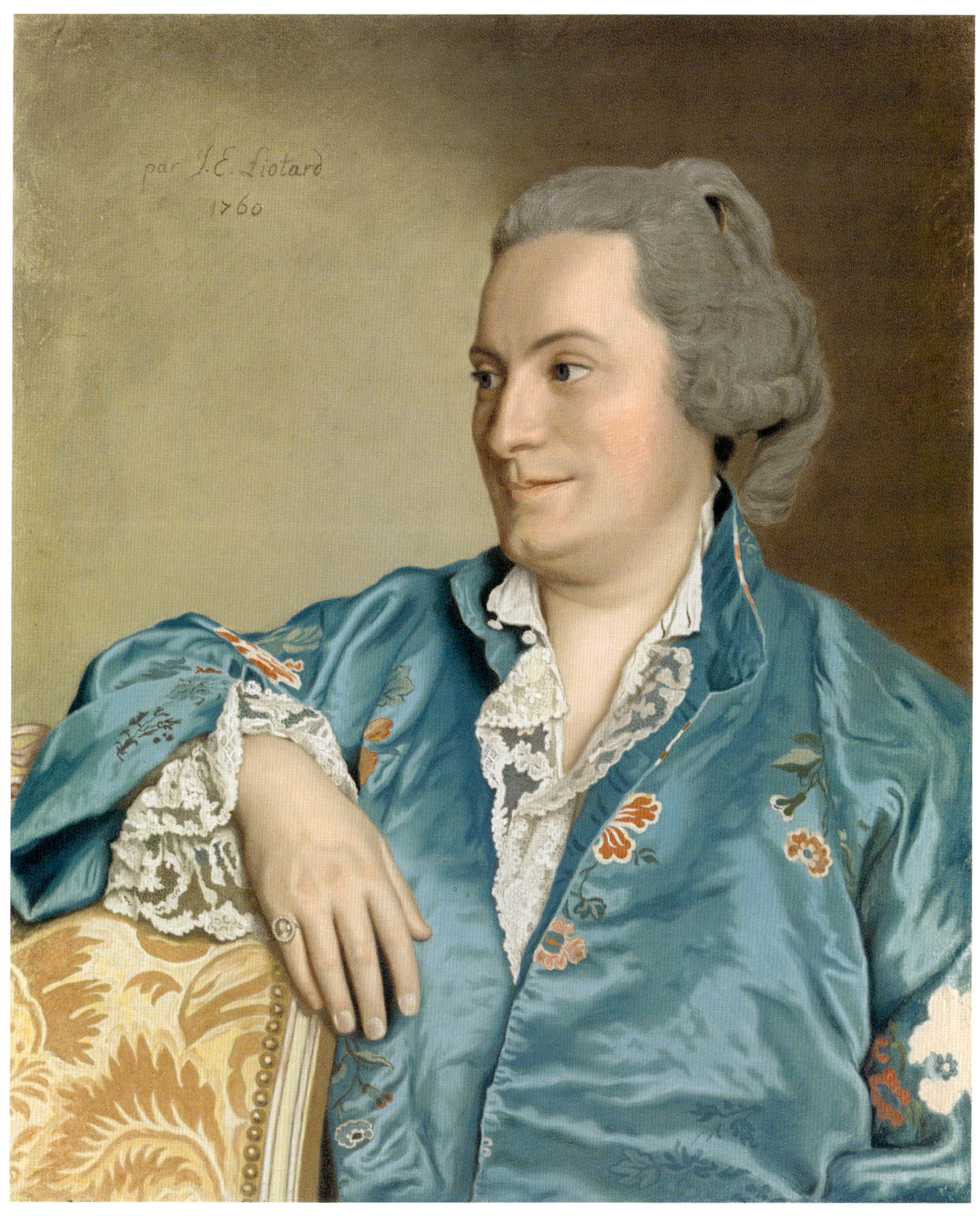
par J.E. Liotard
1760

functions of such works – not merely as commemorative, but as intimate tokens of love.

The dominant palette in these pastels of rich blue set off by a neutral tan background was also employed in an ambitious portrait which probably dates from a year later – Liotard's elegant depiction of Suzanne Curchod (1737–1794) [FIG. 38]. Unlike the Thellussons she was not born wealthy; her father was a Protestant pastor in the Swiss village of Crassier near Lausanne. However, Curchod became exceptionally well educated and her knowledge is perhaps alluded to here by the book she has paused from reading. Its mottled calf cover is lovingly depicted by Liotard, but the still life elements on the table outshine it as a tour de force: the silver tray, glass and carafe with their reflections are comparable with details in *The Chocolate Girl*. There is also the miraculous fruit – in Liotard's hands pastel becomes the ideal medium to replicate the furry texture and lush colours of a peach.

Suzanne Curchod looks up as though she is leaving her studies to engage in conversation and this is entirely appropriate as she was to both form part of and lead highly accomplished, cultivated, intellectual circles in Geneva and Paris where the art of discussion and debate was of paramount importance. At the time Liotard portrayed Curchod she was engaged to the historian Edward Gibbon (1737–1794), the future author of *The History of the Decline and Fall of the Roman Empire*, who spent five formative years based in Switzerland and found her '… learned… lively in conversation, pure in sentiment and elegant in manners'. The engagement was, however, broken off in 1762 because of parental disapproval, as her humble background was considered inappropriate. Two years later she married the financier and statesman Jacques Necker (1732–1804) who was to secure great advancement at the court of Louis XVI in Paris. It was there that she dominated sparkling salons at which many of the great minds of the period gathered to discuss politics and literature and art. As Madame Necker she was portrayed in oil by Joseph Siffred Duplessis (1725–1802) in a splendid formal portrait, now in the Chateau de Coppet in Switzerland, which provides an interesting point of comparison with Liotard's earlier, more unconventional and characterful study. She had one child – Anne Louise Germaine – who is better known as Madame de Staël (1766–1817), the renowned and daring writer and political theorist, who inherited something of her mother's wit and wide-ranging intelligence.

In the spring of 1762 Liotard returned to Vienna after a long absence. The main reason for this visit was to see Maria Theresa again. He was evidently proud of the pastel portrait of Suzanne Curchod and took it with him. He showed it to the Empress who persuaded him to sell it to her along with *L'Ecriture*. This was the beginning of the decade that his own young family was growing and in the same year he also made a quite remarkable series of drawn portraits of the younger members of the Imperial family which distil the abilities he had developed in terms of drawn portraiture and sensitivity to depicting the clothing and attributes of young sitters. He was commissioned to draw eleven of the children of the Emperor and Empress; she had sixteen children in all, thirteen of whom survived infancy, and memorably declared that had she not almost always been pregnant she would have wanted to have gone into battle during the Seven Years War. The Hapsburg drawings were all half-length studies and in most cases Liotard depicted the children engaged in a domestic activity, such as reading, sewing, drawing or playing an instrument. As such they extend the repertoire of activities which had started to be shown in the private Hanoverian court portraits. Such engaging and animated works would at the time never have been displayed in public and these very personal souvenirs were only intended for the Empress; she travelled with them around her vast realm and made it very clear to Liotard what great pleasure they gave her. The intimate function of the drawings is especially well illustrated by the portrait of Archduchess Marie Antoinette of Austria (1755–1793) [FIG. 39], as it is recorded as having been displayed on the desk of the Empress when she was writing to her daughter. She wrote regularly to her children, whom she planned to place through advantageous marriages across Europe in positions that would further the cause and status of the Hapsburgs. She also micro-managed every aspect of their domestic and private lives.

The seven-year-old Archduchess sits bolt upright in her chair looking directly at us and unwinding a thread to use for sewing or knotting. Eight years later she married the Dauphin of France by proxy and in 1774 she was crowned Queen. Her life and the narratives and myths that swirl around it chiefly focus on her adult existence, fabled extravagances, and death by guillotining. Here, however, is a young child, characterful certainly although constrained by the protocols of the Viennese court. She wears a pink silk dress, diamond earrings and her hair is curled and powdered. There is a clear distinction between the intense, precise

FIG. 38
Jean-Étienne Liotard
Suzanne Curchod (1737–1794)
c. 1761
Pastel on four sheets of vellum, 85.5 × 104.7 cm
Schönbrunn Palace, Vienna
Inv. AC 5502

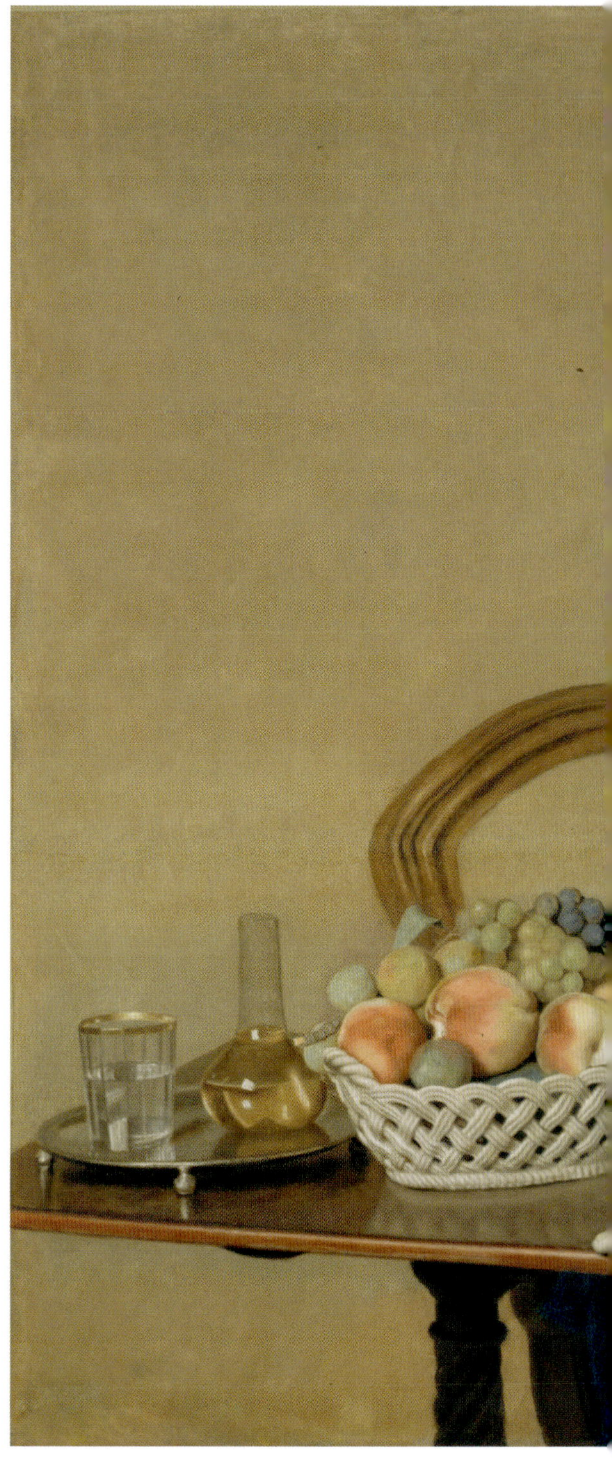

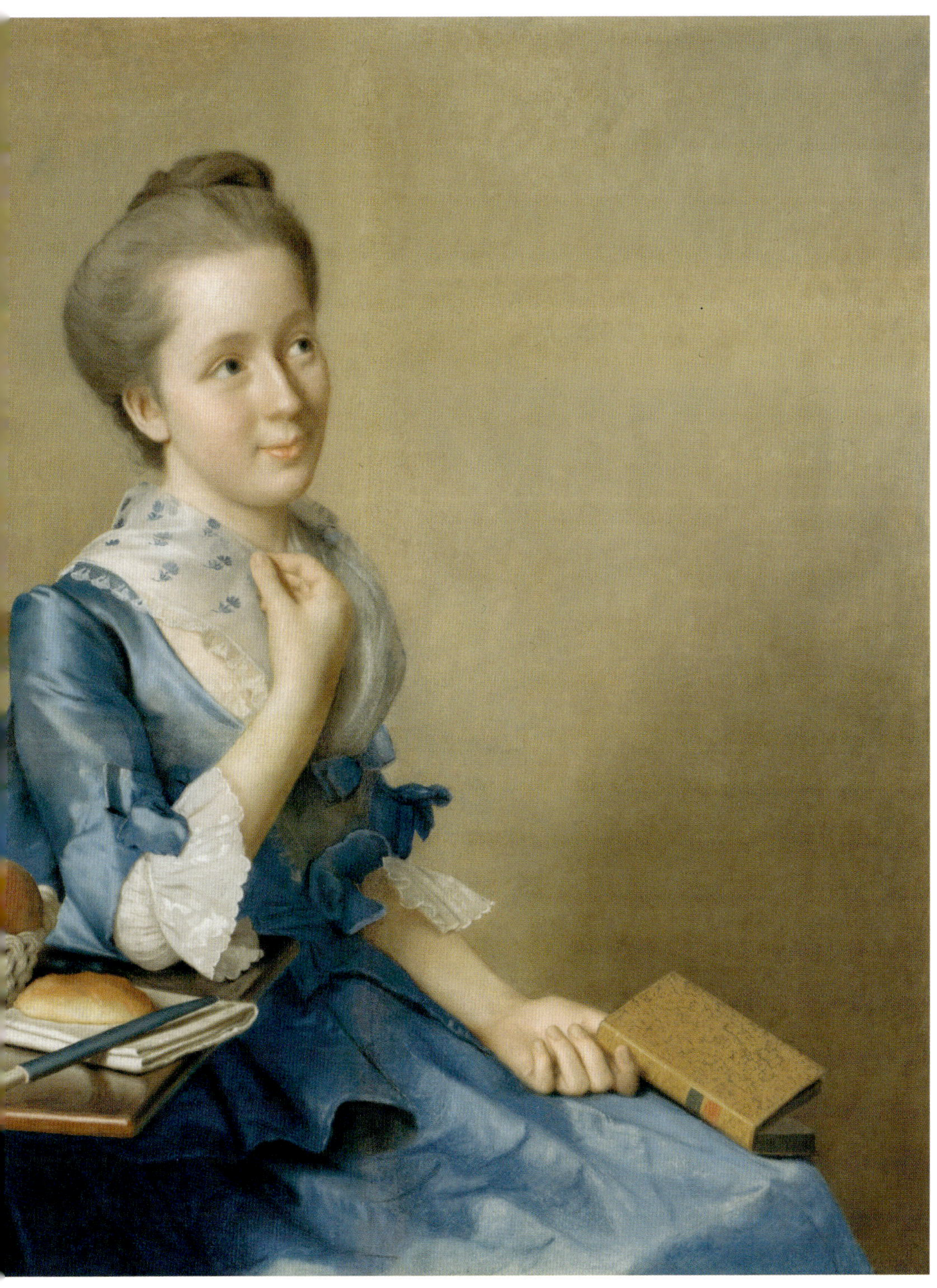

drawing of her face and the much broader, hurried sketching of her dress and chair. Her life was confined at this period and spent either at the Hofburg Palace in Vienna or the Schönbrunn, the Imperial Summer residence. Her governess was Countess von Brandeis (1713–1769) and she received private tutoring, focusing on religion, foreign languages and etiquette, although apparently with limited success. It was in October of 1762, the year Liotard drew her, that the little Archduchess met Mozart, who was the same age and already recognised as a prodigy.

Another example from the Vienna series of drawings demonstrates the range of accomplishments mastered by Marie Antoinette's siblings. Her far less well-known older sister, Archduchess Maria Elizabeth of Austria (1743–1808) [FIG. 40] was drawn in a more animated pose. She was renowned as being somewhat vain because she was considered the most beautiful of the Archduchesses, as well as highly accomplished in terms of musical skills, and it seems that Liotard has depicted her closely reading a score which rests on a stand on the desk at the right. She follows the notes with a pointing gesture and her eyes and so does not look at us. Three years later she performed for the court in an operetta by Christopher Willibald Gluck (1714–1787) at the wedding celebrations of her brother Joseph. Maria Elizabeth was, like all the Imperial children, intended by her mother to forge a beneficial alliance through marriage; however, in 1765 three years after the drawing was made she contracted smallpox and her face was scarred. This thwarted such plans and instead she became a canoness and then abbess of the Convent for Noble Ladies in Innsbruck. Members were permitted freedom to mix in high society and lead a public life and this she did, enjoying hosting receptions and becoming renowned for her sharp wit. The pleasures of such an existence were though curtailed by the invasion of Napoleon in 1806, when she had to flee to Linz.

In 1763, the year after drawing the Imperial children, Liotard built on the increasingly complex and ambitious pastel portraiture he had developed with works such as his depiction of Tronchin, and scaled new heights for the medium with his spectacular depiction of *John, Lord Mountstuart, Later 4th Earl and 1st Marquess of Bute (1744–1814)* [FIG. 41]. Mountstuart is portrayed at the age of nineteen. He was the son and heir of John Stuart, 3rd Earl of Bute (1713–1792) and Mary Wortley Montagu (1718–1794) (the daughter of Lady Mary, author of the famous *Turkish Embassy Letters*). The 3rd Earl had wide-ranging interests, encompassing politics and botany and the collecting of paintings, notably

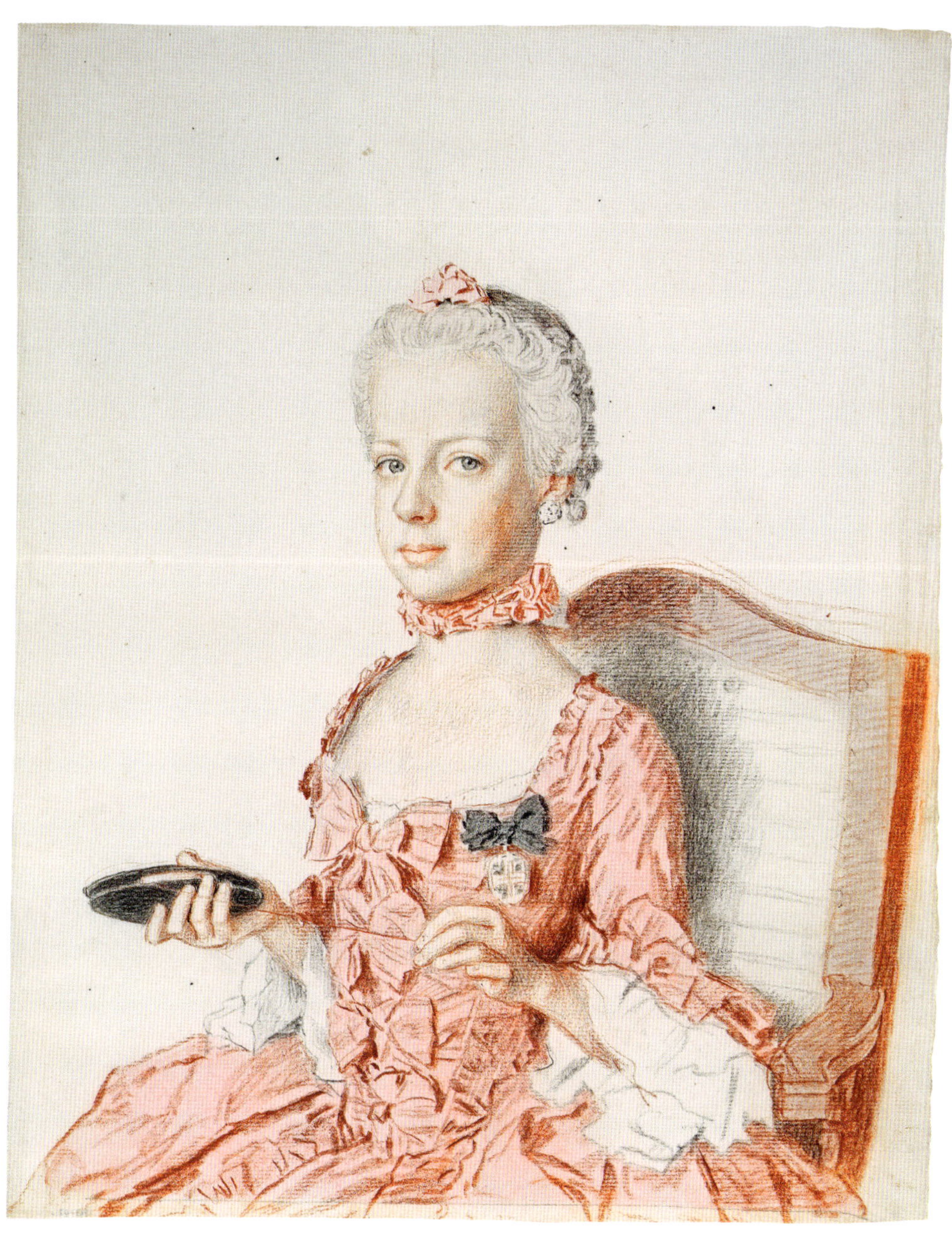

FIG. 39
Jean-Étienne Liotard
Archduchess Marie Antoinette of Austria (1755–1793)
1762
Black and red chalk, graphite pencil, watercolour and watercolour glaze on paper, heightened with colour on the verso, 31.1 × 24.9 cm
Cabinet d'arts graphiques des Musée d'Art et d'Histoire, Geneva
Inv. 1947–0042

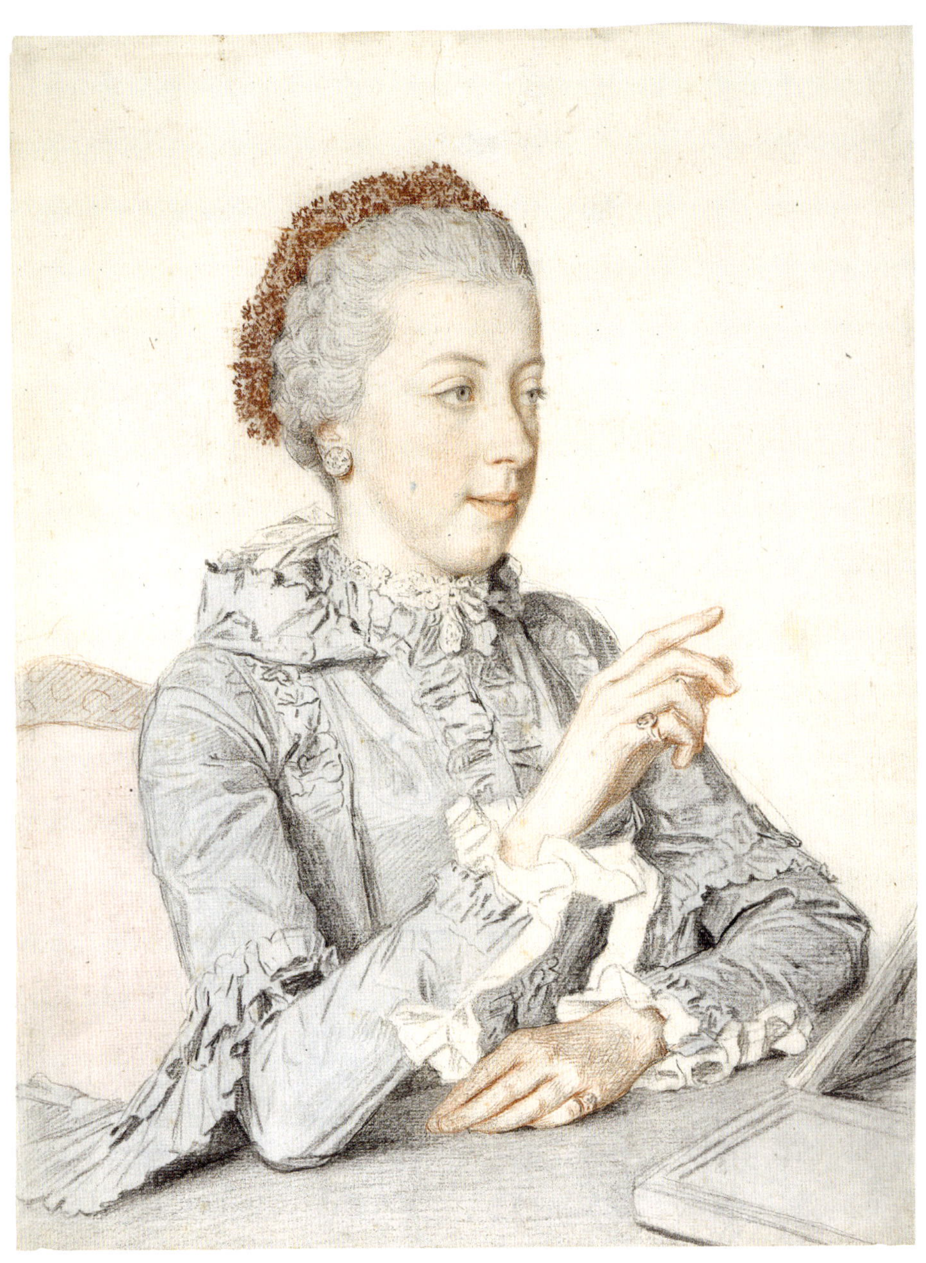

FIG. 40
Jean-Étienne Liotard
Archduchess Maria Elizabeth of Austria (1743–1808)
1762
Black and red chalk, graphite pencil, watercolour and watercolour glaze on paper, heightened with colour on the verso, 31.1 × 24.6 cm
Cabinet d'arts graphiques des Musée d'Art et d'Histoire, Geneva
Inv. 1947–0035

seventeenth-century Dutch and Flemish works, as well as earlier Italian pictures. Later, in 1780, he was appointed first President of the Society of Antiquaries of Scotland. He was a royal 'favourite' and was closely connected with Princess Augusta, whom Liotard had portrayed with her family in the 1750s. The pastel portrait of his son Lord Mounstuart was commissioned when Bute was briefly serving as Prime Minister to King George III, but it was executed in Geneva rather than London, where Mountstuart stayed for three years (1761–3), prior to undertaking an Italian Grand Tour. He was educated there by Prof. Paul Henri Mallet (1730–1807), a historian who had made his name studying Danish literature and Mountstuart visited during this period luminaries such as Edward Gibbon, Suzanne Curchod's admirer, and Voltaire. So we see here a highly sophisticated, cosmopolitan Genevan interior, with gilded andirons and a mirror that both look French in style, a carpet that might be Turkish and a Far Eastern screen. It is interesting to speculate about whether this is a glimpse of Liotard's home life or his sitter's lodgings. The pastel is signed and dated in the shadow beyond the screen.

This work represents a remarkable achievement for a pastel portrait – as a full-length study on an impressive scale. It was executed on vellum and its height is just under 115cm. Liotard's work was not though the largest pastel portrait of the period – that distinction is held by Maurice Quentin de La Tour's sensational *Portrait of the Marquise de Pompadour* in the Musée du Louvre, of 1752–55, which has a paper support and is 178.5cm high. Working on such a large scale and for an important patron required careful planning on Liotard's part: a surviving black and white chalk drawing by him shows how Mountstuart's relaxed pose, leaning against the mantelpiece, was rapidly established. To some extent it echoes the pose his father had adopted in a famous full-length oil portrait by Allan Ramsay (1713–1783) of 1758 (Scottish Government; on loan to the Scottish National Portrait Gallery). Ramsay's painting was becoming widely known just at the period Liotard was working on his composition through engravings after it.

It is the textural details he defined with pastel that are so ingenious – the gilding on the mirror frame, weave of the carpet, silk on the chair, painting on the screen and the dying embers in the fire. Material wealth and international taste are ostentatiously displayed so you are left in doubt about Mountstuart's status. His father was delighted with the result and paid twice the price originally agreed with Liotard. It is perhaps unsurprising because of the work's ambition, that a fine

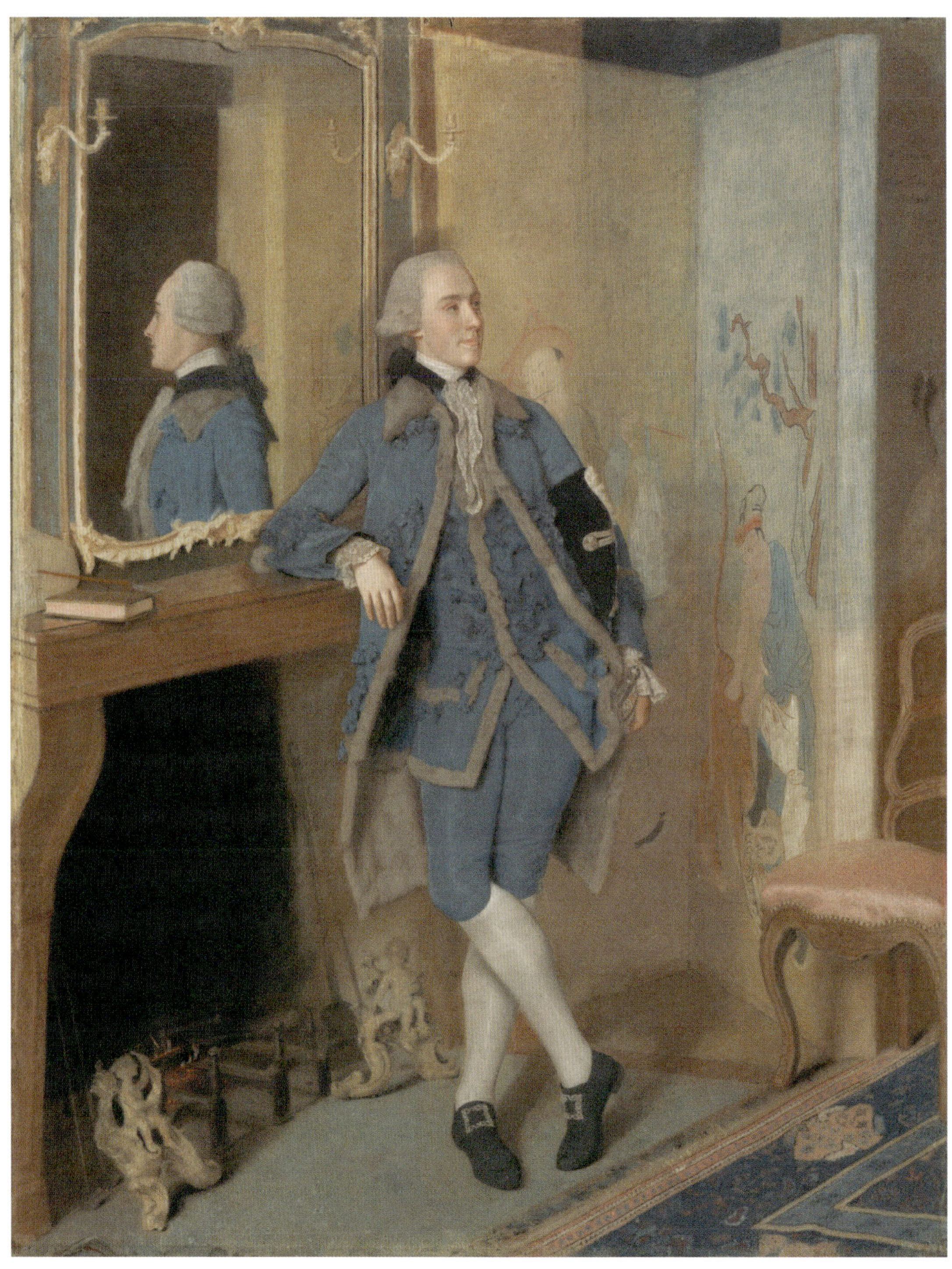

mezzotint was made after the portrait ten years later by John Raphael Smith (1752–1812). By then Mountstuart was a member of parliament. Later, he served as an envoy to Turin and became British Ambassador to Spain. He developed knowledgeable aesthetic tastes; in 1783, for example, he compiled an inventory of seventy-five paintings in the family collection that might be conserved, retained and discarded.

One of the most intriguing aspects of Liotard's pastel which was rare and innovative in the the context of eighteenth-century portraiture was the manner in which Mountstuart is ingeniously depicted reflected in profile, while appearing in three-quarter view in the room he inhabits. The profile view is associated with the contemporary vogue for silhouettes and the long heritage of portraits on coins and medals and gems, while the presence of the sitter in the room simultaneously brings such traditions to life. Liotard was subtly displaying here his ingenuity and knowledge of different strands of portrait practice. Such a pictorial device using mirrors became commonplace in the nineteenth century when it was employed in fashion magazines and was then taken up on more than one occasion by later outstanding and inventive portrait painters, such as Jean-Auguste-Dominique Ingres (1780–1867).

FIG. 41
Jean-Étienne Liotard
John, Lord Mountstuart, Later 4th Earl and 1st Marquess of Bute (1744–1814)
1763
Pastel on vellum, 109.2 × 86.4 cm
The J. Paul Getty Museum, Los Angeles
Inv. 2000.58

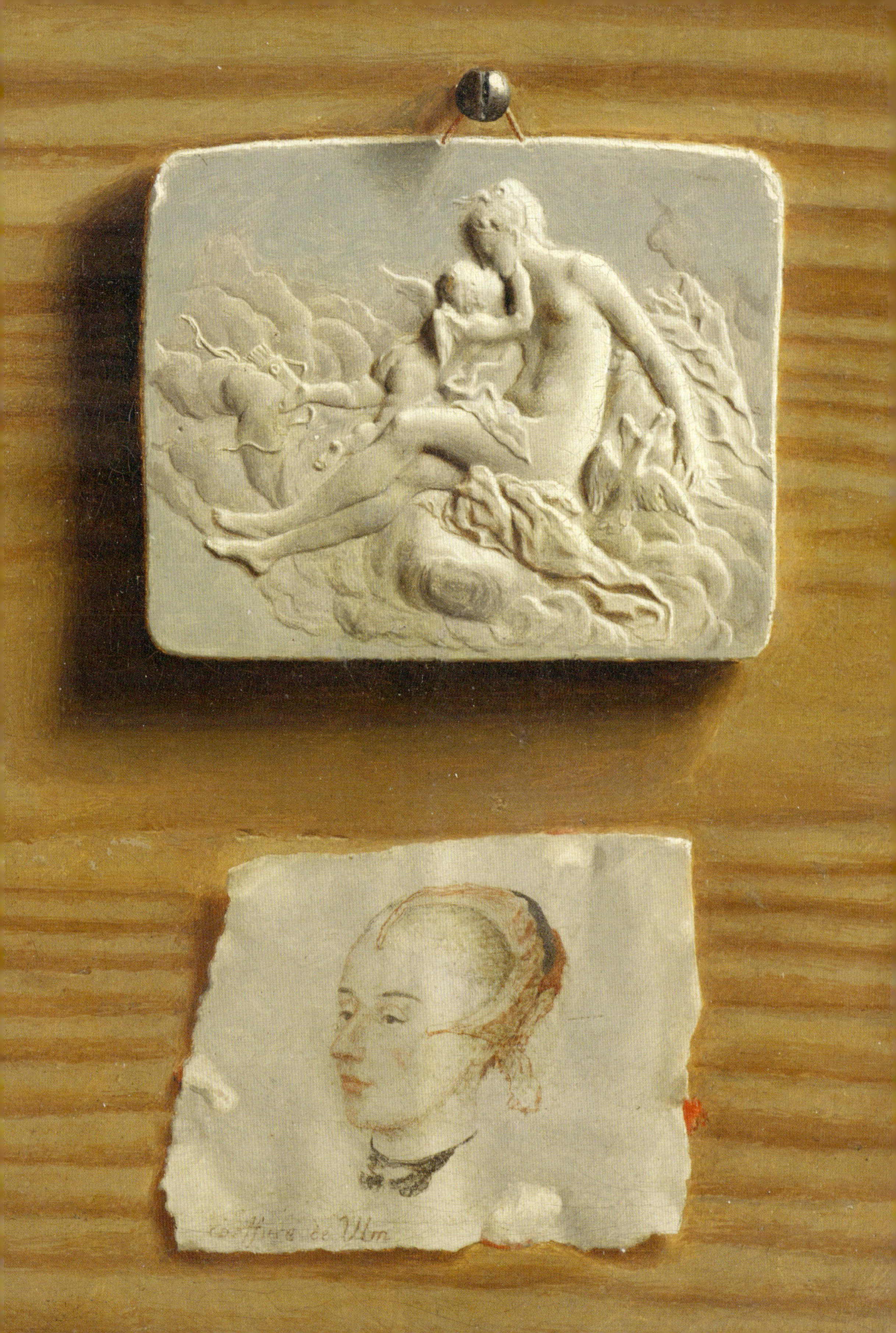

7 Late Innovations
Theory and Practice

IN 1763, AS WELL AS making the splendid portrait of Lord Mountstuart, Liotard was busy on a number of different fronts. He purchased a country house to accommodate his growing family at Confignon, which is four miles south-west of Geneva, within the Duchy of Savoy. He also wrote to his patron in Britain Lord Bessborough the letter referred to earlier about fixing pastels. In it he also reported on the success of his visit the previous year to the Austrian Empress, his sale to her of three works, and her gift for his wife of a porcelain travelling breakfast set. Liotard in addition noted in the letter his ambition to sell to his English contacts works by Jan van Huysum (1682–1749), the renowned Dutch painter of flower pieces. Art dealing and collecting were to gradually become more prominent activities during the latter part of Liotard's life.

He travelled through Turin in 1766, and then back to Geneva where, during the second half of the 1760s, Liotard created his only surviving landscape – his *View from the Artist's House* [FIG. 42]. Executed in pastel and gouache on vellum, it is a work of staggering freshness and modernity. The view is towards the Mont Blanc Massif and is constructed from a carefully orchestrated sequence of horizontal elements that lead the eye into the distance. The cream wall in the foreground has peeling paint on its top. Beyond, a vine and an ornate pergola hint at gardening. A ramshackle shed contrasts with stone arches that appear to support a dam. Water is channelled along a canal and beyond this the ploughing of a field can just be seen. The greys and blues of the mountains are sprinkled with snow. All these muted details contrast with the bright scarlet of the artist's Ottoman tarbush – or fez, a name which refers to the city where the dye used to colour it's felt was sourced. He depicted himself at the lower left both within the space of the picture and engaged in the act of creating it, as he has a porte-crayon in his raised hand. It's a witty

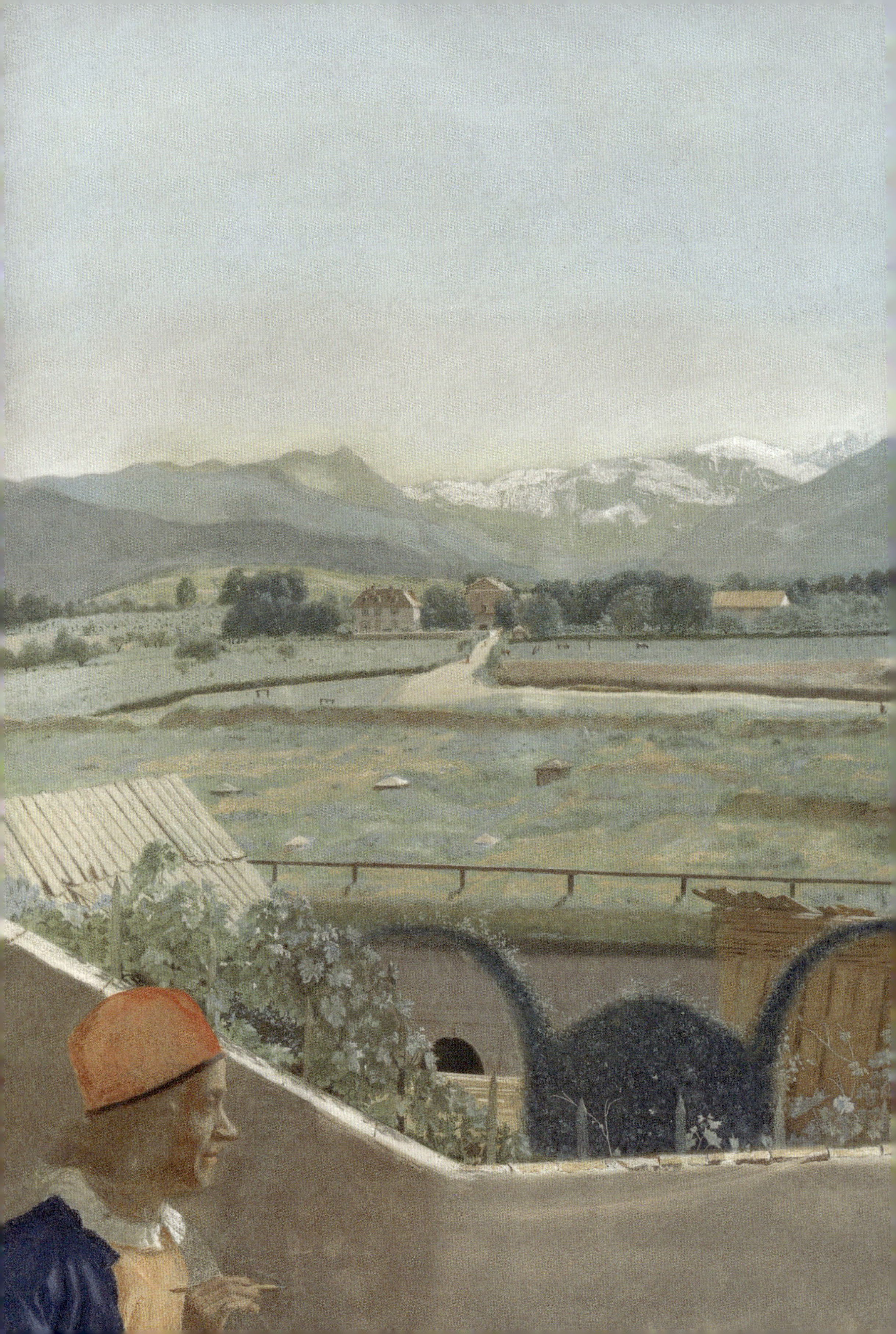

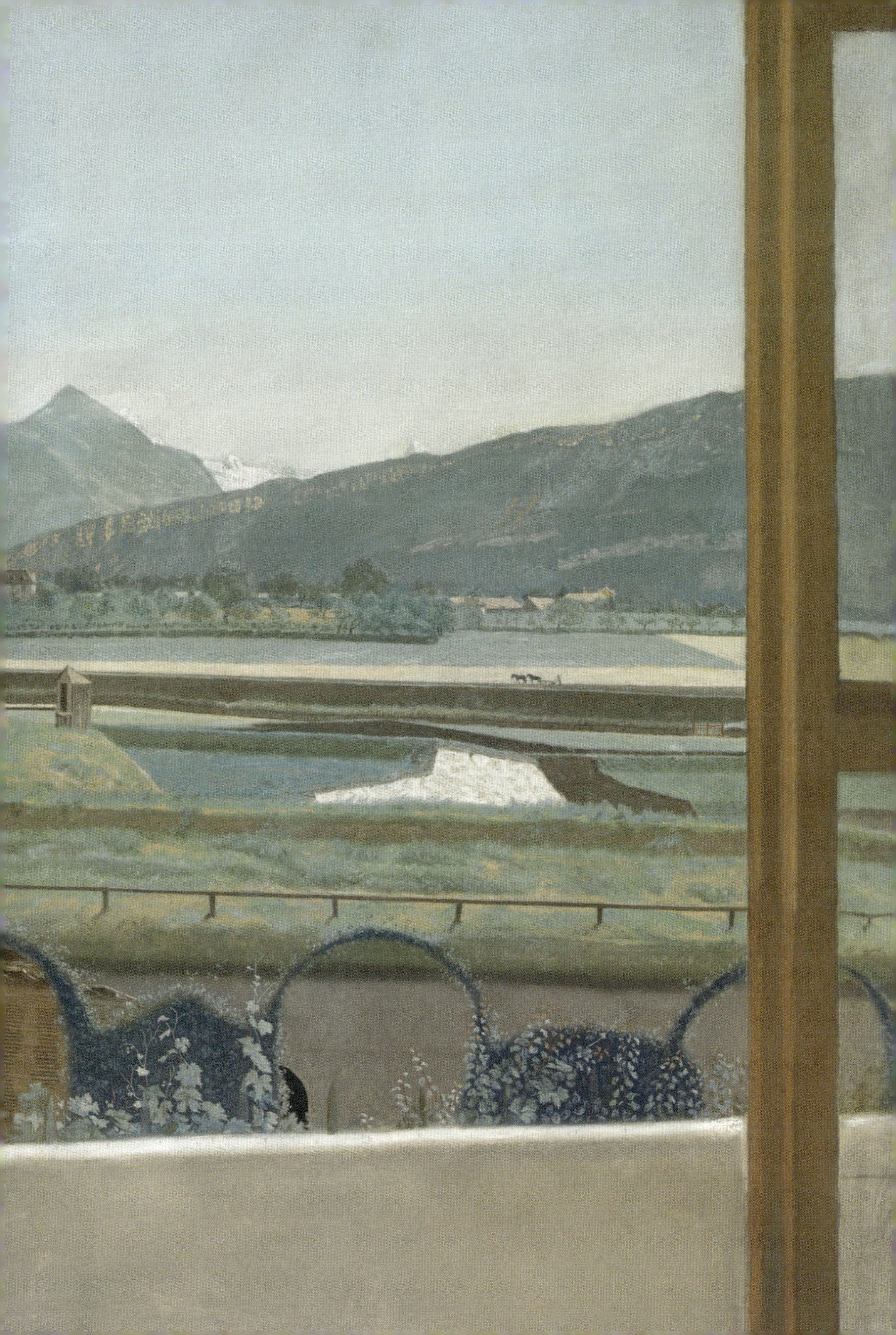

conceit that can be linked with other strands of playful illusionism that become a preoccupation in his late career. Liotard's presence in miniature here also almost acts as a pictorial equivalent of a signature – it's as though we need it to be assured this extraordinary work is indeed his.

It may be the single landscape from Liotard's hand now known today, but it is recorded that he produced other works with such subjects; intriguingly these included a lost enamel landscape that had been acquired by King George III. Landscapes can also be glimpsed in the pastel copies he made of Dutch seventeenth-century paintings. These limited precedents from his own career provide no hint though of the extraordinary innovation that the *View from the Artist's House* represents. In terms of wider art historical prototypes for the 1760s view, the earliest the artist might have known is the depiction of Lake Geneva with mountains beyond used as the setting for Konrad Witz's (1410–1445) famous *Miraculous Draft of Fishes* (Musée d'Art et d'Histoire Geneva). Liotard's use of pastel for his scene has, however, few if any precedents; it stands though at the beginning of a tradition later taken up by Elizabeth Louise Vigée Le Brun (1755–1842), who, between 1807 and 1808, depicted Mont Blanc in pastel, so anticipating by many years the pastel landscapes of the Impressioinsts.

In the early 1770s Liotard returned to Lyons and Paris continuing to pursue portrait commissions. The *View from the Artist's House* gives a strong indication, however, of his ambitions with other types of subjects which provided a vehicle for his virtuosity. This strand of creativity especially found expression from the 1760s onwards in witty *trompe-l'œil* (deceive the eye) paintings, intended to create tantalising illusions, demonstrate his remarkable mimetic skills and no doubt stimulate conversations about his talent and inspire commissions. They form a brilliant prelude to his later more conventional still lifes. Arguably the finest of the surviving examples is Liotard's deeply considered oil on silk study of 1771 now in the Frick Collection [FIG. 43]. The silk support, with its very fine and close weave, provided an especially smooth surface on which to paint. The subject is in effect a self-portrait or curriculum vitae explored through inanimate objects. A piece of wood, perhaps pine, was propped up in the studio and has two plaster bas-reliefs screwed to it and two drawings attached below. This miniature gallery distils both the breadth of Liotard's experiences and influences – from France and Germany to Constantinople – as well as his uncanny ability to replicate in paint (just as he had with pastel) the variety and minutiae of different

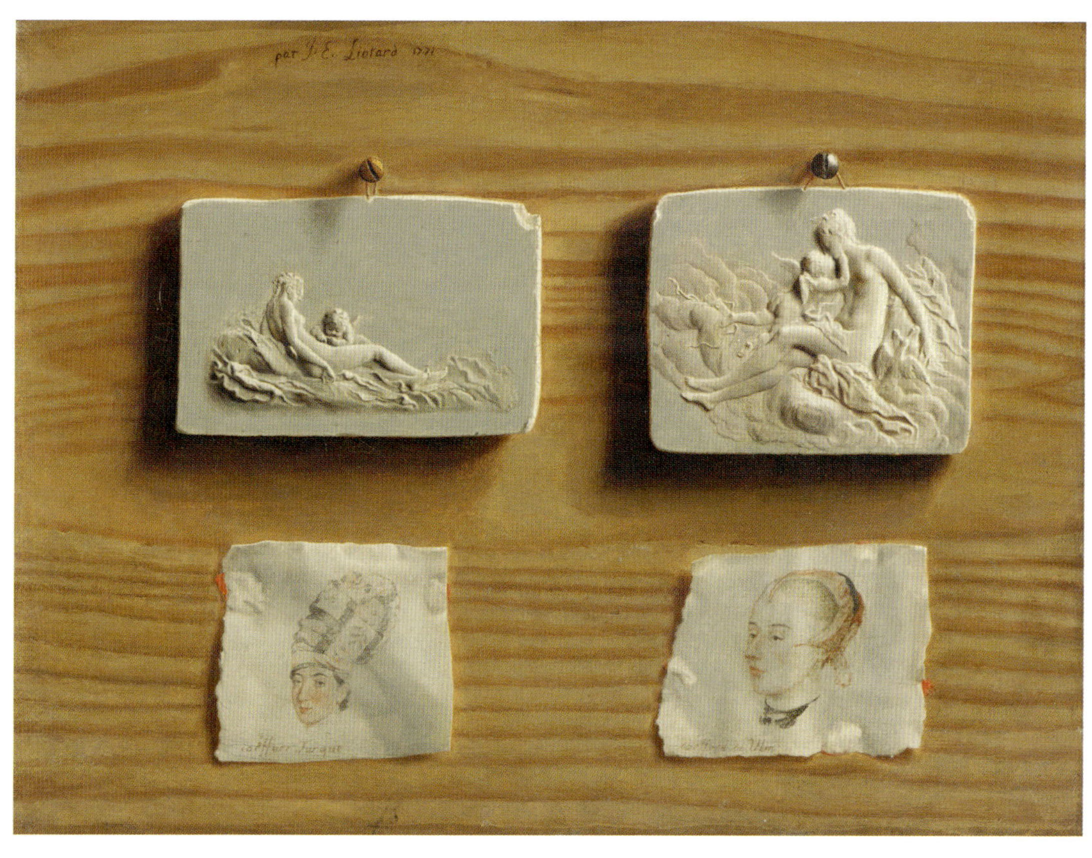

FIG. 42 (pages 128, 129)
Jean-Étienne Liotard
View from the Artist's House in Geneva
c. 1768
Pastel and gouache on vellum, 46 × 59.7 cm
Rijksmuseum, Amsterdam
Inv. SK-A-1197

FIG. 43
Jean-Étienne Liotard
Trompe-l'œil with Two Bas-reliefs and Two Drawings
1771
Oil on silk mounted on canvas, 23.8 × 32.4 cm
Frick Collection, New York
Inv. 97.1.182

materials. The reliefs depict Venus on a drapery at the left and on a cloud at the right; in both cases Cupid accompanies her. The left relief has been identified as following the composition of a print by Michel Aubert (1704–1757) after a 1739 painting by François Boucher – the pre-eminent rococo painter of the age and friend of Favart.

While such plaster reliefs attest to Liotard's ability to assimilate the art of his contemporaries, the drawings below demonstrate his skills at the direct study of people and their fashions: on the left is a Turkish woman, whom he must have drawn between 1738 and 1742, while at the right is a woman from Ulm in Germany, a city he visited in the 1740s and 1760s. The surrounding details are extraordinary: the heads of the screws are depicted as both rusted and clean, the reliefs are chipped, red sealing wax was used to attach the drawings, and the delicate shadows cast are created by light from a window at the upper right. All this illusion is though broken by the tiny signature at the upper left. The result was clearly a matter of pride to the artist and valued by his most loyal patron: it was not a commissioned painting but became an eye-catching advert and was exhibited by Liotard both in Paris and London. He sold it at Christie's in 1774, where it was acquired by the Earl of Bessborough. In the 1773 and 1774 London auctions such pictures were described as 'deceptio visus' ('deceptions of sight').

The rich variety of media explored within the Frick painting was revisited in other contemporary displays of 'deceptions of sight'. For example, Liotard painted a work on glass now in the Museum of Fine Arts in Budapest which engages with similar themes: it shows a plaster plaque decorated with a classical scene featuring Silenus and putti, that is hung from a nail before a blue silk backdrop. The splendour of the silk contrasts with the entirely believable and meticulously depicted cracks which extend across the plaque.

The early 1770s were marked for Liotard not only by the creation of such inventive works, but also by further travels which took him back to cities he was by now very well acquainted with. He returned to Amsterdam and is recorded as acquiring there in a sale in July of 1771 a painting by Ludolf Backhuysen (1630–1708), so building further his collection of Dutch seventeenth-century works. There followed on from this a final visit to London (1772–4) undertaken at the age of seventy. During this period Liotard received commissions from English friends including Bessborough, whom he visited at his country estate, Parkstead House in Richmond Park. Liotard's pastel portrait of Bessborough's son

Frederick (1758–1844), with whom he became friendly, shows him at the age of fifteen, seated and holding a porte crayon (Stansted Park Foundation). Liotard may have given Frederick informal lessons and the boy evidently enjoyed drawing and watercolour painting as an amateur. Two albums of topographical studies by him survive in the British Museum. Later, Frederick married Lady Henrietta Spencer (1761–1821); their daughter was Lady Caroline Lamb (1785–1828), the novelist, wife of Lord Melbourne and lover of Lord Byron.

As well as being engaged with such private artistic projects Liotard also exhibited at the Royal Academy of Arts in 1773 and 1774. The Academy had been in existence for five years and in 1773 he is recorded as exhibiting at its fourth annual exhibition five works 'in crayon'. The catalogue for the exhibition simply refers to him as 'Liotard'. His exhibits included the portrait of Bessborough's son Frederick at the age of fifteen, as well as a now lost depiction of General Cholmondeley (1708–1775). They were all presumably created during the weeks before the exhibition, as was a very austere self-portrait Liotard chose to display (now Musée d'Art et d'Histoire, Geneva). It's particularly of interest as he chose to depict himself beardless – having removed some years before the attribute that so many in London would have associated with his exotic demeanour. The brilliant scarlet hat remained, however, a clear indicator of his identity. The self-portrait was to be yet another purchased made by Bessborough. The 1773 exhibition was most notable in terms of public comment not because of the inclusion of singular works such as this, but rather because Sir Joshua Reynolds, who many years earlier had taken such a dim view of Liotard's achievements, included thirteen paintings – the largest number he was ever to display together in such a setting. In the 1774 Academy exhibition Liotard did not match this level of productivity, but exhibited two oil paintings, including the provocative and curious laughing self-portrait (FIG. 1).

All this activity suggests a concerted effort to recapture something of his earlier newsworthy profile and the sales it inspired. At the same period as his works appeared at the Academy Liotard also organised his own selling exhibitions of his works and old master collection: the first of these ventures was at his house in Great Marlborough Street (1773) and the second at Christie's on Pall Mall (1774). The 1773 sale featured ninety old master paintings, which he had chiefly acquired in Amsterdam. It was described as a 'capital collection' which you could visit between ten o'clock and three every day, except Sundays, and for which you could buy a 'descriptive catalogue'. The prices it appears were considered too high by the market and only twelve works were sold. This poor result led to the Christie's sale the following year, where more reasonable prices resulted in a large number of purchases by collectors. Bessborough bought various works at the Christie's sale by Liotard including his oil of *A Dutch Girl at Breakfast* of 1756–7. The London exhibitions and auctions had been preceded by an exhibition in Paris, which did not inspire purchasers, hence the move across the Channel to a different market.

This period appears to be one where Liotard was chiefly reliant on old connections for income and achieving mixed success as a dealer. Some new and intriguing associations were though forged; for example, in 1773 Liotard made a charming pastel portrait of Mathew Robinson Boulton (Birmingham Museum and Art Gallery), the three-year-old son of the brilliant designer, inventor and industrialist Mathew Boulton (1728–1809). It demonstrates the continuance of his sensitivity when encountering very young sitters and could have led to other works for one of the greatest British polymaths of the age. However, in October of 1774 Liotard had moved on and is recorded as being back in Geneva with his family and engaged in buying land where a new house might be built.

Three years later in July of 1777 the artist was visited in his studio by the Holy Roman Emperor, Joseph II (1741–1790), who was travelling under the alias 'Count of Falkenstein'. This was undoubtedly a great privilege and a measure of Liotard's continuing high status at the Viennese court. The parallel with illustrious precedents stretching back to antiquity – such as the visit Alexander the Great made to the studio of the revered painter Apelles would have been familiar to both parties. The Emperor used this alias in order to give him greater freedom of movement and undertake extensive travels without all the complex and costly ceremonial that usually attended his appearances. Travelling in this manner in the 1760s he had reached the border of the Ottoman Empire in Hungary and visited Italy; in the year he dropped in on Liotard 'Falkenstein' also visited Paris, creating something of a sensation – not least because his relatively modest and 'modern' or enlightened mode of travel was seen as a telling counterpoint to the splendour and decadence of Louis XVI's court. In October of 1777, presumably inspired by the honour he had been afforded, Liotard made his final visit to Vienna.

This journey was perhaps more notable, however, not because of the mutual respect he enjoyed with his Hapsburg patrons, but rather because of the stop he made during the journey in Zurich where Liotard met Johann Kaspar Lavater (1741–1801) and the poet and painter Solomon Gessner (1730–1788). Lavater was also a considerable creative force. Born in Zurich he became a church minister, renowned for his oratory, but he did not confine his intellectual pursuits to those of a religious life, establishing a reputation as a philosopher who engaged with ethics and mysticism, a poet, and, above all, a physiognomist. His *Physiognomische Fragmente* (1775–8) was being published just at the period Liotard encountered him. It developed in a systematic manner ideas which were in wide circulation and are now considered abhorrent, according to which the character or strengths and weaknesses of an individual could be elucidated by studying their 'lines of countenance'. This pseudo-science and the stereotyping and prejudices it inspired proved very potent. In Lavater's lifetime his work became famous as illustrated copies were widely circulated, especially in Germany, France and Britain, and physiognomy undoubtedly formed an important lens through which the portraits of the eighteenth century were perceived.

We have no surviving evidence of Liotard's views on such theories. It was though in the late 1770s that he determined to write and publish a treatise himself. His focus was not, however, on the type of views promoted by Lavater, but rather an attempt to explain the principles and rules he had applied to his art over his career. He worked on the text in Geneva and then had it published in Lyons. Artistic treatises rarely make thrilling reading and Liotard's *Traité des principes et des règles de la peinture* (1781) does not break this rule. It is, however, of interest for a number of reasons: because of the point in his career he decides to work on it, the insights it provides to his practice as an artist and the way in which these have a broader, quasi-philosophical dimension. In 1781 when it was published he was seventy-nine and entering the final phase of his artistic life. So in many respects it represents a statement of values, which we may assume he hoped would be beneficial to others (although there is no evidence to suggest that this was the case), and also a retrospective survey of what he had achieved. There is perhaps a further motivation here: Liotard was not an intellectual, but he had come into close contact with some of the powerful creative minds and thinkers of his age: men and women such as Algarotti, Tronchin, Pococke, Curchod and Lavater. With this company in mind he may have felt a need to some degree to legitimise and celebrate his achievement in literary form and explain and decode what many perhaps considered to be the alchemy of his art.

The Treatise begins with references to Truth and Nature, unsurprisingly in view of the tenor of his work, and a desire that painting will return to its traditional function, by which he meant the imitation of nature. He also refers on a number of occasions to the patrons he clearly regarded as his most illustrious – Maria Theresa and the Hapsburgs. The Treatise then proceeds to establish twelve key artistic 'qualities'. These are: drawing, colouring, judgement, invention, composition, expression, chiaroscuro, harmony, effect, contrast, projection and grace. All of them are shown in various ways to be tied to his overarching ambition of imitating nature. The qualities he outlines along with their benefits are then expanded on and Liotard shows how they might be achieved through the application of twenty 'rules'.

These rules concern: the use of light tones; dark tones; light and dark tones; colour being beautiful in fully lit areas; colour not being piercing; distant objects being painted with vigorous contrasts; avoidance of 'touches'; minimising aerial perspective; dividing compositions equally into light and darks areas; painting neatly; being patient; letting reason guide you; avoiding unsuitable objects for painting; avoiding dryness and hardness in the use of lights and darks; using the best quality pigments; finishing works as highly as possible; seeking harmony in lights and darks; seeking striking effects; using nine classes of colours and tones; and heeding the advice of 'ignorarts'.

What emerges here is a curious mixture of practicality and advice over attitude which is not very logically ordered. The references to fine bright pigments and high finish will be no surprise in view of the approach Liotard had applied many times – both in pastel and oil paint – to his portraits and works in other genres. Especially notable is his emphasis in rule number seven on avoiding 'touches'. What he meant by this was to not allow linear marks, or artistic touches such as hatching remain visible; it is fundamental to his ambition to replicate or mimic nature and distinguishes his work from that of contemporaries such as Carriera.

It is not necessary to go through all his rules in order to acquire a flavour of the practical aspects of the treatise, but one more might usefully be noted. In number eight Liotard advocated minimising aerial perspective: this is an interesting point which goes some way to explaining the crystalline quality of the pastel landscape he recorded seen from his house outside Geneva (FIG. 42).

More philosophically an artist should, Liotard proposed, be both patient and steered by reason. Also, intriguingly, they should heed the advice of 'ignorarts'. This odd statement is particularly striking and gets in many respects to that heart of Liotard's view of the role of art. He expands on it by explaining that even an unskilled or ignorant eye can be as perceptive as that of an artist. Assessing how aesthetic judgements should focus on the relationship between a painted image and its counterpart in nature, he cites the well-known ancient story of the competition between Zeuxis and Parrhasius. The fifth century BC Greek painter Zeuxis was especially renowned for his ability to replicate nature in his still lifes. According to Pliny the Elder's *Naturalis Historia* Zeuxis and his contemporary Parrhasius arranged a competition to determine who was the greatest artist. Zeuxis painted a bunch of grapes so compelling that birds flew down to peck at them. Parrhasius' painting was apparently concealed behind a curtain and Zeuxis was invited to pull it aside. The curtain itself proved, however, to be a painted illusion. Parrhasius was then deemed to have won. Liotard disagreed with this traditional outcome, arguing that the Zeuxis and the grapes should have triumphed – as they were harder to depict convincingly and the birds were a better judge of nature than a painter. So artistic deception and mimetic skill were key in his view to the role and power of art. Liotard in fact painted a bunch of grapes no doubt with this tale in mind (*c.* 1771–4, Kunsthistoriches Museum, Vienna).

Beyond the Treatise, there remains one further intriguing alignment between Liotard and this illustrious ancient precedent. The painter Zeuxis is reputed to have died from laughter and this was said to be because of the way in which he had painted the beautiful goddess Aphrodite; the picture he created was commissioned by an old woman who insisted, inappropriately, on modelling for it. Liotard must have been aware of this quirky biographical detail, which may well have appealed to his own sense of wit and irony and interest in candid representation. It also provides a possible context for decoding his laughing self-portrait (FIG. 1). Is he, in that work, not only steering us to admire all the wonders he created over a lifetime of making portraits, but also poking a little fun at pomposity and the human attribute of pride in appearances? We are being invited perhaps to follow his smile, look beyond the curtain (which links with the Pliny story) and make the judgements of 'ignorarts' that he had come to value.

His views on what might be termed the merits of an 'innocent eye' as opposed to one that was tainted by artistic training or too much thinking about aesthetic matters was not only expressed in print through the

Treatise, but also featured in conversations and correspondence. For example, back in September of 1765 Liotard explained to the philosopher Jean-Jacques Rousseau that 'My greatest pleasure is to try to think purely, naturally and without prejudice of any kind... I try to think like animals, which have neither bad habits nor prejudices.' This is perhaps evidence of his evolving consideration of his own practice, but also an attempt to align himself with the views of the most famous fellow Genevan who placed great value on the 'state of nature'.

The year after his Treatise was published Liotard's wife Marie died. His life from now on became confined to the social circle and support his children provided. In artistic terms his instinct to keep challenging himself did not though abate and Liotard began work on a series of remarkable still lifes. His decision to focus on still lifes in the latter part of his career was logical in various respects. He may have considered it an effective new way of exploring and illustrating themes articulated in the Treatise. On a practical level it also made sense as he could create such works at home, without having to travel, a key consideration as he became older and was not in a position to chase after portrait commissions all across Europe. His still lifes also built on the skills he had developed with his *trompe-l'œil* paintings and earlier genre scenes – such as *The Chocolate Girl*, and *The Lavergne Family Breakfast* (FIGS. 17 and 29).

In addition to these motivations they also allowed for meditative considerations of sometimes profound themes. One of the finest of the late pastel still lifes suggest this and has a strong autobiographical character. This is his *Still-life: Pears, Figs, Plums, Bread Roll and Knife on a Table* (FIG. 44) of 1782. The drawer in the foreground is prominently inscribed: 'peint par J.E. Liotard age'de 80 ans'. It was clearly a matter of importance to the artist that there was no lessening of his remarkable skills at this advanced age; he especially demonstrates here his lifelong sensitivity as a subtle colourist, as the purples and blues and bloom on the fruit provide such a delicate and rich foil for the neutrality of their setting: the creamy grey of the folded napkin on which they rest and the dull brown of the little table. What he is also doing here is perhaps subtly conflating the passage of time across his own life with the *vanitas* element that is a common trope of still life paintings. Natural elements in them, such as fruit, will wither, reminding the viewer of the transient state of nature and by implication our own mortality and the vanity of material preoccupations.

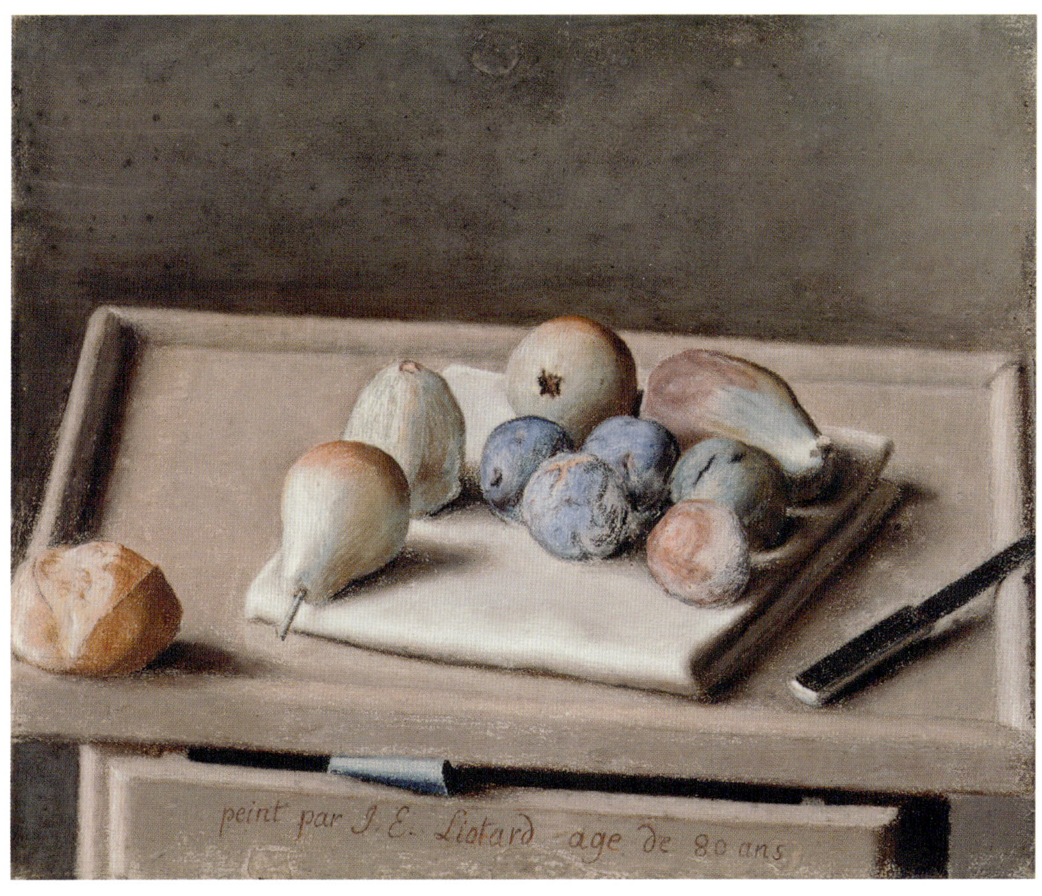

FIG. 44
Jean-Étienne Liotard
Still-life: Pears, Figs, Plums, Bread Roll and Knife on a Table
1782
Pastel on canvas, 33 × 38 cm
Musée d'Art et d'Histoire, Geneva
Inv. 1897–10

FIG. 45 (*overleaf*)
Jean-Étienne Liotard
Still Life: Tea Set
c. 1770–1783
Oil on canvas, mounted on board, 37.5 × 51.4 cm
The J. Paul Getty Museum, Los Angeles
Inv. 84.PA.57

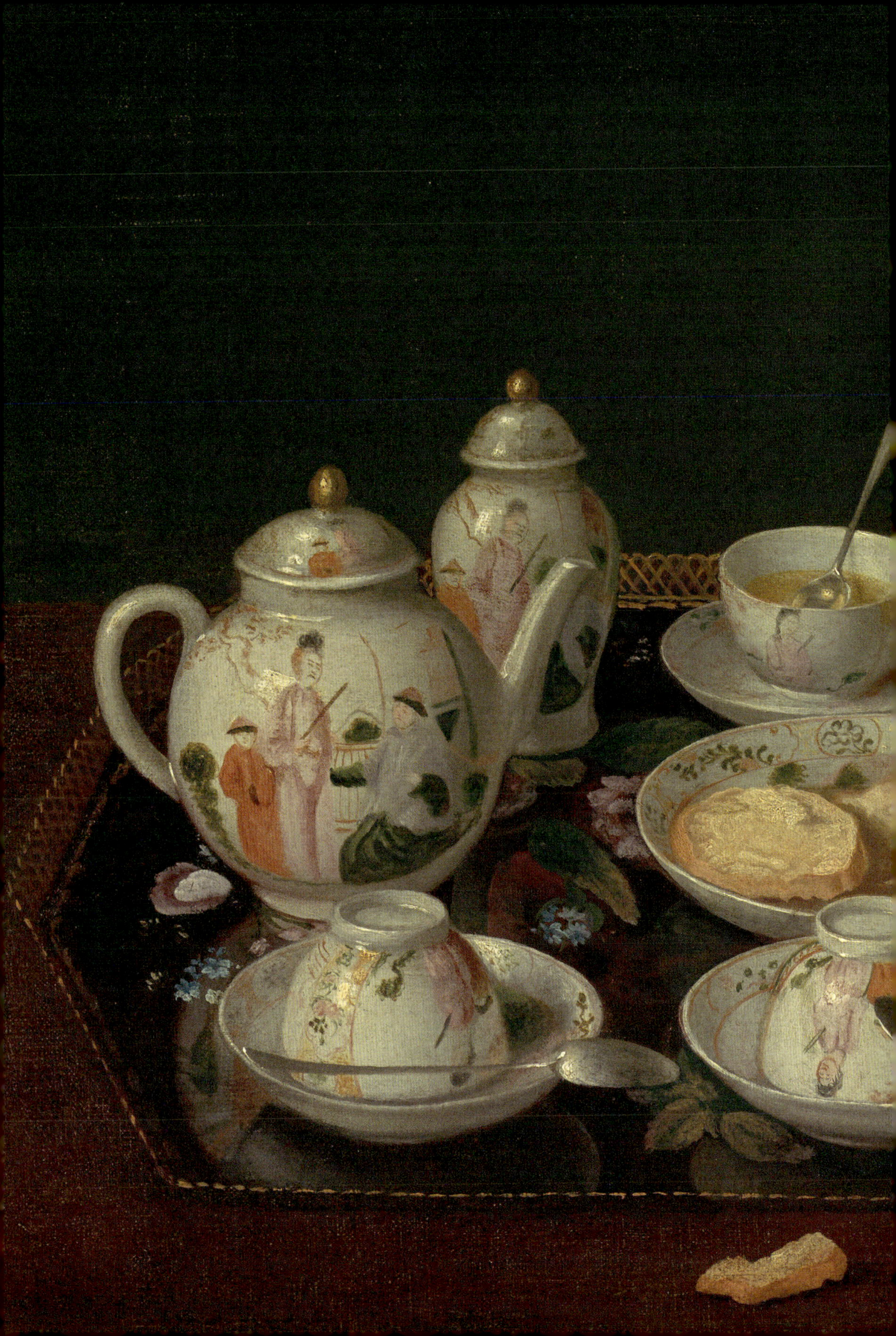

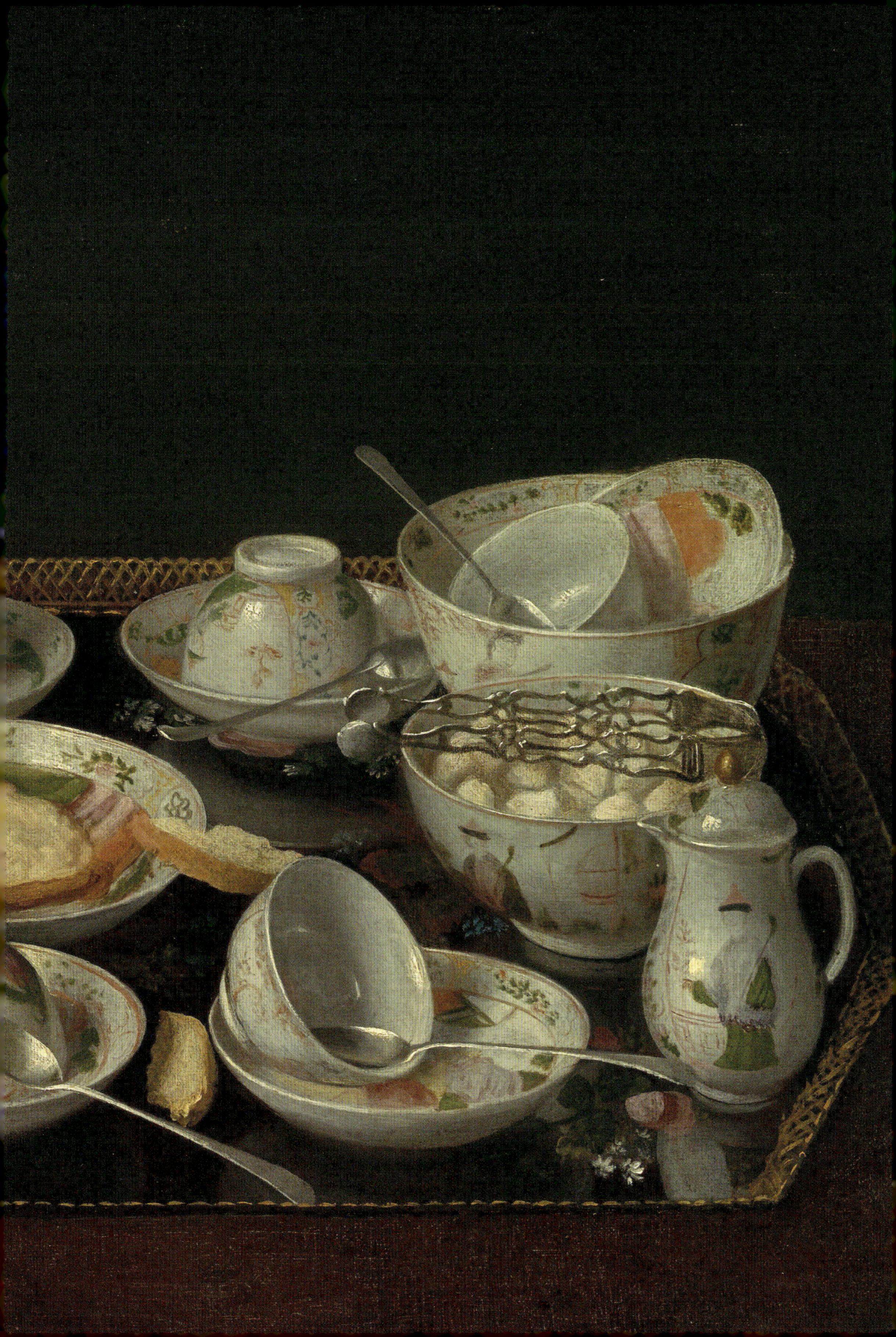

His instinct appears to have been to imply such thoughts through a focus on isolated objects rather than displays of abundance. This is particularly the case with his surviving studies of flowers; although Liotard owned works by Jan van Huysum (1682–1749) which are renowned for their crowded and spectacular floral displays, when he tackled such subjects he confined his pastels to one or two delicate blooms.

As well as exploring still lifes in pastel, Liotard also returned to oil painting in order to consider the visual poetry of inanimate objects. His *Still Life: Tea Set* (FIG. 45) is thought to have been painted in about 1783. Its rather crowded composition shows that the taking of tea is over and the artist appears to have enjoyed the abstract pleasure to be gleaned from scrutinising the regular round forms of the white porcelain tea bowls, which are shown upright, upside down and at an angle, along with silver spoons that are ingeniously dispersed in six different positions across the canvas. The light carefully catches all the objects, including a teapot and sugar tongs. This is not a still life as a statement about the passage of time, but rather one that conveys domestic luxury and international tastes and the pleasure of apparently causal, but actually carefully calibrated artifice. The porcelain is thought to be Chinese export ware decorated in the so-called Mandarin pattern and the tray on which it rests may be made of tole – a term used to describe painted, enamelled or lacquered tin. So Liotard's painting is a quiet essay in chinoiserie. Such tastes, which were widespread across Europe, had been glimpsed earlier in his Genevan work, in details such as the oriental screen behind Lord Mountstuart in his portrait (Fig. 41). It should be emphasised though that although chinoiserie found expression in many contexts – especially the collecting and display of ceramics and the crafting of interior decoration, the painting of a work like this was a novelty. Export ware featured along with other collectables in various artists' paintings but there are few if any direct points of comparison with Liotard's canvas which focuses exclusively on it. Even at this very late stage in his career he was still proving to be an innovator.

Liotard's daughter Marie-Jeanne, in a letter from Geneva to her elder brother in Amsterdam, dated 10 September 1782, wrote: 'He is keeping himself busy my dear Father, he has painted since some time some paintings of fruits which are truly masterpieces… and they are admired by everybody and we are extremely happy because this has resulted in him abandoning printmaking which is so bad for his eyes.' Failing sight was to some extent mitigated by the use of spectacles, which Liotard wears in his last self-portrait; it dates from the period that Marie-Jeanne was writing and shows the artist seated and sketching (Musée d'Art et d'Histoire in Geneva).

He may have had to contend with such challenges, but they did not prevent him continuing to engage in matters of business. In May 1785 Liotard wrote to the Charles-Claude Flahaut de la Billarderie, Comte d'Angiviller (1730–1809) who was in the employ of Louis XVI, offering for sale to the French crown a selection of fifty-three of the finest old master paintings he owned as well as a number of works he had created himself. He had for some years been attempting to dispose of his collection: the sale did not succeed and the works remained with Liotard until his death. The works offered to France included the laughing self-portrait (FIG. 1), which has such an unsettling quality and is difficult to decipher. D'Angiviller sought the advice of a painter called Jean-Baptise-Marie Pierre (1714–1789) to assess the offer Liotard had made and Pierre considered the self-portrait a 'figure horrible'. It remained with the artist's family until the 1870s.

The following year he sold his house in Geneva and moved in with Marie-Jeanne at Begnins, which is twenty miles north-east of the city. A pastel still life by Liotard dated to 1786 featuring pears, an apple, plums and walnuts, all arranged on a white glazed plate survives. It is inscribed by his son Jean-Étienne and described as '… painted by my father at Begnins'.

Liotard died on 12 June 1789. This was no doubt a cause of sadness to his close-knit family, but the timing proved to be from a historical perspective extraordinarily appropriate, as just over one month later on 14 July the Bastille in Paris was stormed. This flashpoint of the Revolution changed forever the *ancien régime* he had been portraying above stairs and below with such brilliance and insight for decades.

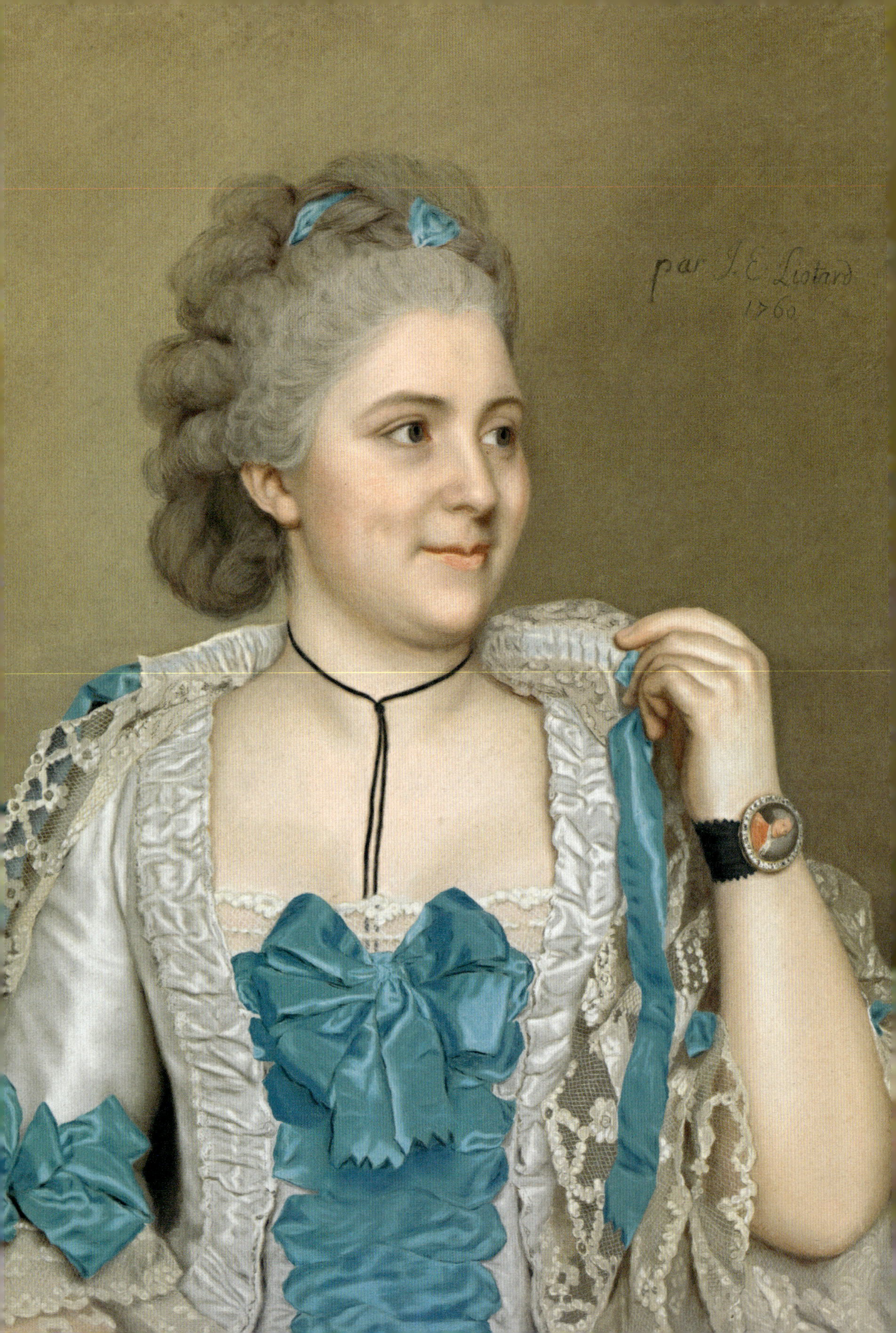
par J.E. Liotard
1760

Conclusion

BY ANY MEASURE LIOTARD had enjoyed a highly successful and richly varied career, which served him and his patrons well. His extraordinary range of clients in terms of geography and social standing has few if any direct parallels in the eighteenth century. He certainly inspired some artistic jealousies and critical commentaries, especially in Britain and France, but the trail he left across Europe was chiefly one of curiosity followed by admiration. The revolution in Paris brought with it, however, not only a profound political upheaval but also a cultural realignment across society which led to a demand for new forms of portraiture and suppression of the arts of the old order. That welcoming smile this account of his career started with was not a motif to be found in paintings after 1789.

So his world and world view was swept away. But this is not the only reason Liotard's work remains relatively little known. Access to it has always been limited. His portraits hung in the drawing rooms, bedrooms and studies of his patrons, or sat on their desks (as was the case with Maria Theresa's drawings of her children). They were confined to country houses or grand palazzi or Parisian and Genevan mansions. Miniatures would be worn, admired in private, or kept in collectors' cabinets. These could be very grand – such as the one in Stawberry Hill outside London where Horace Walpole kept his Liotard self-portrait along with a stunning array of earlier miniatures that demonstrated how it formed part of an illustrious tradition. It was only on rare occasions that his work intruded into the public domain during his life – through occasional exhibitions, for example, in Paris and London, or displays in the sale rooms of auctioneers. Prints after his works also provided some degree of wider visibility.

Relative obscurity was also perhaps unintentionally achieved because Liotard's achievements were so varied. This is most clear because of his

Detail, FIG. 36

far-reaching travels but is also the case because of the wide range of media he mastered: painting in oil, watercolour and enamel, as well as creating splendid pastels; drawing in chalk; and making prints as an engraver and mezzotinter. The consequence of all this is that he later came to play a small part in many narratives about art and its different techniques and materials as well as art in different countries. In a similar vein his work has been used to illustrate particular and separate academic themes, such as the histories of fashion or orientalism. These are entirely appropriate contexts in which it should appear but provide only a partial or segmented view of Liotard's achievement.

Another key reason why Liotard's reputation fell away from public notice was the way in which he worked: he mainly painted and drew in isolation, not regularly employing teams of assistants, so not inspiring a 'school' of followers. There are isolated exceptions to this. In 1743 in Vienna, following new-found success at the Hapsburg court, he employed two artists called Jean-Adam Serre (1704–1788) and Johann Peter Kobler von Ehrensorg (*fl.* 1740–1774). As we have seen, he also gave lessons in the use of pastel to a royal pupil – Princess Caroline Louise; and an aristocratic one – Frederick, the son of the Earl of Bessborough. Twenty years later Liotard took responsibility for his only known apprentice in a more traditional sense: Louis-Ami Arlaud (1751–1829), to whom he was related and who studied with him for two years before moving to Paris. Arlaud later visited Rome and London, becoming a miniaturist. These opportunities for teaching are of interest, but did not result in a new generation Liotardesque artists.

His influence on a few other contemporaries is though measurable. Artists to consider in this regard include the Frenchman François-Xavier Vispré (*c.* 1730–1792), who was in London when Liotard visited the city. Chiefly renowned for printmaking, he was also a pastellist and his 1750 *Portrait of a Man reclining on a Sofa* in the Ashmolean Museum is certainly Liotardesque in manner. Liotard also never had a single institutional base at a time when so many artists were harnessed to a particular court or academy; this further explains why no 'school' of followers emerged around him.

The fact that he spent much of his career travelling had other distinct benefits, however, in terms of the breadth of experience it resulted in. It also meant he came to work for extraordinarily varied clientele. It should be noted though that Liotard's record of European society was inevitably partial and highly selective, being confined to his experiences and ambitions; his European view was chiefly an urban one, focusing on wealthy, literate sitters. There were also many who did not submit to his scrutiny; for example, ecclesiastical figures, grandees of the legal world and other artists come to mind. Furthermore, when he did depict servants, he constructed idealised imagery of their deference, appearance and duties, far removed from the realities of their toil; this no doubt suited the expectations of his aristocratic and regal patrons – hence the acquisition for a royal collection of the supremely polite and restrained *Chocolate Girl*. Having listed all these caveats, it would be difficult to identify another artist of the age who had the breadth of his outlook. Liotard's international connections pre-dated those of travelling painters such as Johan Zoffany (1730–1810) who was born in Frankfurt, chiefly worked in England, but also spent key periods in Italy and India; or Élizabeth Vigée Le Brun (1755–1842), who was born and died in Paris, but visited Flanders and the Netherlands, Lyons, Italy, Austria, Russia and Germany.

IT WAS IN THE LATE nineteenth century that Liotard's reputation began to rise again and his own story was reconstructed, to some extent because the public gained access to his works, which had hitherto been chiefly kept in private collections. When in 1885 the Rijksmusuem in Amsterdam opened its new building, twenty-two works by him were on show. They had been donated by the artist's Dutch descenadants; most of the remaining portraits belonging to his family were purchased in 1934 by the Musée d'Art et d'Histoire in Geneva – hence the wealth of material related to him in that collection. These institutional purchases were paralleled by a growth in scholarship; in 1897 the first monograph on the artist was also published in the Netherlands. More recently, brilliant and comprehensive research by scholars such as Roethlisberger and Loche and Jeffares has put studies of Liotard on a firm foundation.

It is striking that thanks to the work of these art historians Liotard's complex career and work is remarkably well documented: with his family he left a paper trail across Europe, consisting of receipts, letters, notices of births and marriages, inventories of possessions and press cuttings, as well as prompting the commentary of contemporaries. There are still missing links, however: most importantly concerning his training in the art of pastel. Related to this is the curious slow development of the artist during his early years in Geneva and Paris – perhaps his skills did develop in a plodding way; alternatively, there is more to discover here. In addition, some thus far elusive works might still be tracked down – such as the recorded but apparently lost portraits of the Pope or Madame de Pompadour. Having said that, the survival rate is impressive: around three hundred pastels, thirty oil paintings, over one hundred and fifty drawings and fifteen prints allow us to acquire a remarkably rich overview of Liotard's achievement and working processes.

The pattern of loss and reclamation of the artist's reputation outlined here applies to the vast majority of Liotard's works and achievement. There is though one very significant exception to this trajectory. It might be imagined that this would be the *The Lavergne Family Breakfast*; however, for most its life it has been far from the public gaze. The exception is *The Chocolate Girl* (Fig. 17) which has enjoyed and perhaps had to endure a history of scrutiny unrivalled by any other eighteenth-century pastel. This status is explained by a number of interconnected reasons. Firstly, as soon as it was acquired from the artist it found its way into what was one of the most celebrated and extensive collections of works in pastel in Europe: that of Augustus III, Elector of Saxony and King of Poland. It could be seen in his gallery in Dresden, which was built in the former court stables and opened in 1748. Most of the pastels in the King's collection were, following the conventions of the time, portraits or perhaps allegories: a large, austere and beautifully depicted representation of an unnamed serving girl inevitably stood out. Liotard's probable intention to create a stir and prompt admiration in this instance far outlived him. The simplicity of the composition, peculiarity of the subject and admirable artistry resulted in it being replicated many times. Copies in pastel came first. Then from 1782 prints were produced: the first of these was an etching by the Viennese engraver Carl von Pechwell (1742–1789). His print stands at the beginning of an extraordinary, diverse and seemingly never-ending line of reproductions. By the mid-nineteenth century it was estimated that fifty thousand copies or reproductions were created annually. Some were simply made for sale as replicas of the pastel's composition, while others took on different commercial roles, such as packaging for the marketing of chocolate. The image is now ubiquitous, being reformulated in folk art, souvenirs in every conceivable medium and stamps. These reproductions are global rather than being confined to Germany. Liotard, who was in addition to all his other achievements a clever self-publicist would, it might be imaged, be somewhat bemused by all this but perhaps approving. Such a reception history is of interest in its own right but also begs questions; the image has certainly taken on a life of its own, but this did not result in an equally widespread awareness of who Liotard was, what he did and how we should estimate his achievement.

Recent exhibitions organised in the wake of scholarly reappraisal have helped raise his profile so that it features more often in considerations of eighteenth-century art and portraiture. Also at a less elevated level, the candour and intimacy of a number of his most successful works seem to increasingly appeal to modern viewers with their thirst for insights into the private lives and worlds of the past.

Key to the continuance of this attention is direct experience of his work, which when seen continues to amaze gallery visitors because of its technical mastery and psychological insight. Liotard's achievement has long been clear in parts of collections in Paris, Amsterdam and Geneva, but in recent years it has also become part of the narratives told in the great and growing collections of the Getty Museum and the National Galleries in Washington and London. He should now undoubtedly become part of the mainstream of the stories told about *ancien régime* art across Europe, rather than inhabiting a curious tributary.

The *Encyclopédie* described someone who was cosmopolitan as 'a man who is nowhere a stranger'. Through his international experiences and unrelenting curiosity this seems to be an apt description of Liotard. He should also, no longer, be a stranger to us.

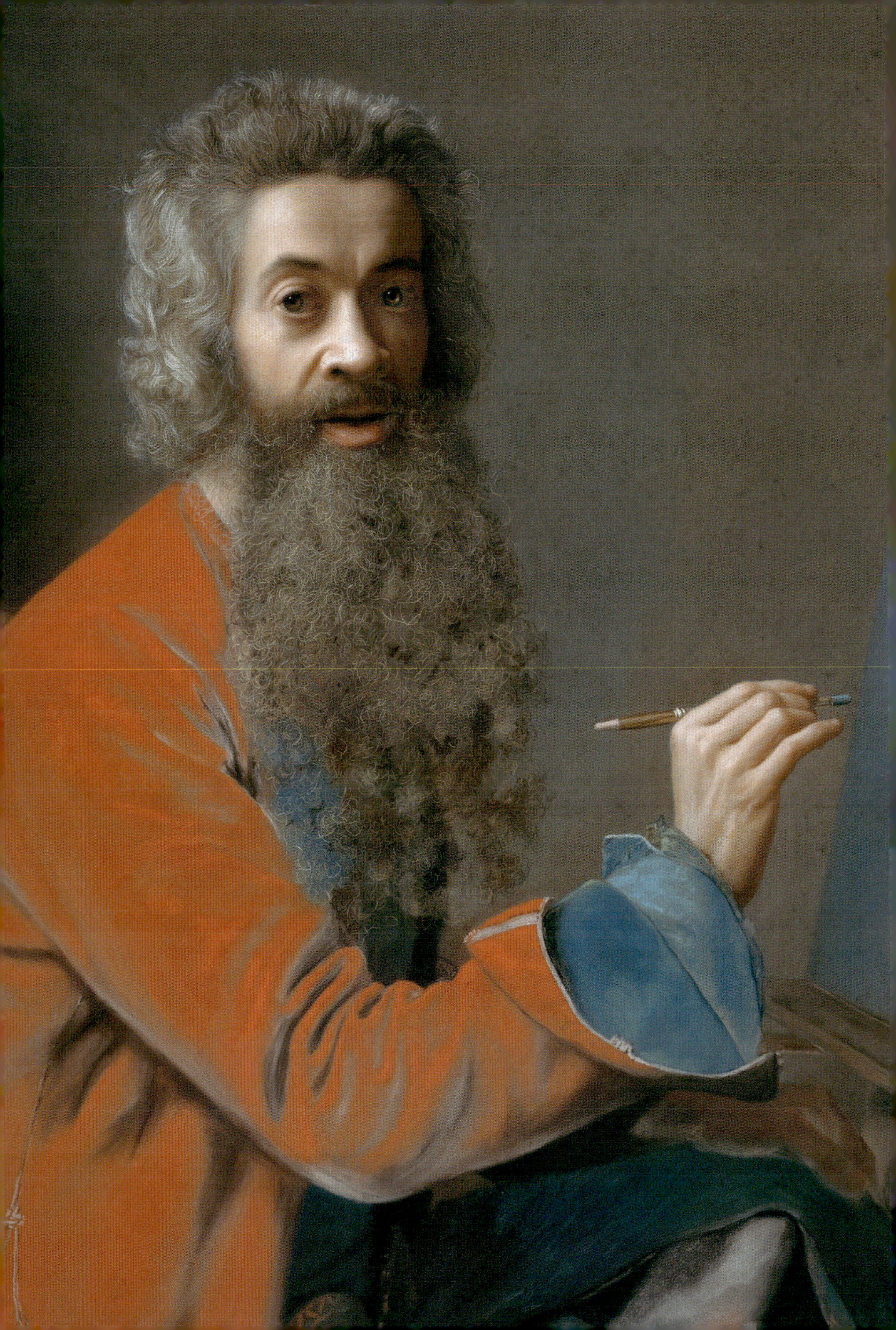

Chronology

Bibliography

Notes on Sources

Detail, FIG. 2

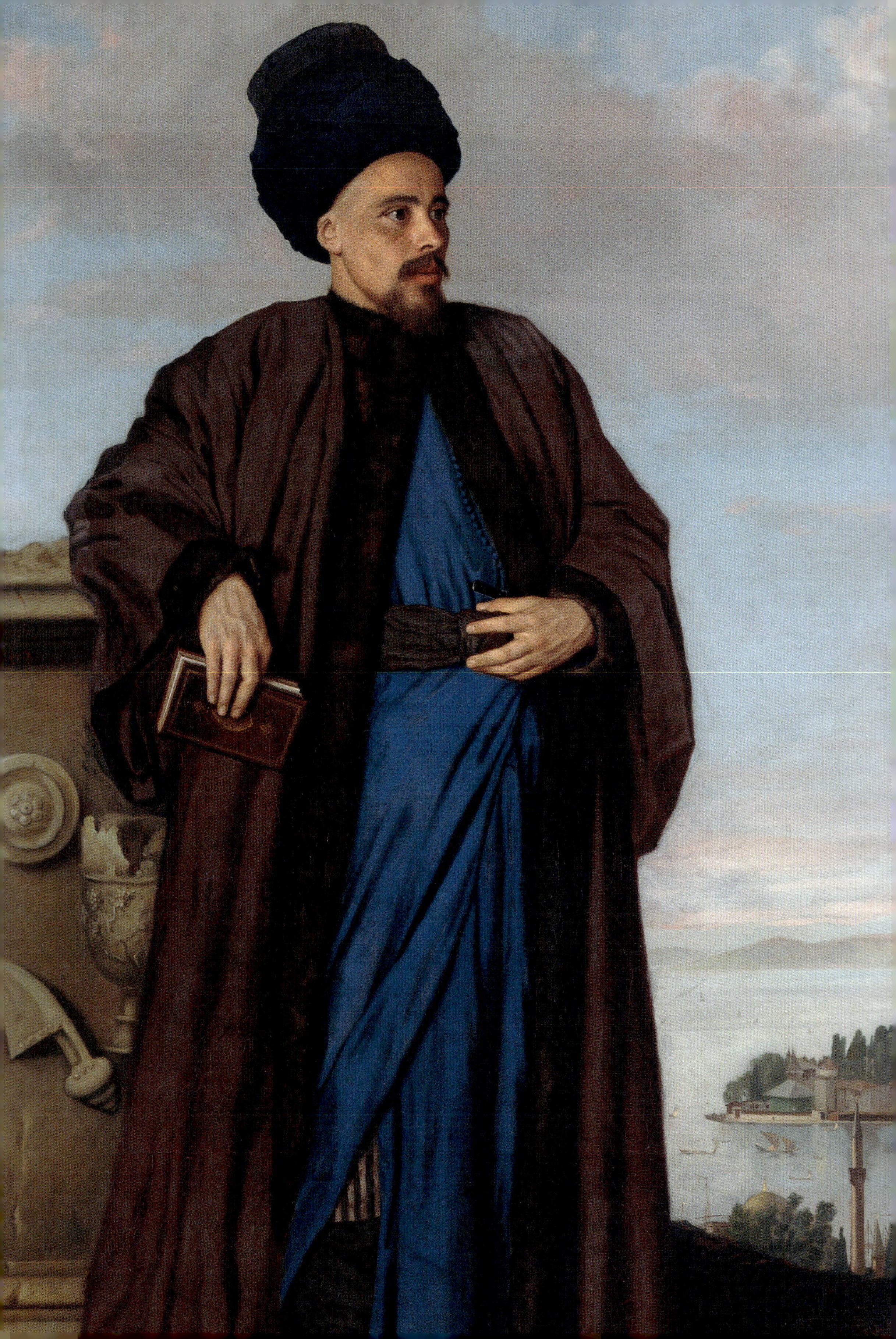

Chronology

1702
Jean-Étienne Liotard is born in Geneva, 22 December.
He has a twin brother, Jean-Michel.
Their parents are French Huguenots: Antoine Liotard and Anne Sauvage.

1715–20
Liotard serves a short apprenticeship with the miniaturist Daniel Gardelle in Geneva.

1723
The artist travels to Paris and takes up his second apprenticeship with Jean-Baptise Massé.
By 1726 Liotard appears to be working independently.

1735
He takes up an opportunity to journey to Naples, accompanying the new French ambassador.

1736
Visits are undertaken to Florence and Rome; in the latter city Liotard meets a group of British Grand Tourists who propose a journey to the Levant.

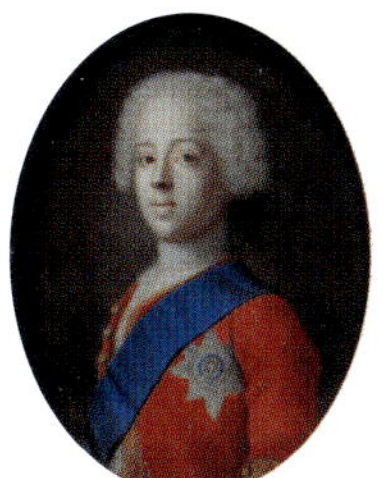

FIG. 6, *Prince Charles Edward Stuart*, 1737

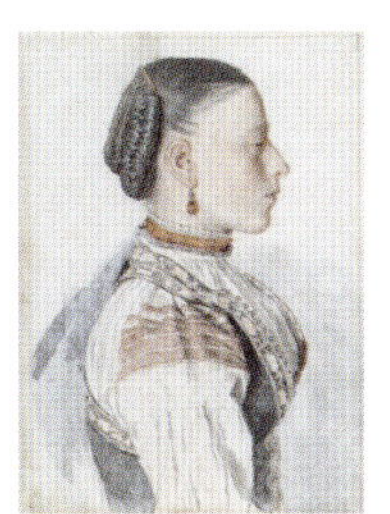

FIG. 7, *Young Roman Woman in profile*, 1737

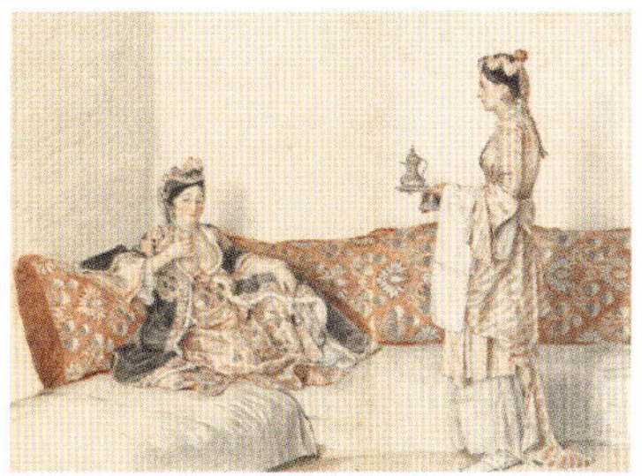

FIG. 9, *Maid Serving Tea*, *c.* 1740–42

1738
They travel to Constantinople, via Malta, the Greek islands and Smyrna.
Liotard makes figurative drawings at each stop.
Liotard remains in Constantinople for four years.

1742
Liotard is invited to the court of Prince Constantine Mavrocordato in Moldavia;
he stays for ten months and is the first western European artist to visit this Ottoman outpost.

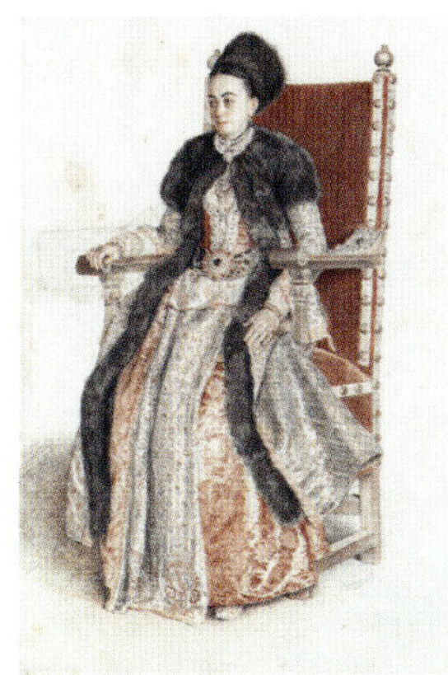

FIG. 15, *Ekaterina Mavrocordato (c. 1715–1775)*, 1742–3

Opposite
FIG. 12, *Richard Pococke (1704–1765)*, 1740, detail

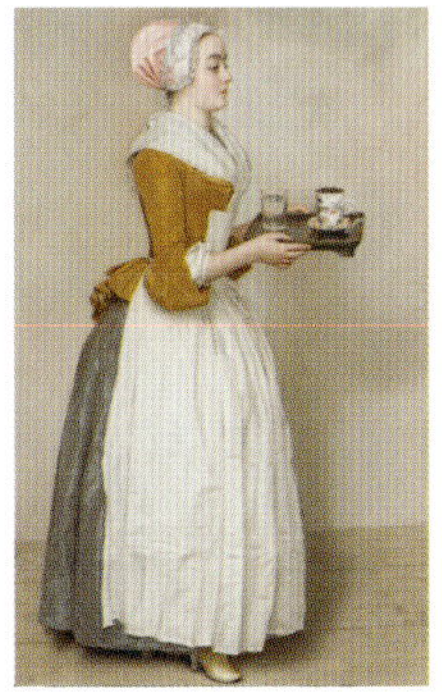

FIG. 17, *The Chocolate Girl*, *c.* 1744

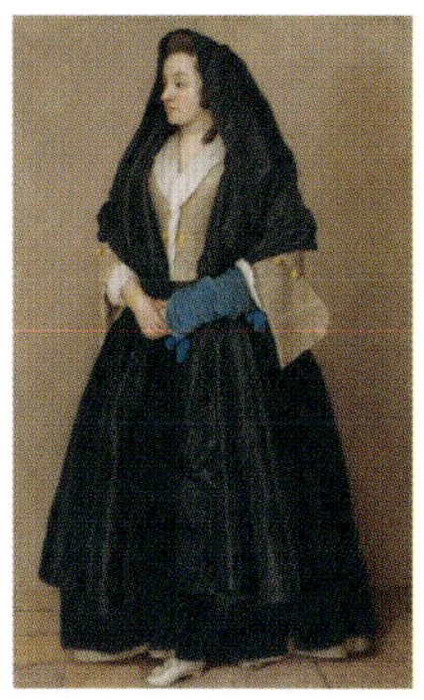

FIG. 8, *An Elegant Young Woman in Maltese Costume*, *c.* 1744

FIG. 19, *Marshal General of France, Maurice, Count of Saxony (1696–1750)*, 1748 (see p. 77)
FIG. 2, *Self-Portrait at the Easel*, 1751–2 (see p. 15)

1753–4

The first of Liotard's visits to London is made; again royal commissions are forthcoming; he depicts Princess Augusta and her children as a private commission.
FIG. 21, *Self-portrait in Profile*, 1753 (see p. 83)
FIG. 22, *Augusta, Princess of Wales (1719–1772)*, 1754 (see p. 84)

1743

Arriving in Vienna, Liotard establishes friendly relations with the Hapsburg court; Maria Theresa and her husband Francis Stephen become important patrons.
FIG. 16, *Maria Theresa (1717–1780) in a Fur-Trimmed Gown*, 1743 (see p. 68)

1745–6

Liotard joins his brother in Venice; he meets Rosalba Carriera and Count Francesco Algarotti and sells him his pastel of *The Chocolate Girl* for the cabinet of the Elector of Saxony in Dresden. Visits are undertaken to Milan and Darmstadt.

1746

He journeys to Basel, Geneva and Lyons before working in Paris, where Liotard succeeds in securing royal patronage. His Bourbon portraits are exhibited.

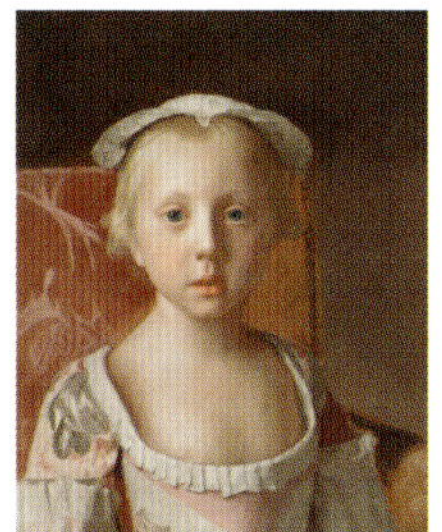

FIG. 23, *Princess Louisa Anne*, 1754

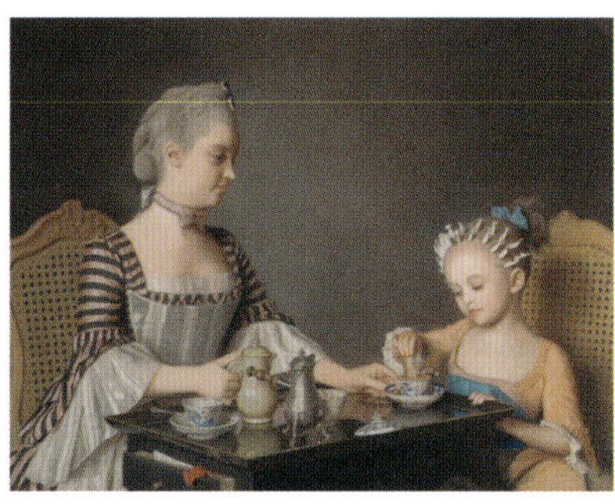

FIG. 29,*The Lavergne Family Breakfast*, 1754

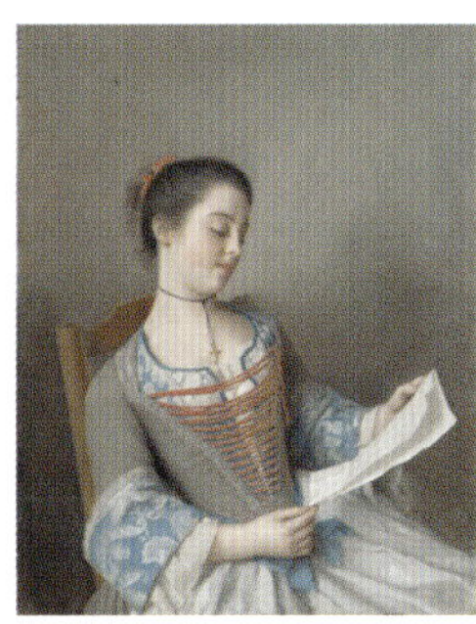

FIG. 18, *La Liseuse (The Reader)*, 1746

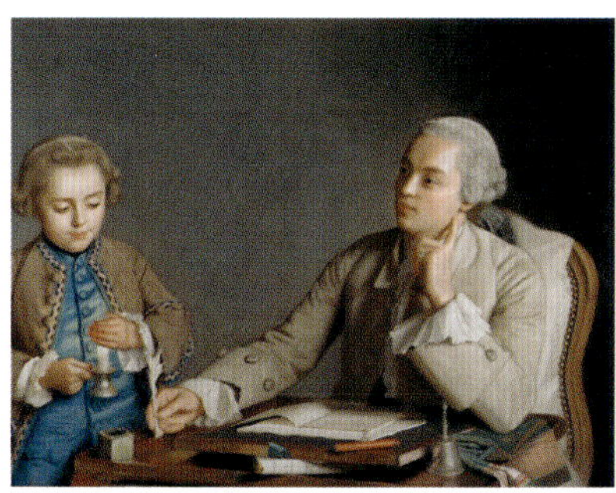

FIG. 28, *L'Ecriture (The Writer)*, 1752

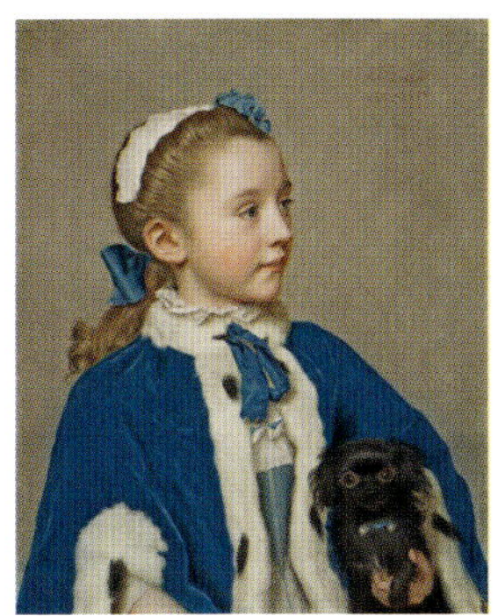

FIG. 33, *Portrait of Maria Frederike van Reede-Athlone at Seven Years of Age*, 1755–6

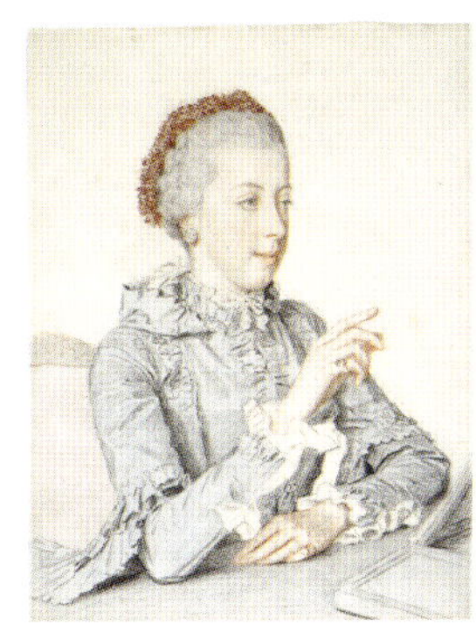

FIG. 40, *Archduchess Maria Elizabeth of Austria (1743–1808)*, 1762

1755

A journey is made to the Netherlands, where he visits Delft, The Hague and Amsterdam. Liotard recieves commissions and starts building his collection of old master paintings.

1756

Liotard marries Marie Fargues in Amsterdam; she is from a French Huguenot family.

1757

A visit is made to Paris and then Liotard returns to Geneva. By this period he has secured wealth and fame and depicts many distinguished local citizens.

FIG. 35, *François Tronchin (1704–1798)*, 1757 (see p. 112)

1758

Liotard and Marie's first son is born.

FIG. 3, *Madame François Tronchin 'Dressed for the Cold'*, 1758 (see p. 18)

FIG. 36, *Julie de Thellusson-Ployard*, 1760 (see p. 114)

FIG. 37, *Isaac-Louis de Thellusson*, 1760 (see p. 115)

FIG. 30, *Marie Liotard-Fargues with Her Eldest Son Jean-Étienne Liotard*, 1761–2 (see p. 104)

1762

The artist travels again to Vienna; during this visit he makes drawings of the Imperial children.

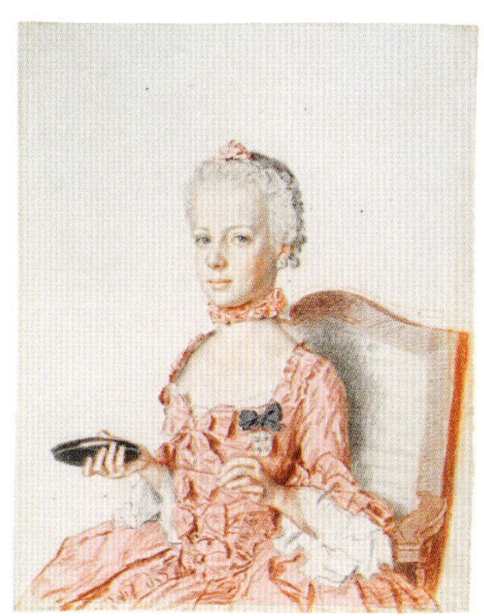

FIG. 39, *Archduchess Marie Antoinette of Austria (1755–1793)*, 1762

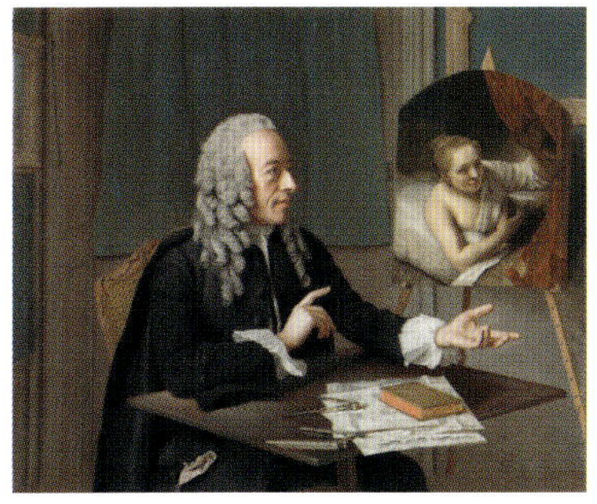

FIG. 34, *Charles-Simon Favart (1710–1792)*, 1757

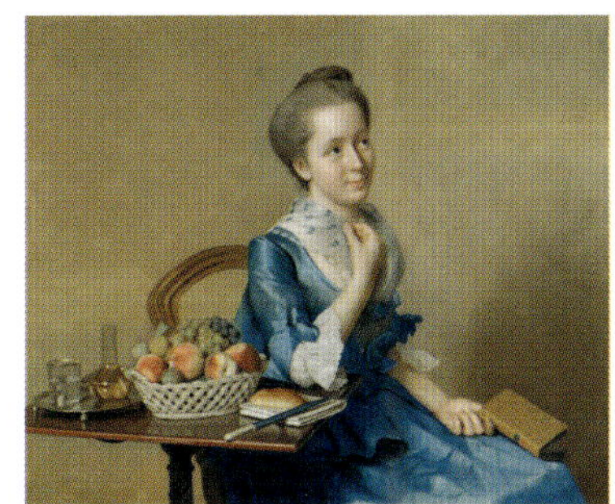

FIG. 38, *Suzanne Curchod (1737–1794)*, *c.* 1761

1763
Liotard buys a country house outside Geneva.

1766
He travels to Turin.
FIG. 42, *View from the Artist's House in Geneva*, *c.* 1768 (see pp. 126, 127)

1770
A journey is made to Lyons.

1770–71
Liotard organises a sale of his works and collection in Paris.
FIG. 43, *Trompe-l'œil with Two Bas-reliefs and Two Drawings*, 1771 (see p. 131)

1771–3
A return is made to the Netherlands.

1773
In London again, Liotard exhibits at the Royal Academy of Arts and organises sales of his work.

1774
In Geneva he plans a new house.
FIG. 31, *Marie-Thérèse Liotard Holding a Doll*, *c.* 1775 (see p. 106)

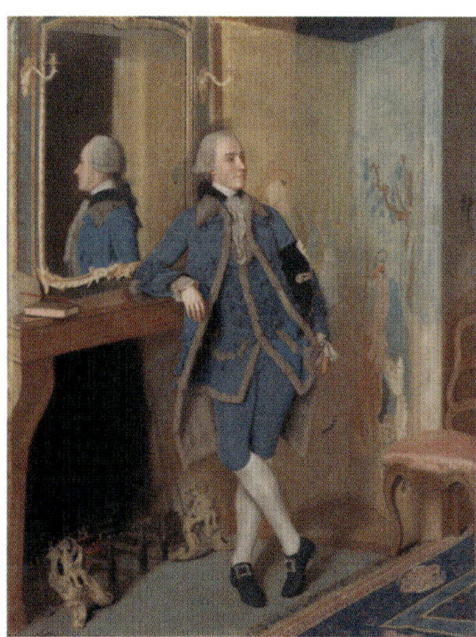
FIG. 41, *John, Lord Mountstuart, Later 4th Earl and 1st Marquess of Bute (1744–1814)*, 1763

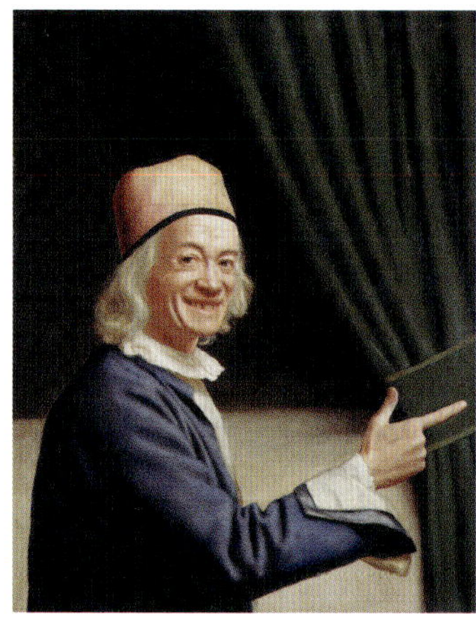
FIG. 1, *Self-Portrait Laughing*, *c.* 1770

1777
Liotard is visited in his studio by the Holy Roman Emperor Joseph II.
He travels to Vienna for the last time and stops in Zurich.

1781
He publishes his treatise in Lyons.

1782
Liotard's wife dies. Portrait commissions are not forthcoming and he focuses on still life compositions.
FIG. 45, *Still Life: Tea Set*, *c.* 1770–83 (see pp. 140, 141)

1786
Liotard moves in with his daughter.

1789
12 June. Liotard dies in Geneva, aged 87.

Opposite
FIG. 44, *Still-life: Pears, Figs, Plums, Bread Roll and Knife on a Table*, 1782, detail

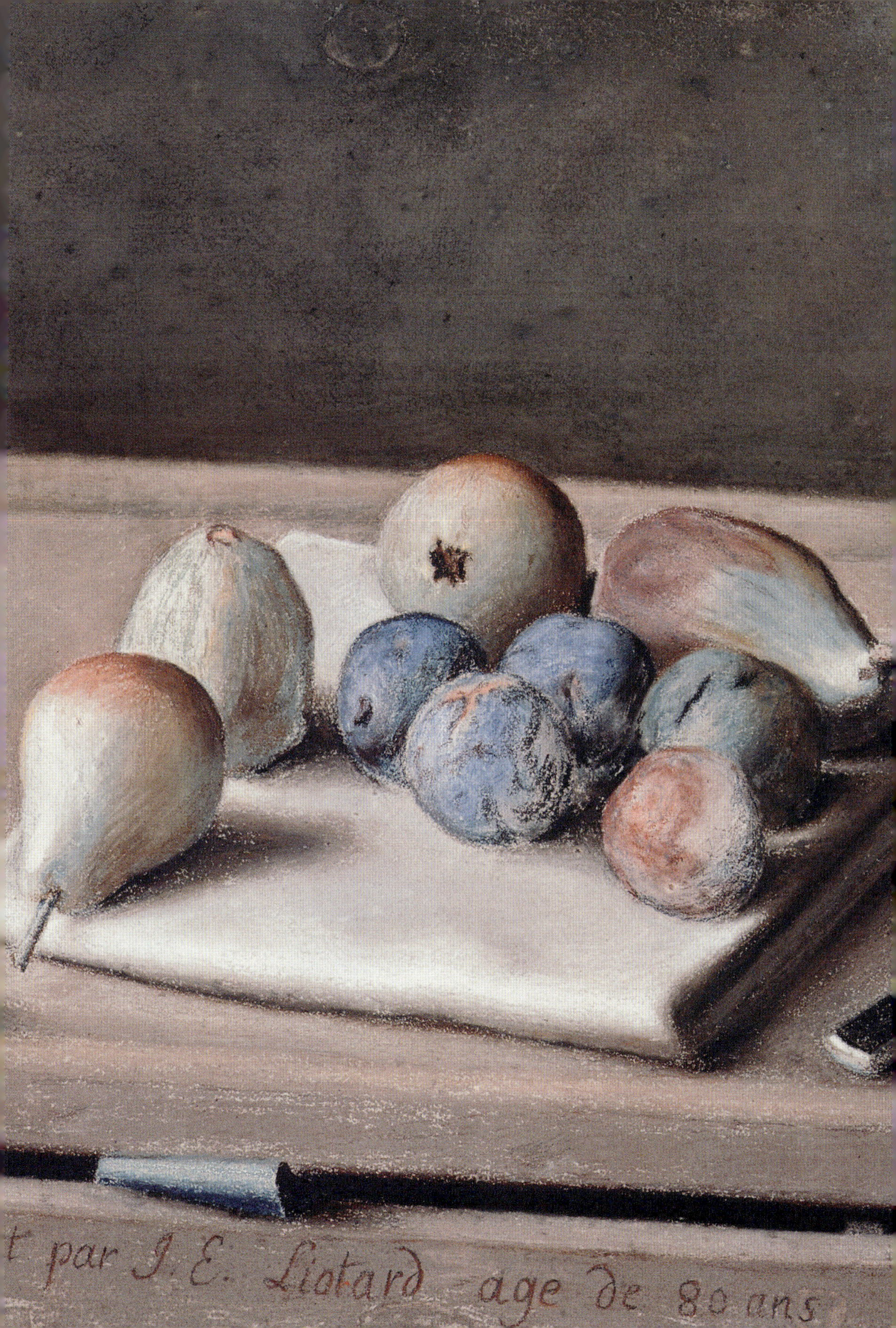
par J. E. Liotard age de 80 ans

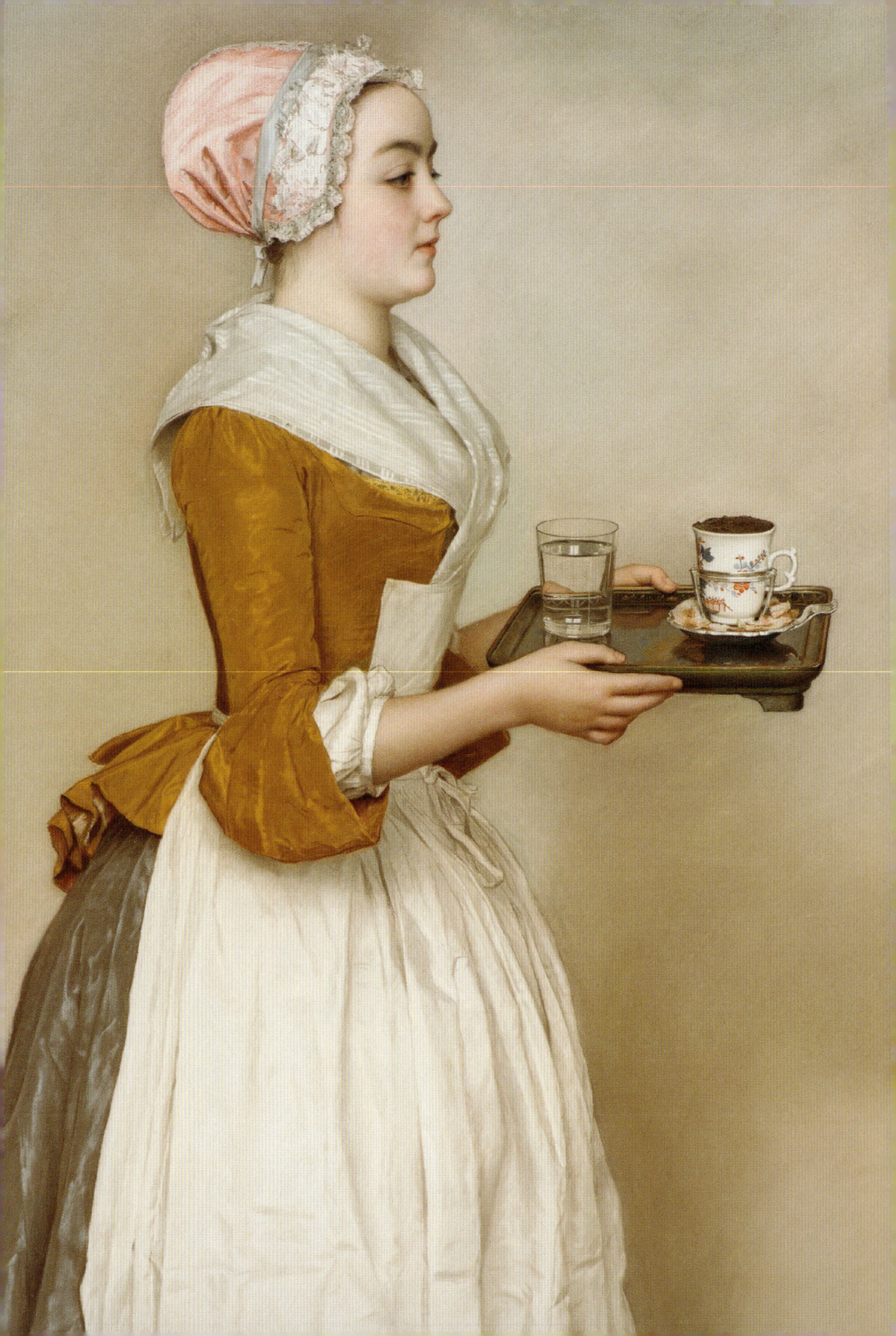

Bibliography

The literature on Liotard is extensive and not always easy to locate; that on eighteenth-century portraiture, pastels, Liotard's sitters and the cities he visited is vast. The bibliography here is highly selective. Fundamental sources for all studies of Liotard's work and career are: Roethlisberger and Loche 2008, and Jeffares 2006, along with the online version of the latter, with its numerous scholarly updates, which are invaluable. There is also a useful bibliography in Edinburgh and London 2015.

ANDERSON 1994
J. Anderson, 'Fixing Pastels: A letter from Liotard to the 2nd Earl of Bessborough in 1763,' *The Burlington Magazine*, 136, 1994, pp. 23–5.

BAETJER AND SHELLEY 2011
K. Baetjer and M. Shelley, *Pastel Portraits: Images of Eighteenth-Century Europe*, New York, 2011.

BAKER 2015
C. Baker, 'Wandering Star', *R.A. (Royal Academy) Magazine*, Autumn 2015, pp. 64–69.

BARK 2007–08
J.M. Bark, 'The Spectacular Self: Jean Etienne Liotard's Self-portrait Laughing,' *Inferno*, Vol. 12, Article 5.

BREWER 1997
J. Brewer, *The Pleasures of the Imagination, English Culture in the Eighteenth Century*, London, 1997.

BULL 2002
D. Bull, *Jean Etienne Liotard (1702–1789)*, Rijksmusuem Dossier, Amsterdam, 2002.

BULL 2008
D. Bull, 'Princess, Countess, Lover or Wife? Liotard's "Lady on a Sofa"', *The Burlington Magazine*, 150, 2008, pp. 592–602.

BURNS AND SAUNIER 2015
T. Burns and P. Saunier, *The Art of the Pastel*, New York, 2015.

COFFIN AND HOFSTETTER 2000
S. Coffin and B. Hofstetter, *The Gilbert Collection. Portrait Miniatures in Enamel*, London, 2000.

CONISBEE 1981
P. Conisbee, *Painting in Eighteenth-Century France*, Oxford, 1981.

DAVIES 2021
N. Davies, *George II, Not Just a British Monarch*, London, 2021.

DRESDEN 2018
S. Koja and R. Enke, eds., '*The most beautiful pastel ever seen': The Chocolate Girl by Jean-*Étienne Liotard, exh. cat., Gemäldegalerie Alte Meister, Dresden, 2018.

EDINBURGH AND LONDON 2015
C. Baker, W. Hauptman and M. Stevens et. al, *Jean-Etienne Liotard 1702–1789*, exh. cat., National Galleries of Scotland, Edinburgh and The Royal Academy of Arts, London, 2015.

FAHY 2005
E. Everett, ed., *The Wrightsman Pictures*, The Metropolitan Museum of Art, New York, 2005.

FORT WORTH, SAN FRANCISCO AND BOSTON 2017–18
F. Ilchmanm T. Michie, C.D. Dickerson and E. Bell, eds., *Casanova, The Seduction of Europe*, exh. cat., Kimbell Art Museum, Fort Worth, The Museum of Fine Arts, Boston, and Museum of Fine Arts, Boston, 2017–18.

GENEVA AND PARIS 1992
A. de Herdt, *Dessins de Liotard*, Musée d'Art et d'Histoire, Geneva and Musée du Louvre, Paris, 1992.

GRASSELLI 2003
M.M. Grasselli, Jean-Étienne Liotard, 'An Elegant Woman in Maltese Costume', *National Gallery of Art Bulletin*, Washington, no. 29, Spring 2003, pp. 15–16.

GRIFFITHS 2016
A. Griffiths, *The Print Before Photography, An Introduction to European Printmaking 1550–1820*, The British Museum, London, 2016.

HASKELL 1980
F. Haskell, *Patrons and Painters, A Study in the Relations Between Italian Art and Society in the Age of the Baroque*, New Haven and London, 1980.

HAUPTMANN 2011
W. Hauptmann, 'Liotard at the Royal Academy, 1773. The Enigmatic "Dr Thomson"', *The British Art Journal*, 12, 2011, pp. 34–43.

INGAMELLS 1997
J. Ingamells, *A Dictionary of British and Irish Travellers in Italy 1701–1800*, New Haven and London, 1997.

JEFFARES 2006 AND ONLINE
N. Jeffares, 'Dictionary of Pastellists before 1800', London, 2006; updated online version with numerous valuable clarifications to our knowledge of Liotard's work: www.pastellists.com

JONES 2014
C. Jones, *The Smile Revolution in Eighteenth-Century Paris*, Oxford, 2014.

KELLY 2009
J.M. Kelly, *The Society of Dilettanti, Archaeology and Identity in the British Enlightenment*, New Haven and London, 2009.

LEVEY 1959
M. Levey, *Painting in Eighteenth-Century Venice*, New Haven and London, 1959.

LIPPINCOTT 1985
L. Lippincott, 'Liotard's "China Painting"', *The J. Paul Getty Museum Journal*, Vol. 13, 1985, pp. 121–130.

LOCHE AND ROETHLISBERGER 1978
R. Loche and M. Roethlisberger, *L'opera completa di Liotard*, Milan, 1978.

LONDON 1985
T. Murdoch et al., *The Quiet Conquest, The Huguenots 1685–1985*, exh. cat., The Museum of London, 1985.

LONDON 2014
D. Shawe-Taylor, ed., *The First Georgian's, Art and Monarchy 1714–1760*, exh. cat, the Queen's Gallery, London, 2014.

LONDON 2023 A
A. Reynolds, *Style & Society, Dressing the Georgians*, exh. cat., The Queen's Gallery, London, 2023.

LONDON 2023 B
F. Whitlum-Cooper and I. Moon, *Discover Liotard and The Lavergne Family Breakfast*, exh.cat., National Gallery, London, 2023.

LONDON AND EDINBURGH 2004
G. Waterfield, A. French and M. Craske, *Below Stairs, 400 years of servants' portraits*, exh. cat., The National Portrait Gallery, London and the Scottish National Portrait Gallery, Edinburgh, 2004.

LONDON AND ROME 1996
A. Wilton and I. Bignamini, eds., exh. cat., *Grand Tour. The Lure of Italy in the Eighteenth Century'*, Tate Gallery, London and Palazzo delle Esposizioni, Rome, 1996.

MARANDET 2003
F. Marandet, 'The Formative Years of Jean-Etienne Liotard,' *The Burlington Magazine*, 145, 2003, pp. 297–300.

MASON 2009
S. Mason, ed., *Matthew Boulton, Selling what all the world desires*, New Haven and London, 2009.

MILLAR 1963
O. Millar, *The Tudor, Stuart and Early Georgian Pictures in the Collection of Her Majesty The Queen*, 2 vols., London 1963.

MURDOCH 2021
T. Murdoch, *Europe Divided, Huguenot Refugee Art & Culture*, London, 2021.

NEW HAVEN AND LONDON 2010
M. Snodin ed., *Horace Walpole's Strawberry Hill*, exh. cat., The Yale Center for Britsh Art, New Haven and the Victoria and Albert Museum, London, 2010.

NEW YORK 2006
C.B. Bailey et. al., *Jean-Etienne Liotard. 1702–1789. Masterpieces from the Musées d'Art et d'Histoire of Geneva and Swiss Private Collections*, exh cat., Frick Collection, New York, 2006.

NEW YORK, SAN MARINO, RICHMOND AND LONDON 1996–7
C. Lloyd and V. Remington, *Masterpieces in Little, Portrait Miniatures from the Collection of Her Majesty Queen Elizabeth II*, exh. cat., The Metropolitan Museum of Art, New York, The Huntington Library, San Marino, The Virginia Museum of Fine Arts, Richmond and The Queen's Gallery, London, 1996–7.

NOON 1979
P.J. Noon, *English Portrait Drawings and Miniatures*, Yale Center for British Art, New Haven, 1979.

OBERER 2018
A. Oberer, *The Life and Work of Rosalba Carriera (1673–1757), The Queen of Pastel*, Amsterdam, 2018.

O'CONNELL 2003
S. O'Connell with R. Porter, C. Fox and R. Hyde, *London 1753*, London, 2003.

OUTRAM 2006
D. Outram, *Panorama of the Enlightenment*, London, 2006.

PARIS 2018
X. Salmon, exh. cat., *Pastels in the Musée du Louvre, 17th and 18th Centuries*, Musée du Louvre, Paris, 2018.

PARMANTIER-LALLEMENT 1996
N. Parmantier-Lallement, 'Liotard, Jean-Etienne,' in J. Turner, ed., *The Dictionary of Art*, 1996, vol.19, pp. 435–7.

POINTON 1993
M. Pointon, *Hanging the Head, Portraiture and Social Formation in Eighteenth-Century England*, New Haven and London, 1993.

POINTON 2009
M. Pointon, *Brilliant Effects, A Cultural History of Gem Stones and Jewellery*, New Haven and London, 2009.

PORTER 2000
R. Porter, *Enlightenment, Britain and the Creation of the Modern World*, London, 2000.

PORTER 2003
R. Porter, *Flesh in the Age of Reason*, London, 2003.

RIBEIRO 2011
A. Ribeiro, *Facing Beauty, Painted Women and Cosmetic Art*, New Haven and London, 2011.

ROBERTSON 2020
R. Robertson, *The Enlightenment. The Pursuit of Happiness 1680–1790*, London, 2020.

ROETHLISBERGER 1985
M. Roethlisberger, 'Jean-Etienne Liotard as a Painter of Still Lifes,' *The J. Paul Getty Museum Journal*, Vol. 13, 1985, pp. 109–120.

ROETHLISBERGER AND LOCHE 2008
M. Roethlisberger and R. Loche, *Liotard. Catalogue, sources et correspondence*, 2 vols., Doornspijk, 2008.

SLIGHT 2016
J. Slight, 'Liotard: a review of the RA exhibition, with a general note on his frames', *The Frame blog* (online).

SMENTEK 2010
K. Smentek, 'Looking East, Jean-Etienne Liotard, the Turkish Painter', *Ars Orientalis*, volume 39, 2010 (Globalizing cultures: art and mobility in the eighteenth century), pp. 84–113.

STEIN 2023
P. Stein, 'Liotard and Boucher: a question of precedence,' *The Burlington Magazine*, 165, June 2023, pp. 612–19.

WALKER 1992
R. Walker, *The Eighteenth and Early Nineteenth Century Miniatures in the Collection of Her Majesty the Queen*, Cambridge, 1992.

WAX 1990
C. Wax, *The Mezzotint, History and Technique*, New York, 1990.

WHITLUM-COOPER 2010
F. Whitlum-Cooper, 'Drawing Distinctions: Jean-Etienne Liotard in Constantinople and Vienna,' *Immediations*, 2011, pp. 2–23.

WILLIAMS 2014
H. Williams, *Turquerie, An Eighteenth-Century European Fantasy*, London, 2014

YALE AND LONDON 2017
J. Marschner, ed., *Enlightenened Princesses, Caroline, Augusta, Charlotte and the Shaping of the Modern World*, exh. cat., Yale Center for British Art and Kensington Palace, London, 2017.

Detail, FIG. 19

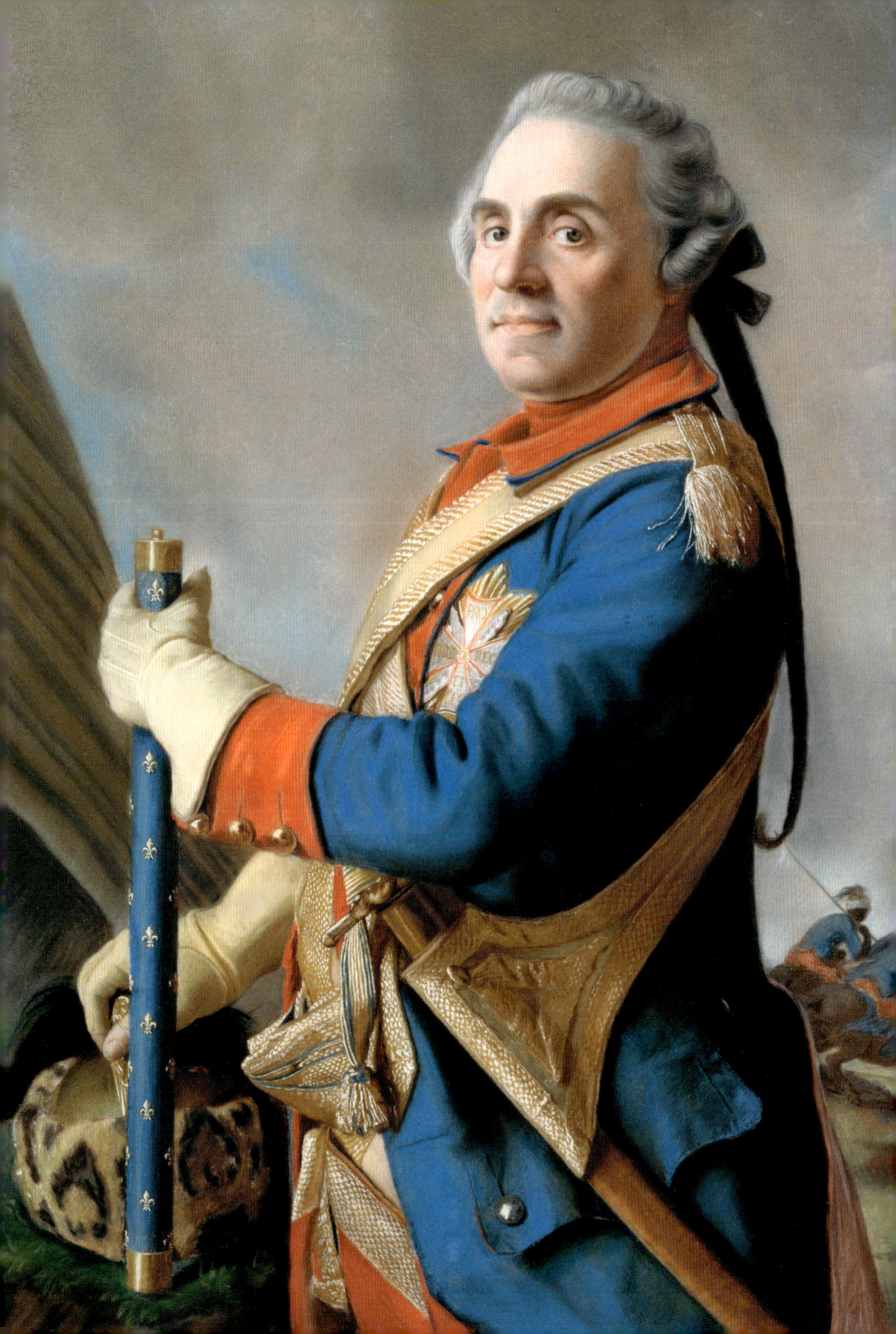

Notes on Sources

For this introductory book detailed physical descriptions of Liotard's works, provenances and exhibition histories are not provided; they can all be found, however, in Roethlisberger and Loche 2008.

INTRODUCTION

For the wider phenomenon of smiling in late eighteenth-century portraiture see Jones 2014.

There are very few points of comparison with Liotard's smiling self-portrait, apart from Joseph Ducreaux's (1735–1802) later *Self-Portrait, Mocking* of *c.* 1793 (Musée du Louvre) which features pointing and grinning and baring teeth.

For the Walpole quotation, see Roethlisberger and Loche 2008, vol. 1, p. 87.

For the 1762 Liotard quotation see Jeffares in Edinburgh and London 2015, p 27.

The Mozart quotation dates from a letter of 11 September 1778.

For the Diderot/Hume interaction and its wider significance see Robertson 2020, p. 600.

Diderot's comment on the dusty medium of pastel is quoted by Hauptman: Edinburgh and London 2015, p. 23.

For the John Russell quotation see Baker in Edinburgh and London 2015, p. 19.

For the number of people engaged in the business of portraiture in London in the mid-eighteenth century, see Noon 1979, p. vii. The population of the city at the time was approximately 675,000.

GENEVA AND PARIS: FAMILY AND TRAINING

For the cultural and artistic achievements of the Huguenot diaspora see London 1985 and especially Murdoch 2021.

For a useful description of the process of making an enamel portrait see Coffin and Hofstetter 2000.

Carriera's presence in Paris was key to establishing a vogue for pastel portraiture there; for the latest study of her career see Oberer 2018.

ITALIAN ENCOUNTERS

For Liotard's British travelling companions see entries in Ingamells 1997, and for the Society of Dilettanti, Kelly 2009.

For the important Bessborough letter see Anderson 1994.

ADVENTURES IN CONSTANTINOPLE

The quotations at the opening of this chapter are from *A Voyage Performed by The Late Earl of Sandwich Round the Mediterranean in the Years 1738 and 1739, Written by Himself* (1799). This book was based on Sandwich's journal and published after his death by his chaplain John Cooke.

For a valuable survey of the cultural interactions between Europe and the Levant see Williams 2014.

See Bull 2008 for a detailed consideration of the various versions of FIG. 10, *Woman in Turkish Dress, Seated on a Sofa* and the complex and vexing issue of who Liotard was and was not portraying in them.

FIG. 14, Liotard's oil of a *Woman on a Sofa Reading* and its related drawings, have been the subject of extensive analysis recently; this has established it influenced works by Boucher, rather than vice versa, as had been previously thought: see Stein 2023.

NEW AMBITIONS: VIENNA, VENICE AND PARIS

FIG. 17, Liotard's *Chocolate Girl*, was the focus of an illuminating exhibition (see Dresden 2018) that considered it in the context of the artist's career as well as its extensive critical fortunes and the numerous reproductions it has inspired.

For Algarotti's wide interests see Haskell 1980.

For the Bourbon series of portraits see Hauptman in Edinburgh and London 2015. For the Philip Yorke quotation see Jeffares online, p. 2.

SENSATIONS IN LONDON AND LYONS

For Liotard's work at the court in London see: Millar 1963, Walker 1992, London 2014 and Hauptman in Edinburgh and London 2015.

The Lord Chesterfield quotation see Jeffares 2006 and online.

FIG. 29, *The Lavergne Family Breakfast* is the centrepiece of London 2023B.

THE NETHERLANDS AND RETURNING TO GENEVA

A detailed family tree for Liotard is provided in Roethlisberger and Loche 2008.

It was Jeffares who correctly identified Marie-Thérèse as the subject of FIG. 31. See his online discussion.

The Getty Museum website has excellent updated entries on its works by Liotard, such as the portrait of John, Lord Mountstuart, FIG. 41.

LATE INNOVATIONS: THEORY AND PRACTICE

For the history of Royal Academy exhibitions see the Paul Mellon Centre's online research project.

There is an especially useful discussion of Liotard's his *Traité des principes et des règles de la peinture* (1781) in Lippincott 1985.

For the 1765 dialogue between Liotard and Rousseau see Fehlmann in Edinburgh and London 2015, p. 71.

CONCLUSION

The unique status of *The Chocolate Girl* and its enduring popularity is discussed in Dresden 2018.

Acknowledgements

This book is intended as an introductory survey of the work of a remarkably sophisticated artist who deserves to be better known beyond the enthusiasm of specialists. It relies on the knowledge and publications of many scholars and curators (see Bibliography). It also emerges from the most enjoyable experience of co-curating an exhibition on Liotard which was shown at the National Galleries of Scotland and Royal Academy of Arts in 2015 and 2016. The key and very generous collaborators of that project were MaryAnne Stevens and William Hauptman, to whom I remain very grateful. The other contributors to the accompanying catalogue for that exhibition also made extraordinarily valuable contributions to it: Neil Jeffares, Aileen Ribeiro, Duncan Bull and Marc Fehlmann. The writing of this study has benefited greatly from the hospitality and excellent resources of the British School at Rome.

Liotard: A Portrait of Eighteenth-Century Europe has been supported with a very generous grant from The Tavolozza Foundation, for which we are extremely grateful. The Tavolozza Foundation provides grants for publications and projects which promote appreciation of artists at work and works on paper internationally.

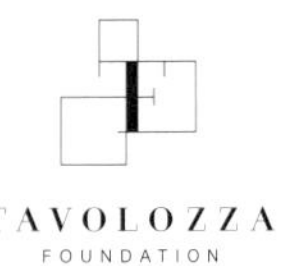

Detail, FIG. 37

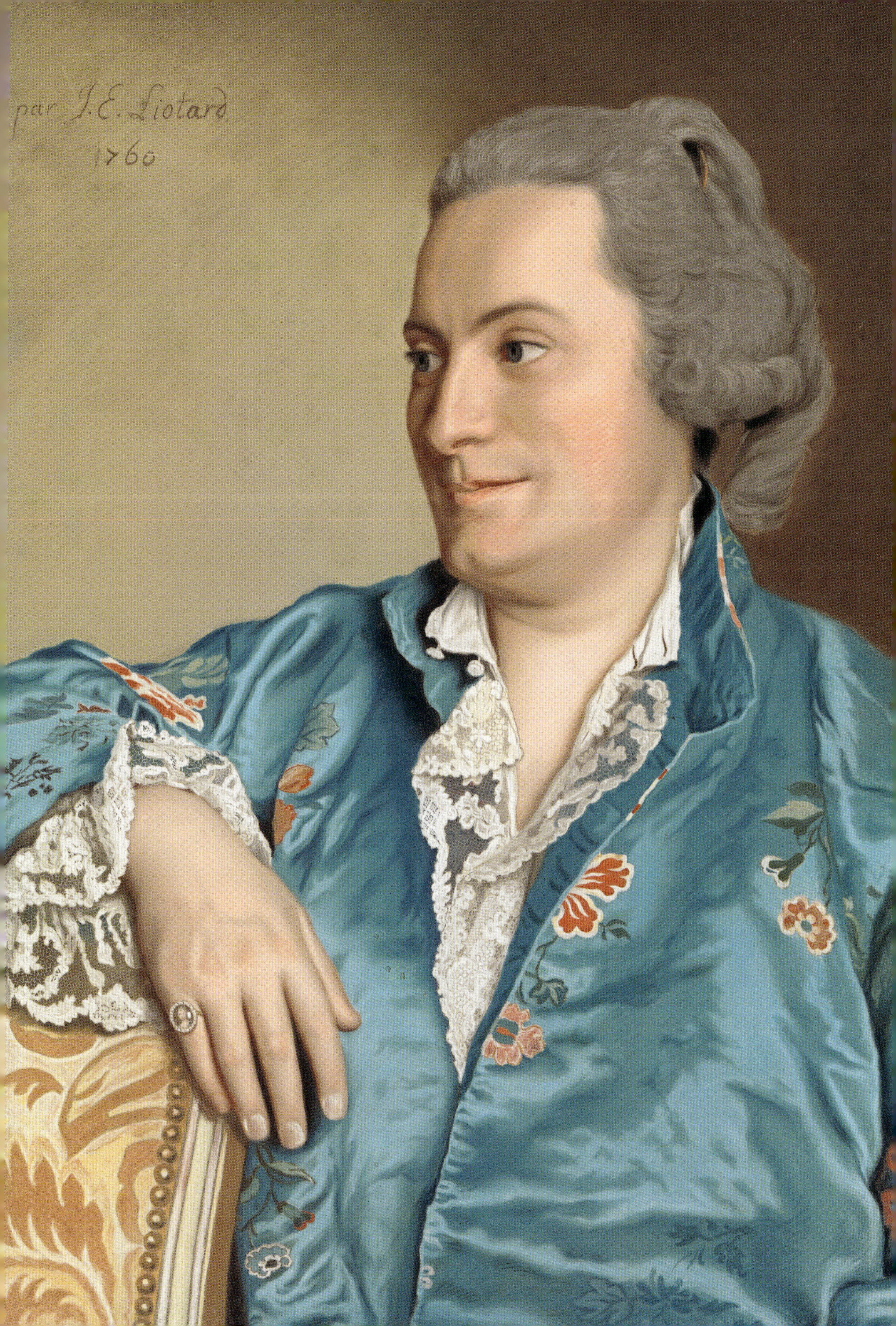
par J.E. Liotard
1760

Photographic Credits

FIGS 1, 2, 3
© Musée d'art et d'histoire, Ville de Genève, photographe: Bettina Jacot-Descombes, Nathalie Sabato, Jean-Marc Yersin (FIG. 3 on permanent loan from the Fondation Jean-Louis Prevost)

FIG. 4
© The Trustees of the British Museum

FIG. 5
The Picture Art Collection / Alamy Stock Photo

FIG. 6
Tomasso, UK

FIG. 7
RMN-Grand Palais / MichËle Bellot / RMN-GP / Dist. Photo SCALA, Florence

FIG. 8
National Gallery of Art, Washington Patrons' Permanent Fund and New Century Fund

FIG. 9, 36, 37
Kunst Museum Winterthur, Stiftung Oskar Reinhart © SIK-ISEA, Zürich (Philipp Hitz)

FIG. 10
The Metropolitan Museum of Art, New York, Bequest of Mrs. Charles Wrightsman, 2019

FIG. 11
The Picture Art Collection / Alamy Stock Photo

FIGS 12, 30, 39, 40
© Musée d'art et d'histoire, Ville de Genève, photographe: Bettina Jacot-Descombes (FIG. 40 on permanent loan from the Gottfried Keller Foundation)

FIG. 13
© Fitzwilliam Museum / Bridgeman Images

FIG. 14
Christie's Images, London / SCALA, Florence

FIG. 15
Staatliche Museen zu Berlin, bpk / Kupferstichkabinett, SMB / Volker-H. Schneider

FIG. 16
Private Collection, Photo © Fine Art Images/Bridgeman Images (On permanent loan to Schloss Schönbrunn, Vienna)

FIGS 17, 19
© Gemäldegalerie Alte Meister, Staatliche Kunstsammlungen Dresden Photo: Hans-Peter Klut, Wolfgang Kreische

FIG. 18
Heritage Image Partnership Ltd / Alamy Stock Photo

FIG. 20
Fondazione Ordine Mauriziano, Stupinigi, Turin, Archivo Nicola Restauri

FIGS 21, 22, 23
Royal Collection Trust / © His Majesty King Charles III 2023

FIG. 24
© Ashmolean Museum, University of Oxford

FIGS 25, 26
The Devonshire Collections, Chatsworth
Reproduced by permission of Chatsworth Settlement Trustees/Bridgeman Images

FIG. 27
Compton Verney, Warwickshire, UK
© Compton Verney/Bridgeman Images

FIG. 28, 38
Bundesmobilienverwaltung Vienna, Photo: © Schloß Schönbrunn Kultur- und Betriebsgesellschaft m.b.H./Edgar Knaack (FIG. 28 on loan from the Kunsthistoriches Museum, Vienna)

FIG. 29
The National Gallery, London
Accepted in lieu of Inheritance Tax by HM Government from the estate of George Pinto and allocated to the National Gallery, 2019

FIG. 31
Wikimedia Commons / Christophe André

FIG. 32
Private collection

FIGS 33, 41, 45
The J. Paul Getty Museum, Los Angeles, digital image courtesy of Getty's Open Content Program

FIG. 34
Private collection

FIG. 35
The Cleveland Museum of Art, John L. Severance Fund

FIG. 42
Penta Springs Limited / Alamy Stock Photo

FIG. 43
Copyright The Frick Collection
Bequeathed by Lore Heinemann in memory of her husband, Dr Rudolph J. Heinemann, 1997
Photo: Joseph Coscia Jr.

FIG. 44
DeAgostini Picture Library/ SCALA, Florence

Index

Figures are shown with a page reference in *italics*.

Published in 2023 by Unicorn
an imprint of Unicorn Publishing Group
Charleston Studio, Meadow Business Centre,
Lewes BN8 5RW
www.unicornpublishing.org

Images – see photographic credits page 168

ISBN 978-1-911397-59-5

10 9 8 7 6 5 4 3 2 1

Book design by Philip Lewis
Cover design by Felicity Price-Smith

Printed in the EU by
FineTone Ltd, Riga